Hitler's Thirty Days to Power: January 1933

Henry Ashby Turner, Jr

D0709113

BLOOMSBURY

MANY OF THE DESIGNATIONS USED BY MANUFACTURERS AND SELLERS
TO DISTINGUISH THEIR PRODUCTS ARE CLAIMED AS TRADEMARKS. WHERE
THOSE DESIGNATIONS APPEAR IN THIS BOOK AND ADDISON-WESLEY WAS
AWARE OF A TRADEMARK CLAIM, THE DESIGNATIONS HAVE BEEN PRINTED
IN INITIAL CAPITAL LETTERS.

First published in Great Britain 1996
This paperback edition published 1997
Bloomsbury Publishing Plc, 38 Soho Square,
London W1V 5DF

First published in the USA 1996 by Addison-Wesley Publishing
Company, Inc.

A CIP catalogue record for this book is available
from the British Library

ISBN 0 7475 3171 4

10 9 8 7 6 5 4 3 2 1

Printed in Great Britain by Clays Limited, St Ives plc

TO

Patrick Herbst

CONTENTS

PREFACE

EVERYONE HAS HEARD OF HITLER. Most know he was the dictator of Germany who caused the Second World War and the slaughter of millions of Jews. But how Hitler got power is another matter. Few understand the way in which his dictatorship came about. Because Germany was a republic when Hitler became chancellor, many assume that he was democratically elected by a majority of the German people. Such was not, however, the case. His rise to power was far more complicated and, above all, more chancy. It was, in fact, a very near thing that could have been thwarted at numerous points. Much of Hitler's story has been ably recounted in previous books, but no one has yet subjected to thorough scrutiny the dramatic events of the crucial month of January 1933, at the end of which Hitler became head of the German government. To tell that story is the task of this book.

THIS work has benefited greatly from the generous help of others, for which I am very grateful. William Sheridan Allen, Peter Gay, Richard F. Hamilton, and Peter Hayes read drafts of the manuscript and provided valuable suggestions. In addition to commenting on the manuscript, William L. Patch, Jr., shared with me relevant documents from his own research, as did Larry Eugene Jones and Hagen Schulze.

Pertti Ahonen obtained copies of other useful evidence for me. Renate Köhne-Lindenlaub spared me thousands of miles of travel by providing me with a copy of a document from the Krupp archive. Mary E. Sarotte helped me to obtain some of the photographs. George O. Kent and Mary R. Habeck provided invaluable assistance in locating and obtaining a copy of the "Moscow Document" described in the Appendix. My editor, Henning P. Gutmann, provided unwavering encouragement as well as helpful guidance, and Lynne Reed faithfully shepherded the manuscript into print.

HITLER'S
THIRTY DAYS
TO POWER

PROLOGUE:

The Field Marshal, the Corporal, and the General

O N   T H E   F I R S T   D A Y of 1933, a chorus of relief and rejoicing arose from defenders of Germany's beleaguered Weimar Republic. For three years the young state had been subjected to mounting assault by antidemocratic forces, the strongest and most threatening being Adolf Hitler's National Socialist Party. Now the tide appeared to have turned. "The mighty Nazi assault on the democratic state has been repulsed," proclaimed the New Year's editorial of the prestigious *Frankfurter Zeitung*. "The republic has been rescued," announced a staff writer for the *Vossische Zeitung,* a venerable Berlin daily. *Vorwärts,* the newspaper of the Social Democrats, the party most responsible for the republic's creation fourteen years earlier, headlined its editorial "Hitler's Rise and Fall." A major Catholic paper in Cologne, the *Kölnische Volkszeitung,* pointed out that whereas its prediction a year earlier that Hitler would never get power had seemed daring at the time, that view had now become commonplace. Ruminating about what to tell future grandchildren about his own times, a writer for the *Berliner Tageblatt* suggested: "Everywhere, throughout the whole world people were talking about—what was his first name?—Adalbert Hitler. Later? Vanished!"

In light of the knowledge that Hitler would be legally installed as German chancellor within less than a month, these expressions of republican optimism look in retrospect like a collective delusion. Yet an examination of what had gone before reveals that the hopefulness of Nazism's opponents was at the time by no means unfounded.

THROUGHOUT its turbulent fourteen years, the first German republic, founded in the city of Weimar in 1919, had to struggle against heavy handicaps. From the start, millions of Germans despised it. Extreme leftists rejected it as a mere bourgeois democracy and called for its overthrow by a proletarian revolution. On the Right, die-hard monarchists regarded as treason the revolution, in the wake of Germany's defeat in the First World War, that overthrew the Hohenzollern dynasty of Prussia, under which the country had been united into the Empire created in 1871. Along with other enemies of democracy, they denounced as un-German a republic whose institutions had been created by a national assembly freely elected on the basis of universal suffrage. The militarists who had led the country into the war added to the republic's foes by falsely claiming that the army had not been defeated in the field but had instead been struck down by a 'stab in the back' on the home front by the politicians who established the republic. The new regime thus bore for many Germans the stigma of treason and national humiliation. The victorious Western democracies further heightened the Weimar Republic's unpopularity by forcing it to accept a punitive peace settlement. The Versailles Treaty severed sizable portions of Germany's prewar territory, saddled the country with sole guilt for causing the war, made the republic liable for heavy reparations to the victors, and restricted its sovereignty in numerous ways, including tight limitations on its military forces.

It was a tribute to Germany's republicans that the new government survived its early years despite these liabilities, as well as a hyperinflation that destroyed the currency, attempts at forcible overthrow by extremists of both Right and Left, and occupation of parts of the country by the victorious powers of World War I. By the middle of the '20s democracy seemed to have taken root in Germany, and the country enjoyed a half-decade of something approaching stability and prosperity. But with the onset of the Great Depression, which struck the German economy harder than that of any other European country, the Weimar Republic fell upon hard times. In 1930 parliamentary rule ceased to function when the moderate political parties deadlocked over how to finance unemployment benefits for the growing legions of jobless Germans. As a consequence of that crisis, decisive political power shifted from the parliament to the presidency, with the result that the republic no longer functioned as intended by its founders.

The president in whose hands great power now became concentrated was Paul von Hindenburg, who as field marshal had commanded the German army during the First World War. Elected in 1925, he was reelected to a second seven-year term in 1932 at the age of eighty-five. A legendary figure because of his wartime role, the venerable Hindenburg personified for millions of Germans some of the proudest chapters of their country's past. He was a Junker, a descendant of one of the aristocratic families that had settled Germany's eastern frontier regions centuries earlier. As a young officer in the Prussian army he participated in the wars of unification and was present at the proclamation of the Empire in 1871. Having retired in 1911 after an unexceptional career as an officer, he was recalled to service at the outbreak of war three years later. When the forces under his command halted the advance of Russian forces into German territory, he quickly became a national hero, even though the extent of his personal contribution to that victory was exaggerated for purposes of propaganda on the home front. Later elevated to supreme commander of the army, he managed to emerge from the German defeat in the war with his heroic status intact, in considerable measure by virtue of the stab-in-the-back legend, which he himself played a key role in propagating.

Tall and robust, Hindenburg was an imposing figure. Well into his ninth decade he retained the ramrod bearing of a Prussian officer. Courtly and gracious in manner, he evoked nostalgia for the previous century. His broad, square visage, crowned by a close-cropped military haircut and punctuated by a long, wispy mustache, seemed frozen in an expression of pensive sadness. For many Germans this visage conveyed profound gravity and resolute devotion to arduous duties. Although his public image was one of imperturbable strength, Hindenburg lacked a strong, independent will and seldom took initiatives on his own. Throughout his career, he depended heavily upon the advice of those around him, a trait that became more pronounced with advancing age.

Contrary to his stolid appearance, Hindenburg was subject, at moments of stress, to outbursts of emotion that caused his voice to falter and sent tears coursing down his cheeks. He tended to see political relationships in terms of comradeship and professed to value loyalty above all else, even though throughout his life he repeatedly turned his back on associates who had faithfully served him. Having no intellectual interests outside of military affairs, he rarely held more than simplistic views on other matters, including politics. But despite persistent rumors of senility, all reliable accounts indicate that, although ponderous and slow, Hindenburg remained lucid until the final illness that ended his life near the close of his eighty-seventh year in 1934, well after Hitler's dictatorial rule had reduced him to a figurehead. To the very end, Hindenburg's sheer physical bulk, his aloof dignity, and the living link he provided to past glories imbued him with an aura that awed most contemporaries.

As head of state, President von Hindenburg occupied a position at first sight similar to that of the crowned heads of Europe's parliamentary monarchies, but the republic's constitution bestowed upon his office far greater powers than those of the remaining monarchs. The president exercised ultimate authority over the armed forces and had at his disposal sweeping emergency powers that authorized him to curtail civil rights and enact laws by decree if he thought such measures necessary. Only the president could appoint the head of government, the chancellor, and the other ministers who made up the cabinet. As in other European democracies, the chancellor was required to retain the support of a majority of the national parliament, the Reichstag, and had to resign in the event of a majority vote of no confidence. The president could, however, at any time dismiss the chancellor and cabinet; he could also dissolve the Reichstag prior to expiration of its normal four-year term and schedule a new election. As the events of January 1933 would demonstrate, these powers made the president the crucial figure in a time of political instability and put him in a position to exercise a decisive influence on the course of events.

Initially elected as the candidate of conservative and reactionary rightists, Hindenburg for a time pleasantly surprised defenders of the republic, although he never renounced his monarchist sentiments. For five years he dutifully presided over the republic in the manner of a constitutional head of state. He appointed chancellors and cabinets either nominated by majority coalitions of parties or acceptable to a majority when coalitions failed to form. But the old field marshal became increasingly impatient with the recurrent bargains and machinations among the parties, which produced a shifting succession of seventeen cabinets under nine different chancellors during the republic's first eleven years. He was particularly displeased by resistance to military expenditures on the part of the largest republican party, the left-of-center Social Democrats, whose ranks included many pacifists. His deeply conservative outlook was also offended by the Social Democrats' lip service to the Marxist ideology of their past, which they had in practice long since put aside in favor of pragmatic reformism.

When the political deadlock of 1930 brought down a Social Democrat–led cabinet and left the Reichstag incapable of agreeing on a replacement, the group of high army officers who served as Hindenburg's closest advisers prevailed upon him to break with the parliamentary system and exclude the Left from positions of authority. With the proclaimed goal of elevating the government above politics, Hindenburg began the practice of appointing chancellors of his personal choice who were not beholden to parliamentary majorities. He thus initiated what came to be known as a system of government by presidential cabinets. To enable the chancellors who presided over those cabinets to circumvent the Reichstag's legislative authority, he placed at their disposal the sweeping emergency powers conferred on the presidency by the Weimar constitution. Beginning in 1930, virtually all national laws—including those authorizing taxes and government appropriations—were enacted not by parliamentary action but rather by presidential decrees issued at the request of chancellor and cabinet. The president's authority was not absolute. By majority vote, the Reichstag could rescind his emergency decrees or pass a vote of no confidence against the chancellor and his cabinet. But to discourage such assertions of parliamentary prerogatives, the president could arm the chancellor with a decree dissolving the Reichstag, thus forcing the political parties to face the voters in a new national election.

The first of the presidential chancellors was Heinrich Brüning, a respected parliamentarian of the Catholic Center Party, which had been one of the bulwarks of republican cabinets. For two years, beginning in May 1930, Brüning governed with the acquiescence of the staunchly republican Social Democrats, who had been excluded from his cabinet. Fearing that opposition to Brüning would lead to a more rightist cabinet, their party refrained from no-confidence votes and left unchallenged the presidential decrees with which the chancellor governed. The Social Democrats thus linked their fortunes to Brüning's. This had unfortunate consequences for the republican cause, since the chancellor's deflationary fiscal policies aggravated the effects of the unusually severe and sustained depression. By early 1932 more than one in three wage earners was jobless, and Brüning had become the 'hunger chancellor' for millions of Germans. In the spring of that year Brüning played a major role in Hindenburg's reelection campaign and brought to the verge of success negotiations for an end to Germany's reparation payments to the victorious powers of World

War I. Nevertheless, prodded by conservative advisers, the president had become dissatisfied with the chancellor's unwillingness to bypass the Social Democrats in favor of rightist support. At the end of May 1932 Hindenburg curtly dismissed Brüning.

Instrumental in bringing about Brüning's fall was the man who by the spring of 1932 had become the president's closest adviser, General Kurt von Schleicher. A member of the minor nobility of western Germany rather than of the Junker aristocracy of the East that predominated in the upper echelons of the officer corps, Schleicher had nevertheless enjoyed a rapid rise as a career officer. Admitted at an early age to the army's elite brain trust, the General Staff, he spent most of World War I dealing with problems of supply and transportation that brought him into contact with civilian authorities. After the war he was pressed into service by the Defense Ministry as the army's liaison with the republican government. Since the essentially unreformed military establishment had managed to retain a large measure of autonomy from civilian control despite the republican revolution, this was a role of considerable importance.

By the end of the '20s Schleicher had established himself as an important behind-the-scenes figure in German politics. He had gained early promotion to the rank of general and presided over a special political affairs office subordinate only to the minister of defense. That arrangement placed him beyond the control of generals considerably superior to him in rank. It also led to his inclusion in the small circle of military leaders President von Hindenburg increasingly relied upon for political advice. In 1930 he was one of those who encouraged Hindenburg to break with the parliamentary system. Schleicher had a hand in selecting Brüning as the first presidential chancellor and then played a major role in driving him from office two years later.

At Schleicher's urging, Hindenburg appointed as Brüning's successor Franz von Papen, a politically obscure fifty-two-year-old aristocrat aligned with the extreme right wing of the Catholic Center Party. At the beginning of June 1932, Papen took office at the head of what quickly became known as the 'cabinet of barons' because of the predominance of conservative aristocrats among his ministers. Papen's qualification for the chancellorship was questionable, since he had no experience in national politics. As a Catholic Center deputy in the legislature of the federal state of Prussia during most of the republican period, he attended sessions infrequently and never took the floor to speak. He was, however, an old friend of Schleicher's, who had known him since their days as junior army officers. The general expected Papen to serve as an elegant figurehead who would rely on him for guidance. In order to be in a position to exert his influence within the new cabinet, Schleicher assumed the post of defense minister, resigning his general's commission and becoming, at least nominally, a civilian in order to qualify for the post.

Upon assuming the chancellorship, Papen faced the problem of finding political backing for his cabinet. Like Brüning, he had been appointed as a presidential chancellor, which put him in a position to govern by means of emergency decrees issued by Hindenburg. But he still needed to gain sufficient parliamentary backing to avoid a no-confidence vote in the Reichstag. In that respect, his position was from the outset far more precarious than Brüning's had been, for he promptly lost the support of his own party upon becoming chancellor. The leaders of the Catholic Center saw him as implicated in the ouster of their colleague Brüning and were outraged by his acceptance of the chancellorship without the party's permission. Only by resigning his party membership did he escape expulsion from the Catholic Center, which now disowned him and joined the opposition. In keeping with the president's wish for a break with the Left, Papen set out to replace his predecessor's reliance on the Social Democrats with support from the political Right. This meant courting the dynamic and rapidly growing Nazi movement led by Adolf Hitler.

Officially known as the National Socialist German Workers' Party since early 1920, the movement over which Hitler had soon thereafter gained control provided a political home after the First World War for socially marginal, racist nationalists who scorned both the old imperial regime and the new democratic republic. It remained an insignificant Bavarian fringe group until the notoriety resulting from Hitler's unsuccessful attempt in 1923 to overthrow the republic, the so-called beer hall putsch in Munich, helped it gain representation in the Reichstag the next year in alliance with similar groups. During the republic's period of prosperity and stability Nazism faded to insignificance, tallying 2.6 percent of the vote and winning 12 of 491 seats in the Reichstag in 1928 only by virtue of the republic's system of proportional representation. But when the Great Depression brought widespread privation and unemployment to Germany, the Nazis began to capitalize on the distress and anxiety of millions.

Unburdened by government responsibility, the Nazis gained popularity by blaming the republicans for all the country's ills and holding out the prospect of sweeping remedies without having to make good on any of their promises. They won the support of anti-Semites by conducting an unbridled campaign of slander against the small Jewish minority. In the streets of Germany they manifested their militancy through their stormtroop auxiliary, the SA. By engaging in bloody street battles with Social Democrats and Communists, each of which parties also maintained paramilitary organizations, the SA contributed to a violent political atmosphere that aroused the anxiety of many citizens. This enabled the Nazis to win over some voters by promising to restore order. In the election of 1930, held just as the effects of the economic crisis were becoming acute, their vote increased eightfold, giving them 107 of 577 Reichstag seats. In the spring of 1932 Hitler challenged Hindenburg for the presidency. Although he lost, he made a sufficiently strong showing to force a second round of balloting in which he tallied an impressive 36.1 percent.

By the summer of 1932 Hitler was Germany's most successful politician. This was an impressive achievement for someone who had arrived in Germany nineteen years earlier from Austria, a failed artist with minimal formal education, in flight from Vienna's shelters for homeless men, where he had been reduced to living for several years. From the moment Hitler joined the fledgling Nazi movement in 1919, after serving in the German army as a corporal on the western front, until his suicide a quarter century later in the ruins of Berlin, politics occupied the center of his life. He soon established himself as the party's leader—*Führer*—and gained absolute authority within it. Exercising a messiah-like hold over his followers, he forged a ragtag collection of radicals and reactionaries, intellectuals and thugs, unsuccessful professionals and restless war veterans, into a formidable organization that effectively combined charismatic leadership and bureaucratic discipline.

Nazism was no ordinary political party but rather, as Hitler tirelessly insisted, a movement that demanded total, unquestioning commitment on the part of its members. After his failed putsch landed him in prison for more than a year, Hitler emerged undaunted and rebuilt his shattered party. Abandoning hope of overthrowing the republic by force, he set out to do so legally, through the ballot box. During the latter half of the '20s, when economic stabilization enabled the embattled republic to consolidate under moderate political auspices, Hitler held the party together on the fringes of national politics by the sheer force of his personality. When the Great Depression brought anxiety and despair to millions, he built a mass following by means of unbridled demagogy and calculated mendacity.

The key to the future dictator's success lay in his own persona. Physically Hitler resembled, in the eyes of those who remained immune to his appeal, the popular stereotype of a barber or waiter. But by crafty manipulation of public perceptions—among other things by allowing himself to be portrayed only in flattering poses by an accomplished photographer dedicated to his cause—he constructed an image of himself that conveyed profundity and self-denying dedication to millions of troubled Germans. In action as a politician he radiated an extraordinary intensity of conviction and certitude that many found irresistible, particularly in unsettled times. Hitler's talents as an orator made him the greatest demagogue of his age. With a psychic energy unlike anything most contemporaries had encountered, he brought susceptible audiences to the brink of mass hysteria with lengthy, passionately delivered speeches that skillfully exploited their inse-curities and prejudices. In conversations with followers, he achieved much the same effect, overwhelming them with torrents of words and disarming them with his utter lack of self-doubt.

What ultimately made Hitler a formidable political threat was, however, his ability to mask his brutal fanaticism behind a facade of conventionality whenever that served his purposes. When he found it advantageous to cultivate the favor of influential persons, he could appear polite and deferential, even humble. When he sought to win over those he knew did not share his extremist views, he concealed his real intentions. By 1932 these characteristics had enabled Hitler to become a major force in German politics, even though he had never been elected to any governmental post.

In hopes of gaining Nazi support, Chancellor von Papen, with the concurrence of Schleicher, entered into what he took to be a deal with Hitler upon taking office in June 1932. When queried about cooperating with the new cabinet, the Nazi leader indicated his readiness to comply if two conditions were met: a lifting of the ban imposed on his stormtroopers by the Brüning cabinet and the disso-lution of the Reichstag elected in 1930 to clear the way for a new election, even though two years of the legislature's term remained. Papen at once gained President von Hindenburg's agreement to both requests. In addition, Papen seized upon an outbreak of bloody political violence between Nazis and Communists as a pretext to invoke the president's emergency powers and depose the govern-ment of Prussia. By far the largest of the seventeen federal states of the republic, Prussia was a major political factor, comprising as it did, three-fifths of Germany in terms of both area and population. The takeover of its government by the Papen cabinet rendered impotent the pro-republican Social Democratic–Catholic Center cabinet in Prussia, which had long been a thorn in the side of rightists, espe-cially the Nazis.

The new national election, which was held at the end of July 1932, proved a catastrophe for the moderate parties. It took place at the very nadir of the depression, when a combination of despair and anger made millions acutely vulnerable to extremist demagogy of the Right and Left. The Communists cut deeply into the strength of the Social Democrats, while the Nazis more than doubled their showing of 1930. Tallying 37.4 percent of the vote and winning 230 seats, Hitler's party now replaced the Social Democrats as the largest party in the Reichstag.

After the July election, Hitler reneged on his assurances of cooperation with the Papen cabinet and demanded the chancellorship for himself. Buoyed by his election triumph, the arch-foe of democracy now invoked democratic principles, contending that as leader of the strongest party in the parliament he had a right to head the government. Instead, Papen offered him the post of vice chancellor in his own cabinet, as well as ministerial posts for other Nazis. But recognizing that the vice chancellorship was an empty title that carried no constitutional authority, Hitler indignantly declined. When President von Hindenburg personally received the Nazi leader in mid-August and inquired whether he and other members of his party would be willing to enter Papen's cabinet, Hitler reiterated his demand for the chancellorship. Hindenburg, whose two previous meetings with the man he referred to in private as "the corporal" had left him profoundly mistrustful, rejected that demand in no uncertain terms. Moreover, his office released to the press a version of their meeting that dealt Hitler a public rebuke by giving the impression that the Nazi leader had demanded total power and by intimating that Hitler had broken a personal promise to the president to cooperate with the Papen cabinet. Neither Hindenburg's conscience nor his duties to the state would, according to the official announcement, permit the president to turn over power to a Nazi movement that was intent upon using it for partisan purposes. A furious Hitler responded by declaring all-out opposition to the Papen cabinet.

Hindenburg's rejection of Hitler's bid for power was reassuring to Germany's republicans. Most had supported the old field marshal's reelection in the spring, but only because no other candidate capable of defeating Hitler was available. They did so with misgiving, because of fears that Hindenburg's use of presidential emergency powers to circumvent the legislative authority of the Reichstag was eroding the constitution. Whereas the republicans had respected Chancellor Brüning, they were appalled by Hindenburg's appointment of Papen as chancellor of a reactionary cabinet with virtually no support in the Reichstag. The president's expression of willingness after the election to accord subordinate roles in the cabinet to Hitler and other Nazis aroused additional concern. Now, however, despite the Nazis' electoral triumph, Hindenburg had ruled out the possibility of Hitler's becoming chancellor, and the two had parted as political opponents. Republicans could therefore at least take consolation in the belief that, however far the president might stretch the constitution, he would never betray it by calling Adolf Hitler to the head of the government.

The trust republicans placed in Hindenburg would have been badly shaken if they had known what the president agreed to out of public view only two weeks after his rebuff of Hitler. The Nazi leader's declaration of opposition left the Papen cabinet facing a certain vote of no confidence when the new Reichstag convened. Papen had the backing of only one significant party, the reactionary German-Nationals, who had occasionally allied with the Nazis in the past but had broken with them acrimoniously over the presidential election and other issues. Altogether, less than 10 percent of the chamber stood behind Papen. There was even the possibility that negotiations under way between the Nazis and the Catholic Centrists, who together constituted a majority in the new Reichstag, might lead to a revival of the parliament's authority and yield a Catholic-Nazi coalition cabinet that would force Papen out of office. Hindenburg was nevertheless unwilling to part with Papen. At the end of August he therefore granted the chancellor's request for a decree that empowered Papen to dissolve the Reichstag at his discretion. Since another election could not be expected to produce a parliament of significantly different composition, the Papen cabinet also requested and obtained the president's agreement not to schedule a new round of balloting, which the constitution stipulated must take place within sixty days following the dissolution of the parliament. This would enable the cabinet to govern dictatorially by means of presidential decrees without fear that the Reichstag would rescind those decrees or adopt a vote of no confidence. In order to keep a cabinet of his choice in power, that is, Hindenburg gave his consent to a violation of the constitution he had sworn to uphold.

WHEN the new parliament convened in September, Chancellor von Papen's plan to circumvent the constitution was derailed by an unexpected turn of events. Papen intended to dissolve the chamber before it could vote no confidence, then have the president declare a state of emergency as justification for not scheduling another election. But when Papen sought to head off a vote on a Communist no-confidence motion by submitting the dissolution decree, the newly elected presiding officer of the Reichstag, Hermann Göring of the Nazi Party, ignored the chancellor and carried out the tally on the motion. The result was the most humiliating parliamentary defeat ever suffered by a German cabinet, with 512 deputies casting ballots in favor of the motion and only 42 supporting the Papen cabinet. Over Göring's protests, President von Hindenburg ruled afterward that the chamber had been legally dissolved by the chancellor before the no-confidence vote carried, but the damage had been done. With the vulnerability of the Papen cabinet now fully exposed, the chancellor and most of his ministers concluded that the time was not ripe for the risk-laden plan to violate the constitution. Instead, the second national parliamentary election of 1932 was scheduled for early November, well within the required sixty days.

The November election dealt a staggering blow to Hitler and his party. After an unbroken succession of dramatic gains over the previous three years, the Nazi juggernaut faltered. Many voters who had cast their ballots for the Nazis in July in the expectation that they would soon come to power and provide quick, decisive remedies to Germany's plight, defected in frustration at the failure of Hitler's bid for the chancellorship. Others became alienated when the Nazis dashed hopes for a broad, rightist, 'nationalist opposition' by denouncing the Papen cabinet as a reactionary clique and excoriating the German-Nationals for their support of the cabinet. Still others were appalled by the increasing violence of the Nazi stormtroopers. Some of those who had earlier found Hitler's party attractive because of its militant rejection of the parliamentary republic recoiled when the Nazis began invoking democratic principles in order to exploit their control over the largest bloc of Reichstag seats. Many conservative Germans who had voted for the Nazis in July took offense at their vitriolic agitation against not only Papen but also President von Hindenburg. Altogether, on election day more than two million fewer voters cast their ballots for the Nazis than in July. The party emerged with 196 of 584 seats in the new Reichstag, a loss of 34. It still commanded the strongest delegation in the parliament, but in what was to prove the last national election prior to Hitler's appointment as chancellor, more than two-thirds of the Germans who went to the polls rejected Nazism.

The outcome of the balloting of November 1932 eliminated the possibility of a Nazi-Catholic Reichstag majority, but the parliamentary situation otherwise remained basically the same. The bulk of those who deserted Hitler's party stayed home on election day rather than shifting their votes. Only the Communists appreciably increased their strength, emerging as the third-strongest party with 100 seats. Their gains came largely at the expense of the second-strongest party, the Social Democrats, the chief defenders of the republican cause. Still the largest party in terms of members, the Social Democrats saw their seats dwindle to 121. Together, the two leftist parties would have constituted a major political force, but they stood irreconcilably opposed to each other. At the direction of the Soviet Union, the Communists placed their highest priority on winning over the much larger following of the Social Democrats by denouncing them as 'social fascists' more inimical to the interests of workers than the Nazis.

The two Catholic parties, the Center and the Bavarian People's

Party, suffered marginal losses in November but together still commanded a bloc of 90 seats. Reduced to insignificance by heavy losses over the previous three years, the two liberal parties salvaged 13 seats between them, while splinter parties spawned by the republic's system of proportional representation held another 12. The German-Nationals, who were Papen's principal supporters, scored gains and emerged with 52 seats, mainly by profiting from disillusionment with the Nazis. But this did not alter the fact that nearly 90 percent of the voters who went to the polls in November again cast their ballots against Papen's cabinet. After consultations with party leaders confirmed this lack of support, Papen submitted his resignation but agreed to remain as chancellor on a caretaker basis.

When Hindenburg sounded out Hitler after the November election about the possibility of his party's participating in a cabinet, the Nazi leader indicated his readiness to seek the support of other parties if the president commissioned him to form a cabinet as chancellor. Assuming that no Reichstag majority could be found for a Hitler cabinet, Hindenburg engaged in a maneuver designed by his advisers to discredit the Nazi leader in the eyes of the public. Calling Hitler's bluff, the president asked him to report within three days whether he could find a workable majority in the Reichstag ready to support him as chancellor of a parliamentary cabinet. Hindenburg attached, moreover, a number of stipulations to that offer, including selection by himself of the defense and foreign ministers.

As expected, Hitler declined Hindenburg's proposal. The terms, he complained, were incompatible with the republican constitution, which assigned selection of cabinet ministers to the chancellor. As an alternative, he suggested that Hindenburg agree to appoint him chancellor and give him access to the emergency powers of the presidency if he could quickly present a satisfactory government program and an acceptable list of cabinet members, which would, he pledged, include Papen's conservative foreign minister and Schleicher as defense minister. As this proposal revealed, Hitler's real goal was to become a presidential, rather than a parliamentary, chancellor. As such, he would be free of dependence on a coalition with other parties and be able to govern by means of presidential emergency decrees, just as Brüning and Papen had done. Hitler's proposal was, however, ignored by the president and his advisers, so that he ceased to be a candidate for the chancellorship.

This second rebuff of Hitler by Hindenburg reinforced the growing belief among Germany's republicans that the venerable president would never turn over the chancellorship to Hitler. Especially heartening was the open letter the president's office sent to the Nazi leader to conclude the November negotiations. After clarifying the difference between parliamentary and presidential cabinets, the letter announced that the president "believes he cannot answer to the German people for giving presidential powers to the leader of a party that has over and over emphasized its exclusivity and has opposed him personally and the political and economic measures he has regarded as necessary. The president must under these circumstances fear that a presidential cabinet led by you would inevitably develop into a party dictatorship with all of its consequences for a heightening of the contradictions in the German nation, something he could never reconcile with his oath and his conscience." When the question of Hitler's possible appointment as chancellor arose again two months later, the defenders of the republican cause would take heart in recalling those words.

With Hitler's recalcitrance confirmed by late November, Papen stood ready to stay on as chancellor, although his political unpopularity had continued to increase. One member of his cabinet reportedly quipped that its motto had become "declarations of war accepted here!" The only success he could claim was the agreement of the victorious powers of the First World War to cancel Germany's reparation debts. Knowledgeable observers knew, however, that his predecessor, Chancellor Brüning, deserved most of the credit for that. At home, Papen's economic policies had thoroughly alienated organized labor. His cabinet had added to the hardships of those most victimized by the depression by reducing the level of unemployment compensation and subjecting applicants to a strict means test. Businesses, by contrast, were accorded tax relief and, as an incentive to hire more employees, were authorized to reduce wages set earlier by collective bargaining contracts. Papen's takeover of the Prussian state government had outraged the two principal parties that sought to defend the republic's institutions, the Social Democrats and the Catholic Centrists. These parties saw that move as an unconstitutional expansion of the national government's authority and smarted at losing control of patronage in the large Prussian civil bureaucracy.

Papen further compounded his unpopularity by publicly proclaiming dictatorship as his goal and endorsing proposals to alter the constitution so as to curtail its democratic character. As a result, he faced another humiliating no-confidence vote when the new chamber convened, should he be retained as chancellor. But, as Papen informed his cabinet in the last week of November, none of this mattered, since President von Hindenburg was "firmly resolved to take all measures that might become necessary" to support him. Hindenburg was again prepared, that is, to grant Papen a decree to dissolve the Reichstag without scheduling a new national election as required by the constitution. Once that step was taken, Papen could govern in dictatorial fashion by means of presidential decrees without having to answer to the parliament.

Whereas Papen enjoyed the support of the president, he had lost that of his patron and defense minister, Kurt von Schleicher. In selecting Papen for the chancellorship, Schleicher had assumed he would be able to control him for his own purposes. "I'm not the soul of the cabinet," he reportedly boasted, "but I am perhaps its will." The general was therefore unpleasantly surprised when his protégé displayed a mounting assertiveness after assuming office. To Schleicher's annoyance, Papen soon made himself increasingly independent of him by ingratiating himself with President von Hindenburg. By late November, although Schleicher had concurred in most of the Papen cabinet's policies, he had become apprehensive about the risks involved in keeping such a widely despised chancellor in office by circumventing the constitution. Forgoing a new election after a dissolution of the Reichstag, Schleicher feared, would unite virtually all the political forces of the country, including the legions of organized labor, in militant opposition to the government. Only weeks earlier, collaboration of the Nazis and the Communists in a transit strike in Berlin had sufficed to bring the capital to the brink of paralysis on the eve of the Reichstag election.

Concerned that Papen's reappointment might lead to civil war, Schleicher set about undermining the man he had made chancellor only six months earlier. At the same time, he made himself a candidate for that office by dissociating himself from the Papen cabinet's most unpopular policies in discussions with political and labor leaders. When Hindenburg nevertheless held to the plan to violate the constitution to keep Papen in office, Schleicher's efforts nearly failed. But he finally succeeded in turning the chancellor's own cabinet against him by revealing the results of a Defense Ministry study which concluded that the army would be unable to cope with a civil war that might pit both Communists and Nazis against the government. On December 2, 1932, an embittered Papen submitted his resignation to Hindenburg, who reluctantly accepted it. The next day, Schleicher was sworn in as chancellor, having received assurances of full support from the president. With only two exceptions, his cabinet consisted of his predecessor's ministers. He himself remained defense minister and also succeeded Papen as commissar for Prussia, a post created when that state's government had been stripped of its authority in July.

FIFTY years old at the time of his appointment, Kurt von Schleicher almost invariably made a strong impression on those who encountered him. He did so, moreover, despite an unprepossessing physical appearance. Of middling stature, he had a sallow complexion, was prematurely bald and tended to paunchiness in middle age. A lively and adept conversationalist, he excelled at winning over others in one-to-one exchanges, his preferred mode of communication. "He has the gift," one journalist observed, "of giving whoever visits him the impression that he completely shares their opinion." Through quickness of mind and a gift for turning a phrase, Schleicher also passed as something of a wit. He was a master at light banter and achieved humorous effects by salting his speech with slang expressions delivered in the rakish dialect of plebeian Berliners. Jaunty and buoyant of bearing, unfailingly optimistic and seemingly unflappable, he possessed a goodly portion of the nonchalant, dashing quality so admired among German officers.

Detractors regarded Schleicher as overbearing and supercilious, a cynical master of intrigue ruthlessly bent on self-advancement. His penchant for behind-the-scenes manipulation gave rise to references to the literal meaning of his family name, which translates into English as "creeper." His repeated abandonment of close associates in order to salvage his own position in times of crisis led to charges of untrustworthiness. What no one doubted was the general's self-confidence. In the spring of 1932, at a dinner party in a fashionable Berlin restaurant, he was overheard to exclaim in his penetrating nasal voice, "What Germany needs today is a strong man." Lest anyone fail to recognize who best fit that role, he tapped himself on the chest.

At once garrulous and reticent, Schleicher remained something of a political riddle as he took office. A republican journalist labeled him a "sphinx in uniform," and the dissident Russian Bolshevik Leon Trotsky once characterized him as "a question mark with the epaulettes of a general." But although many on the political Left as well as the Nazis denounced him as a reactionary, that label did not entirely fit him. Unlike many of his fellow officers, Schleicher neither mourned the overthrow of the Empire nor yearned for a restoration of the monarchy. On pragmatic grounds, he accepted the political realities created by the collapse of the old regime and its replacement by the republic. Recognizing that disputes about the form of government could only divide and weaken Germany, he had by the mid-'20s concluded: "Republic or monarchy is not the question now, but rather what should this republic look like." As was true of most military leaders, however, his loyalty lay not so much with the republic as with what he regarded as the abiding interests of the German state, which transcended particular regimes. For him, the army represented an independent force, above politics, whose function was to serve as a balance wheel, keeping the state on an even keel and ensuring its ability to defend Germany's security interests in the international sphere.

During his first weeks as chancellor in December 1932 Schleicher enjoyed something of a political honeymoon as a result of widespread relief at Papen's departure. By making it known that he had no intention of pursuing his predecessor's plans to alter the constitution, he calmed the defenders of the republic. The two Catholic parties adopted a conciliatory stance toward his cabinet. So did the leaders of the Christian trade unions, who were encouraged by promises on his part of decisive measures to put the unemployed back to work. The Social Democrats, who feared losses to the Communists if they collaborated with a military leader, retained an oppositional stance stiffened by their memory of Schleicher's involvement in the Papen cabinet's deposition of the Prussian state government led by one of their number. But the leaders of the Social Democrats' trade union affiliate, the country's largest, viewed Schleicher as a lesser evil than Papen and responded favorably to his pledges of measures against unemployment. Heartened by the positive responses from organized labor, the new chancellor concluded with relief that he had succeeded in dispelling the danger of a broad, popular revolt against the government that had developed under Papen. There remained, however, the problem of how to avoid a no-confidence vote by the Reichstag.

Schleicher placed his hopes for averting a collision with the parliament on gaining political backing from the Nazis. If their 196 Reichstag delegates supported him or at least refrained from opposition, that would be a major step toward blocking the formation of a hostile majority. Like most army officers, Schleicher admired the militaristic patriotism of Hitler's movement, even while disdaining its demagogic populism. The Nazis were, in his eyes, a useful if unruly counterpoise to the leftist parties. He regarded them, he confided to a friend earlier in the year, as "troublesome types" who had to be "enjoyed with the utmost caution." Like quite a few other prominent conservatives, including former chancellor Brüning, and even a number of respected Jewish figures, he believed the Nazis could be 'tamed' by saddling them with a share of governmental responsibility. But whereas others saw themselves reluctantly driven to that view and would have preferred the destruction of Nazism, Schleicher never seriously considered the latter option. Fearing that if the Nazi Party broke up, its most dynamic elements would flock to the Communists and greatly augment the strength of the revolutionary Left, he opposed repressive measures against Hitler's followers. "If they did not exist," he wrote to his friend, "it would be necessary to invent them."

Schleicher based his optimism about taming the Nazis in part on a parallel he saw with the history of an earlier mass revolutionary movement, the Social Democratic Party. The unsuccessful attempt by the architect of the German Empire, Chancellor Otto von Bismarck, to suppress that party a half-century earlier through persecution proved for Schleicher that repression only added to the militancy and popularity of mass-based radical movements. From the Social Democrats' moderation and declining popularity after they gained a share of power through the revolution of 1918 he concluded that the Nazis would be similarly moderated if they were brought into the government. Once they had to cope with the intractable realities of the economic crisis, he assumed they would become realistic, while their failure to make good on their exaggerated promises would cost them much of their mass support. Like the Social Democratic Party, Nazism would, if burdened with a share of responsibility for the often unavoidably unpopular measures of government, cease to be a rapidly growing militant movement that threatened the state and become instead just another political party. These expectations were grotesquely flawed, of course, by Schleicher's failure to recognize the vast difference between the republican Social Democrats and the totalitarian Nazis.

The Nazis also fit into Schleicher's plans in his capacity as defense minister. After lengthy negotiation with the victorious powers of World War I, Germany was on the verge of securing acceptance by those nations of the principle of armaments parity for Germany. Since there was no likelihood that the victors would join in the general disarmament foreseen by the Versailles Treaty, the achievement of parity would clear the way for realization of the German military's long-standing goal of expanding the armed forces. That had long been one of Schleicher's paramount projects, and he was resolved to start the process of rearmament as soon as possible. But rather than risk alarming the victors by suddenly increasing the size of the army, he intended to move toward universal conscription by creating a militia that would provide military training for large numbers of civilians. For the initial source of manpower, he looked to the paramilitary organizations that had proliferated since the war. Prominent among these unarmed but uniformed and regimented organizations was the Nazi SA. With over four hundred thousand stormtroopers in uniform by 1932, the SA outnumbered by a ratio of more than four to one the small army to which Germany was limited by the Versailles Treaty. In hopes of smoothing the way for an eventual recruitment of Nazi stormtroopers for his planned militia, Schleicher had for some time maintained covert contact with the leadership of the SA through his staff at the Defense Ministry.

Schleicher recognized that Hitler was the key to Nazi support and hoped to strike a deal with him. In several personal encounters over the previous two years, he had failed to discern that Hitler was an implacable fanatic, bent upon a radical transformation of Germany. After their first meeting, Schleicher described the Nazi leader as "an interesting man with unusual rhetorical gifts," who "gets easily carried away with his own plans." Even allowing for Hitler's skill at playing down or leaving unmentioned his fanatical anti-Semitism and other extremist views when talking with members of the conservative establishment, Schleicher's assessment betrayed a frivolous underestimation of the future dictator. The previous summer, following the Nazis' strong showing in the July Reichstag election, he had even been ready to see Hitler installed as chancellor until Hindenburg ruled that out. In late November, knowing of the president's willingness to accept the Nazi leader into the government in a subordinate capacity, he had sounded out Hitler about becoming vice chancellor in a Schleicher cabinet. But, as before, the Nazi leader had made it unmistakably clear that he would participate only in a cabinet he himself headed.

With Hitler unyielding, Schleicher turned his attention to the head of the Nazi Party's elaborate administrative apparatus, Gregor Strasser. A veteran leader whose popularity within the movement was second only to Hitler's, Strasser was regarded by many outside the party as the most reasonable Nazi leader. As an erstwhile pharmacist, he had practical business experience, something conspicuously rare among the top Nazis. In comparison with that assemblage of eccentrics and fanatics, he seemed a sober, levelheaded pragmatist. Because Strasser was widely regarded as a Nazi who took the word 'socialist' in the party's name seriously, he even commanded grudging respect in trade union circles. Schleicher could thus hope to collaborate with him without alienating organized labor. At the time, some observers erroneously concluded from Schleicher's interest in Strasser and his conciliatory gestures toward trade union leaders that the new chancellor was seeking to put together a 'labor axis' (*Querfront*) by splitting off the wing of the Nazi Party associated with Strasser and aligning it, along with organized labor, behind his cabinet. There is, however, no evidence to support this view, which has colored most interpretations of Schleicher's strategy ever since.

Strasser's well-known doubts about Hitler's all-or-nothing strategy made him potentially useful to Schleicher. More realistic than most prominent Nazis, Strasser had concluded from the outcome of the November election that the party was unlikely ever to gain sole control over the government by winning a majority through the ballot box. He therefore regretted that Hitler's refusal to settle for anything less than the chancellorship had prevented the Nazis from gaining a place in the Papen cabinet while their bargaining power had been strongest following the electoral triumph of the previous summer. Strasser's knowledge of conditions at the grassroots level of the party led him to forecast declining morale and mounting financial difficulties if the rank-and-file Nazi activists did not soon receive the rewards of at least a share of power. Under such conditions, he feared the party would suffer devastating losses if another confrontation with the cabinet led to dissolution of the Reichstag and a new election. Learning of Strasser's misgivings through intermediaries, Schleicher hoped to draw him into his cabinet. His goal was not, however, to split the Nazi movement, as some observers assumed, but rather to win the backing of the entire party.

On December 4, a day after taking office, Schleicher met secretly with Strasser in Berlin. Neither left any record of what they discussed, but circumstantial evidence indicates that Schleicher had in mind an elaborate scheme. Its key element was the minister-presidency of Prussia. Nazi and Communist gains in a state legislative election there the previous April had eliminated majority support for the Prussian cabinet led by Otto Braun, a prominent Social Democrat who had dominated that large state's politics throughout the republican period. Since the parties could not agree on a replacement, Braun's cabinet remained in office on a caretaker basis but was stripped of its authority in July by the Papen cabinet—with the concurrence of Schleicher. By the late autumn, it seemed possible that the Prussian impasse might be broken by formation of a new cabinet based on a majority coalition of Nazis and the Catholic Center Party. Strasser was frequently mentioned as minister-president of such a cabinet, since he was thought to be acceptable to the Catholics. If he became Prussian minister-president, Schleicher could offer to restore the authority of that office on condition that Strasser also enter the Reich cabinet. Such an arrangement would resolve the friction-ridden relationship between the Prussian and national governments that had led to the deposition of Braun's cabinet. It would also make it very difficult, if not impossible, for the Nazis to oppose a Schleicher cabinet in which one of their party's most prominent leaders sat.

Hitler swiftly scotched this scheme. He insisted that the Nazi candidate for the Prussian minister-presidency must be his obedient confidant Hermann Göring rather than Strasser. Göring was, however, unacceptable to both the Catholics and to Schleicher. To consider their next move, the leading Nazis met in Berlin on December 5, the eve of the new Reichstag's opening session. The day before, their party had suffered another crushing setback at the polls, this time in local elections in the state of Thuringia. There the Nazis lost nearly 40 percent of the votes they had tallied in the Reichstag election of July and almost a quarter of their reduced showing of November. Coming on top of losses in local balloting in three other states since the disastrous November Reichstag election, the Thuringian debacle provided compelling evidence that the party's support among the electorate was rapidly eroding.

In view of the Nazis' declining fortunes, Strasser argued at the meeting of Nazi leaders on December 5 in favor of cooperating with the Schleicher cabinet. The new chancellor had warned, he reported, that if he faced a hostile majority he would dissolve the new chamber. For the Nazis that would mean the third costly national election campaign within six months and, from all indications, bring more heavy losses. Unmoved by Strasser's arguments, Hitler held to his position of all-out opposition unless he himself became chancellor. Following the leadership meeting, Hitler took his case to a caucus of the Nazi Reichstag deputies. As a stony-faced Strasser looked on silently, Hitler denounced compromise as unworthy of the honor of the party. Rejecting democratic procedures as un-German, the Nazis did not reach decisions by majority votes, but by the close of the caucus it was clear that none of the deputies was willing to challenge the party leader. Even those who sympathized with Strasser submitted to Hitler's will. It was agreed to seek a respite by avoiding an immediate showdown with the Schleicher cabinet and accepting an early holiday recess of the new Reichstag. But the party's leadership ranks remained committed to Hitler's uncompromising course.

When the new Reichstag convened on December 6, the Nazis'

behavior heartened Schleicher, who did not know the extent to which Hitler had bested Strasser. At the opening session the Nazi deputies helped to defeat a Communist motion to make a vote of no confidence the first item of business. They then agreed to an abbreviated agenda that would permit the chamber to recess for a holiday truce of indefinite duration after only four days in session. The Schleicher cabinet raised no objections to the few bills on the agenda, which included an amnesty for persons convicted of political violence and recision of an emergency decree issued by the Papen cabinet that had particularly offended labor. On December 7, Schleicher confidently predicted to his cabinet that the Nazis would refrain from opposing him. He held out the prospect of a Reichstag majority consisting of Nazis, the two Catholic parties, and a group of splinter parties that would acquiesce in the cabinet's governing by means of presidential emergency decree. Such an arrangement would functionally replicate the formula by which former chancellor Brüning had governed for two years, but with the vital difference that whereas Brüning had relied on the republican Social Democrats, Schleicher now proposed to rely on the Nazis.

The day after Schleicher's prediction to his cabinet, December 8, Hitler was staggered by receipt of a letter from Gregor Strasser announcing his resignation as head of the party's organizational apparatus. The immediate reason Strasser gave was Hitler's obstruction of his efforts to tighten his administrative authority over Nazism's regional units. But Strasser also revealed that he was no longer willing to go along with the party leader's all-or-nothing strategy, which he characterized as akin to a wager on chaos. It was time, he maintained, to accept a share of power by becoming part of a broad-based, constructive national front. Strasser nevertheless assured Hitler that he remained a loyal member of the party and had no intention of becoming the focus of opposition within it. To discourage any such expectations, he announced that he was leaving Berlin and going abroad. His assurances were thrown into question, however, when Hitler learned that before submitting his letter Strasser had denounced Hitler's all-or-nothing strategy at a meeting with a group of senior Nazi officials and warned that if they waited until their leader captured the chancellorship on his terms, the party would collapse. Also, within hours Hitler received a similar letter from another veteran Nazi, the economic theorist Gottfried Feder, who had been instrumental in Hitler's entry into politics. The vaunted unity that had been one of the key elements of Nazism's success seemed to be crumbling.

In the face of these developments, Hitler came as close to panicking as he ever did. Having by that time heard reports that Strasser had met secretly with Schleicher and been offered the vice chancellorship, he feared there might be truth to rumors that his erstwhile lieutenant intended to join the cabinet and split the party by taking his followers with him. "If the party falls apart," a shaken Hitler confided to his future propaganda minister, Joseph Goebbels, "I'll finish myself off with a pistol within three minutes." Assembling the Nazi officials who had heard Strasser's denunciation of his strategy earlier in the day, he delivered an impassioned appeal to their loyalty. The consequence of disobedience on the part of his followers, he intimated, would be his suicide.

This melodramatic performance quelled whatever wavering Strasser might have occasioned among the senior Nazi officials, who unanimously reaffirmed their loyalty to Hitler. Bolstered by their support, Hitler brought the Nazi Reichstag deputies to heel on the afternoon of December 8 with a similar harangue. In an effort to discourage speculation about a breakup of the party, he released to the press a statement in which he announced that he had, at Strasser's request, granted him sick leave for three weeks. To Hitler's relief, there were no further defections. Just as he had promised in his letter, Strasser departed for a vacation in northern Italy. For the remainder of the year he would remain out of public view and refrain from political activity. Deserted by Strasser, Gottfried Feder quickly recanted and was readmitted to the Nazi fold. Hitler himself took over as Strasser's successor at the head of the party's bureaucracy and installed men subservient to him in key positions. To bolster morale, he hurried about the country, speaking to gatherings of Nazi functionaries.

Although Hitler's worst fears had not materialized, Strasser's defection was just one of many signs that the would-be dictator's fortunes were ebbing as 1932 drew to a close. Because of his unwillingness to settle for anything but the chancellorship, he was further from power than he had been during the summer, when his party's strength had reached its peak. The heavy election losses since then revealed increasing disillusionment among those Germans whose votes had made him a major political factor. The high office he sought was in the hands of a general who had long been a confidant of the ultimate arbiter of power, President von Hindenburg. He himself had twice been emphatically denied the chancellorship by the president, who had taken a pronounced dislike to him.

To add to Hitler's woes, the economic depression that had propelled him to prominence had begun to wane. Since the spring, the value of shares and bonds traded on the Frankfurt stock market had risen by over 30 percent. "The slump has ended," observed Germany's most prestigious economic research institute at the close of 1932, "and the bottoming out has taken place, following which a new upswing can begin." "Land in Sight!" proclaimed a headline in the business section of the New Year's edition of the *Frankfurter Zeitung*. As 1933 opened, Hitler seemed politically isolated, with no tangible results to show for a year of frenetic political activity, and losing ground with Germany's voters. He had reached a low point that seemed fully to justify the optimism reflected in the New Year's editorials of republican journalists. As Goebbels gloomily noted in his diary, "1932 has been one long streak of bad luck."

2

A Conspiracy
against the Chancellor
Is Hatched

O N   T H E   E V E N I N G   O F   New Year's Day 1933 Adolf
Hitler attended a performance of Richard Wagner's opera
Die Meistersinger von Nürnberg at Munich's Court Theater
under the baton of the celebrated conductor Hans Knappertsbusch. In
his youth, Hitler had become a passionate Wagnerian with an insatia-
ble appetite for the composer's operas. This later brought him to the
attention of the Wagner family, who welcomed him as a kind of
political mascot at the festivals of the master's music in Bayreuth. In a
country justifiably proud of its musical heritage, that association lent
the Nazi leader an aura of high culture seldom, if ever, enjoyed by
German politicians. Hitler's enthusiasm for Wagner's operas also
helped to gain him access, early in his political career, to well-to-do,
aesthetically inclined reactionary circles in Munich. It was at social
gatherings in the homes of these patrons that he learned how to
comport himself in polite society and how to dress for formal occasions. And it was by mixing with the cultural elite of the Bavarian
capital that he acquired a sufficient veneer of refinement to make him

appear a plausible candidate for high political office in the eyes of many Germans, despite his humble origins and minimal formal education.

Following the performance of *Die Meistersinger,* Hitler joined a New Year's celebration at the home of one of his wealthy patrons, the Munich art dealer Ernst "Putzi" Hanfstaengl, a Harvard College graduate who had become an active Nazi. Hitler was the star attraction, the other guests having obviously been invited to please him. These included two of the rough-and-ready attendants who served him as bodyguards and factotums, his personal photographer Heinrich Hoffmann, and his party secretary Rudolf Hess, who was accompanied by his wife. Rounding off the gathering were several young, single women Hanfstaengl and his wife had invited, knowing how Hitler enjoyed being surrounded by attractive but unassertive members of the opposite sex. One of these that evening was Eva Braun, the pert blonde assistant in Hoffmann's studio who later became Hitler's mistress during his years as dictator until their marriage minutes before they committed suicide in April 1945. Gathered about Hanfstaengl's hearth over coffee, this assemblage listened to a phonograph recording of a Rachmaninoff piano concert and conversed until the early hours of the morning, with Hitler contributing a critique of Knappertsbusch's direction of the evening's opera. Hanfstaengl later recounted that, as Hitler was signing the guest book before leaving, the Nazi leader "looked up at me and said in a tone of suppressed excitement: 'This year belongs to us. I will guarantee you that in writing'."

By January 1933 Hitler was, at forty-three, a quite prosperous man. Royalties from sales of his best-selling book *Mein Kampf* provided him with a substantial income that was supplemented by gifts from wealthy patrons. He resided in a large, comfortable apartment in a fashionable district of Munich. The headquarters of the once obscure party he had joined as an unknown ex-Bavarian army corporal occupied a lavishly appointed neo-Renaissance palace prominently located in the center of the city the Nazis referred to as the "capital of the movement." He traveled about in an expensive Mercedes-Benz limousine, driven by his own chauffeur. His frequent holidays were spent at a picturesque chalet he owned in the Bavarian alps. On his numerous and often prolonged visits to Berlin, he resided with his retinue of attendants in the ornate Kaiserhof Hotel in the center of the capital, half a block from the Reich Chancellory. Free of fixed obligations, Hitler lived a self-indulgent, semi-bohemian existence. Rarely rising before noon, he habitually lingered long over afternoon coffee and cake at stylish cafés, surrounded by slavish retainers and fawning admirers. His evenings were frequently spent in choice seats at the opera or as guest of honor in the homes of wealthy admirers like Hanfstaengl. He led, in short, a life of ease and luxury that most Germans could only dream of in those depression-ridden times.

Despite the setbacks of 1932, Hitler was still potentially in a position to wield considerable political influence as the new year began. Even after his party's heavy losses in the November election, it commanded the largest delegation in the Reichstag and was backed by its pugnacious stormtrooper legions. As Hitler had repeatedly been given to understand, high positions in the government and great influence over its policies awaited him and other Nazi leaders. All he had to do was renounce his demand for the chancellorship and agree to share power with the conservatives placed in charge of the state by President von Hindenburg.

Sharing power was, however, impossible for Hitler. No ordinary politician, he was a fanatic with a grandiose sense of mission. He saw himself destined to become nothing less than the creator of a radically new Germany. To achieve a mission of that magnitude, only absolute power, free from all compromise with others, would suffice. From the time he joined the fledgling Nazi movement in 1919 until his suicide a quarter century later, pursuit of that mission consumed Hitler. With little by way of a private life, he sublimated the normal human drives by single-mindedly pursuing what he unquestioningly believed was the destiny foreordained for him by what he referred to as "providence." Incapable of imagining a reality that did not conform to his vision of the future, Hitler proceeded through life, as he himself put it, "with the certainty of a sleepwalker."

Hitler's vision of Germany's future derived from the dark subcurrents of nineteenth-century thought. An autodidact who read voraciously in newspapers and inexpensive popular publications during the idle years of his youth in Vienna and Munich, he would later impress many better educated persons with his command of an impressive range of information, particularly about history. His vigorous, retentive mind was, however, disciplined by neither systematic analysis nor self-skepticism. As a result, he uncritically imbibed many pseudoscientific notions then in circulation. These he shaped into a worldview that guided his thinking throughout his career. It amalgamated the social Darwinist doctrine of a struggle to the death for survival with the racialist proposition that humanity was irrevocably segmented into mutually hostile ethnic groups. The world was, for him, a jungle, where might made right and races either prevailed and grew stronger or weakened and perished. From this, he drew the conclusion that mortal combat between races was a dictate of nature, its way of assuring progress of the species. In his eyes war thus seemed not only unavoidable but ennobling.

Hitler had no doubts about which ethnic group must triumph in this all-out struggle for survival. Steeped in bogus ethnological doctrines then popular in Central Europe, he believed that the Germans belonged to an 'Aryan' master race. As he saw it, they could realize their high destiny only by crushing the lesser peoples who stood in their way, the most dangerous being the Jews, who had, he was convinced, infiltrated German society and were undermining it. Germany was, in his eyes, doomed if it succumbed to the alien and debilitating doctrine of democracy, which recognized Jews as citizens and accorded decisive political power to the ignorant masses. Another source of debility was for him Marxism, a doctrine that enfeebled the German people by fragmenting it into mutually hostile classes. National Socialism's goal was therefore to unite the German nation under a new racially pure elite, headed by himself, that would establish its right to total power by vanquishing all other political forces and destroying the democratic republic. Once the elements that had weakened the nation were eliminated, the new leadership would rid the country of ethnic impurities, launch an all-out war to establish dominance over Europe, and ensure Germany's future growth for the next millennium through the conquest of 'living space' in the fertile regions of Russia.

By the early '30s Hitler had ceased to trumpet these megalomanic plans in public, although evidence of them could be found in the turgid pages of *Mein Kampf,* which few members of the German political elite bothered to read. After the failure of his attempt at a putsch in 1923, he had pursued power by using the extensive civil and political liberties guaranteed by the republic's democratic constitution in order to destroy democracy itself. Since this entailed attracting as many voters as possible, he found it expedient, in his public statements, to conceal his ultimate aims. Pledging to seek power through the constitution and dampening even his virulent anti-Semitism, Hitler increasingly concentrated his fire on the republicans. They had, he charged, traitorously sold out the German people to Marxism and to the victorious wartime enemies that had imposed the Versailles Treaty on the country.

By 1930 Hitler had recognized that he could not succeed in the face of opposition from the entire political establishment. He therefore sought to mollify the military leadership by asserting personal control over the strong-arm auxiliary of his party, the SA, and thwarting its leaders' ambitions to infiltrate the army with the goal of ultimately taking it over. He also set out to harness for his own purposes the hostility toward the republic of other rightist forces. As the Nazis' electoral strength grew, they gained entry into several state governments by joining in coalitions with conservatives. Those arrangements proved unsatisfactory from Hitler's viewpoint, however. They left his party dependent upon coalition partners who could limit its influence on personnel and policy and, by withdrawing their support, drive it from government. Other attempts to find allies also yielded disappointing results, mainly because of Hitler's imperious claims to primacy.

Such setbacks did not daunt Hitler. He occasionally experienced black moments, as when his chief lieutenant Gregor Strasser deserted him in December 1932, but he never lost his messianic conviction that he was destined to become Germany's absolute ruler. His relentless drive for power was fueled as well by a sense of urgency arising from the fear—fed by chronic hypochondria—that he might not live long enough to accomplish his historic mission. "I have no time to wait!" he explained to a follower. "I can't lose another year. I must get power soon in order to accomplish my gigantic tasks in the time remaining to me. I must! I must!" The many attempts to probe Hitler's mind retrospectively have produced a bewildering array of inconclusive, conflicting diagnoses. But whatever the wellsprings of his mentality may have been, he was drawn onward throughout his strange political career by the unshakable conviction that reality would eventually conform to his will. He was, in his own eyes, a man of destiny.

Despite the setbacks he had suffered during 1932, Hitler approached the new year defiantly resolved to hold to his all-or-nothing course. He spent the last days of December at his alpine retreat, dictating a New Year's statement and then reading it aloud to Joseph Goebbels and other members of his retinue to get their reactions. Its primary purpose was to provide a defense of the all-or-nothing strategy that had left him empty-handed at the end of 1932. With the shrewdness that made him such a formidable political tactician, Hitler gave his analysis of the motives that had led President von Hindenburg in November to offer him the chancellorship if he could muster a majority coalition in the Reichstag: "They want to give us a share of government, burden us with responsibility, but withhold from us a really decisive role. . . . For if our opponents invite us to take part in such a government, then they do it not with the intention of slowly and gradually giving us power but rather in the expectation that they will thereby forever wrest power from us."

Hitler's pronouncement left no doubt about his determination to hold to the same course in the new year. "Any compromise," he warned, "bears within it the seeds of destruction of the party and therefore of Germany's future. . . . I am unalterably resolved not to purchase the thin gruel of participation in a cabinet by selling out our movement's entitlement to power." Without mentioning Gregor Strasser by name, he likened those Nazis who favored settling for a mere share of power to the "traitors on the home front" who had, he alleged, at the end of World War I led the Germans to believe they would receive a just peace settlement from the treacherous foreign foes who then imposed the Versailles Treaty. Goebbels, who enthusiastically endorsed his leader's no-compromise strategy, extolled the pronouncement in his diary: "Scathing toward the defeatists . . . Struggle to the knife . . . Radical to the utmost."

ALTHOUGH on New Year's Day Hitler's defiant "Battle Message for 1933" dominated the front page of his party's newspaper, *Völkischer Beobachter,* the Nazis were not ready for an early showdown with the Schleicher cabinet. This became evident on January 4, when the Reichstag's agenda committee met to decide when to reconvene the chamber. Attending the meeting on behalf of the cabinet, Schleicher's chief chancellory aide, Erwin Planck, struck a confident pose. The cabinet was prepared, he announced, to appear before the Reichstag at any time in order to state its policies. When that time came, Planck added, the cabinet would expect a clarification of the political situation on the part of the chamber and would oppose another adjournment before votes were taken on no-confidence motions. In response to this challenge, the spokesmen of the Communists and the Social Democrats presented motions calling for resumption of the chamber's sessions early the following week. Since those parties had already gone on record in favor of a no-confidence vote, they thus indicated their determination to topple the cabinet. By contrast, the Nazi spokesmen showed no interest in a quick test of strength. They proposed leaving the decision on when to reconvene to the presiding officer of the Reichstag, the Nazi Hermann Göring, an arrangement that predictably found no support from any other party.

The reason for the Nazis' lack of eagerness to reconvene the

Reichstag seemed obvious to observers outside the party. An early meeting of the parliament would predictably result in no-confidence motions. Given the Nazis' denunciations of the Schleicher cabinet, they would have to support those motions or lose all credibility. If, as all signs indicated would be the case, the chancellor then responded by dissolving the Reichstag elected in November, the Nazis would face the daunting prospect of further losses in a new election. Anxious to stave off that possibility, the party's spokesmen on the agenda committee therefore withheld their votes from the motions of the Communists and Social Democrats, both of which failed. The issue was finally resolved when the spokesmen of the two leftist parties backed a Catholic Center Party motion to reconvene the parliament on January 24, with the proviso that the agenda committee meet again to review the matter on January 20.

That same day, January 4, Hitler arrived in the Rhenish university town of Bonn early in the morning by overnight train from Munich, accompanied by several other prominent Nazis. This destination left his press secretary, Otto Dietrich, baffled. He had been informed that the purpose of Hitler's trip was to deliver speeches in the campaign for the local legislative election in the tiny state of Lippe, which lay considerably to the north and east of Bonn and would have been more easily reached by a different rail route. The traveling group was met at the Bonn station by Hitler's large chauffeured Mercedes-Benz limousine and driven to one of his favorite hostelries, the Hotel Dreesen in nearby Bad Godesberg, for breakfast. Disclosing nothing about his intentions, Hitler, accompanied by three of his companions, was then picked up by a second car with drawn shades. His destination remained unknown to Dietrich and the others, who followed his instructions to proceed northward later with his limousine to a point on a highway two miles north of the city of Cologne, where they were to await him.

That afternoon the car that had picked up Hitler and his three companions delivered them to the specified rendezvous point. From the conversation on the drive to Lippe, Otto Dietrich later recounted, it could be assumed that a meeting with some important political figure had been the cause of Hitler's secretive behavior. Indeed, what had happened would soon occasion a national sensation, for the politician in question had, only a few months earlier, been the target of some of the Nazis' most vitriolic invective. He was former chancellor Franz von Papen.

Papen's background made him an unlikely candidate for a crucial role in high politics. Descended from a venerable but obscure Catholic noble family from Westphalia in western Germany, he, like his grandfather and father, had initially embarked upon a military career. An accomplished horseman who excelled as a steeplechase rider, Papen trained as a cavalry officer before attending the Berlin War Academy and gaining admission in 1913 to the General Staff. In the course of his military career he befriended his fellow officer Kurt von Schleicher, who was three years younger than he. Through family connections Papen met and married the daughter of a successful manufacturer whose wealth enabled the young officer to travel widely and become fluent in both English and French. Assigned to the German embassy in Washington, D.C., as military attaché shortly before war broke out in 1914, Papen gained notoriety when he was expelled from the United States a year later for complicity in attempts to foment strikes by workers of German and Austrian origin at American factories producing armaments for sale to the British and French. During the war he served on the western front and with the German forces that fought alongside the Turks against the British in Palestine. By the end of the war he had risen to the rank of major.

After the revolution of 1918–19 Papen aligned himself politically with a reactionary, agrarian minority in the Catholic Center Party that disapproved of the party's participation in republican coalition governments with the Social Democrats. In 1921 he gained election to the Prussian state parliament as the deputy for a rural constituency in Westphalia which reelected him for another four-year term in 1924. Backed by the financial resources of conservative Catholic noblemen, he gained control of his party's newspaper in the capital, *Germania*. He moved in aristocratic social circles in Berlin but played no prominent political role until Schleicher secured his appointment as chancellor in June 1932. The Catholic Center's hostile break with Papen after he accepted that office without its leadership's permission left him without the support of a party.

Describing in his memoirs the reaction to the news of Papen's appointment as German chancellor, the French ambassador, André François-Poncet, wrote: "No one wanted to believe it, and then, when the news was confirmed, everyone either laughed or smiled." The ambassador, who knew Papen at first hand, described him tellingly: "He has the distinction of not being taken at all seriously either by his friends or his enemies. His face bears the mark of an ineradicable frivolity of which he has never been able to rid himself. As for the rest, he is not a personality of the first rank. . . . He is regarded as superficial, mischief-making, deceitful, ambitious, vain, crafty, given to intrigue. One quality he clearly possesses: cheek, audacity, an amiable audacity of which he seems unaware. He is one of those persons who shouldn't be dared to undertake a dangerous enterprise because they accept all dares, take all bets. If he succeeds, he bursts with pleasure; if he fails, he exits with a pirouette."

Following his initial meeting with Chancellor von Papen in November 1932, the Swiss envoy in Berlin wrote: "I left Herr von Papen with the impression of having spoken with a really glib man who cannot be blamed if one gets bored in his presence. Whether this should be the principal trait of the man who today governs Germany is, to be sure, another question." After a conversation with Papen during January 1933, the British ambassador, Sir Horace Rumbold, expressed "the wonder of an observer that the destinies of this great country should have been, even for a short time, in charge of such a light weight." Konrad Adenauer, the first chancellor of the postwar West German republic, who first met Papen in the early '20s as a fellow Center Party politician, later recalled: "I always gave him the benefit of mitigating circumstances in view of his enormous limitations."

Despite these unflattering assessments, Papen cut a fine figure in Berlin society circles. There his impeccable manners and his cosmopolitan flair combined with his linguistic facility and endless store of light conversation to make him sought after. Those qualities also won him admission to the circle of officers that included Kurt von Schleicher, and the two spent many leisure hours together during the latter's rise to prominence. Within that group Papen was frequently addressed as "Fränzchen," a playfully condescending diminutive. As ambassador François-Poncet observed, "Papen sometimes served as the butt of their jokes; they enjoyed making fun of him and teasing him, without his taking offense."

After his elevation to the chancellorship, Papen quickly ingratiated himself with President von Hindenburg. Among the numerous contemporaries who noticed this was Ambassador François-Poncet. In his memoirs he observed: "It's he who is the preferred one, the favorite of the marshal; he diverts the old man through his vivacity, his playfulness; he flatters him by showing him respect and devotion; he beguiles him with his daring; he is in [Hindenburg's] eyes the perfect gentleman." Only with great reluctance and a tearful scene did the president part with Papen at the end of his chancellorship. In a break from past practice with departing chancellors, Hindenburg expressed his sense of loss in a personal letter to Papen and presented him with an autographed photograph of himself embellished in his own hand with the refrain from a well-known sentimental soldier's song about a fallen comrade.

The friendship between Schleicher and Papen came under increasing strain during the latter's chancellorship and ended with his fall at the hands of his patron. The general had proposed Papen for that high office in the belief that he would be able to control him. His personal opinion of his protégé's abilities was not high. When, upon Papen's appointment, an acquaintance of both men pointed out to Schleicher that his choice for the chancellorship was not renowned for having a good head on his shoulders, the general reportedly responded: "He doesn't need a head; he's a hat!" The assertiveness that

Papen began to display once he was in office therefore surprised and annoyed Schleicher. On one occasion, after talking with Chancellor von Papen on the telephone in his capacity as defense minister, the general turned to his aides and quipped in rueful fashion: "What do you say about that, Fränzchen has discovered himself."

After engineering Papen's fall and taking his place as chancellor, Schleicher sought to mollify his discarded protégé. In a December radio address to the nation, he praised his predecessor as a "knight without fear or blemish." In a New Year's telegram he extended felicitations to "my dear Fränzchen," apostrophizing him as "the banner-bearer in decisive battles of the old year." But although Papen concealed his feelings behind outward forms of cordiality, friendship on his side had given way to seething enmity toward the man who had propelled him into the limelight and then discarded him.

Having tasted power, Papen wanted it again. He also thirsted for revenge against his former friend and patron Schleicher. Counting on Hindenburg's continuing affection, Papen saw himself returning to office and realizing the mission the president had originally assigned him by becoming chancellor of a cabinet that would unite conservatives and Nazis. In pursuit of that goal he had, during the final stages of his chancellorship, established communications with the Nazi leadership through intermediaries. By way of enticement, he led them to believe that he would be willing to see the leadership of a rightist cabinet eventually assigned to Hitler. Knowing of Hindenburg's outspoken aversion to the Nazi leader, Papen could assume that a Hitler chancellorship would never come to pass. That would leave Nazi support for his return to the chancellorship as the only feasible means to achieve a rightist cabinet of the sort the president wanted.

In mid-December Papen glimpsed an opportunity to arm himself for a political comeback. Following a speech to the exclusive Gentlemen's Club of Berlin—the Herrenklub—in which he expressed regret that attempts to form a cabinet including the Nazis had failed, he fell into conversation with one of the audience, Baron Kurt von Schröder, a banker from Cologne and a Nazi sympathizer. Papen revealed to Schröder his resentment toward Schleicher. The ex-chancellor reported, moreover, that the general's underhanded methods had offended Hindenburg, whereas he himself still enjoyed the confidence of the president. Despite the Nazis' attacks on him during his chancellorship, Papen indicated to the banker his readiness to meet with Hitler.

These disclosures by Papen set in motion the developments that led to his meeting with Hitler in Cologne on January 4, 1933. Baron Schröder at once telephoned news of what Papen had told him to a Nazi intermediary, who then conveyed the report to Hitler. The Nazi leader recognized in the unexpected proposal a chance to escape from the political dead end he had reached. By conspiring with Papen he could hope to make use of the former chancellor's influence with President von Hindenburg for his own purposes. It was even conceivable that Papen might be an emissary from the president. But regardless of who was behind the invitation, it opened enticing possibilities. Beforehand, Hitler's only available move was to have his party join in a vote of no confidence against the Schleicher cabinet when the Reichstag reconvened. If, as expected, a majority ranging from Nazis to Communists supported such a move, thereby bringing about a dissolution of the chamber and new parliamentary elections, he had to face the very real possibility of further losses at the polls. But if, with Papen's help, he could become chancellor before a new election, he would escape from his predicament and attain his goal. If that could be accomplished, he need no longer fear another round of national balloting. Indeed, an election campaign conducted with the formula 'Hindenburg-Hitler' promised handsome gains.

Hitler therefore agreed to meet with the former chancellor. During the last week of December intermediaries for the two men made arrangements for a rendezvous at Schröder's residence in Cologne. That location fit the travel plans of the two former political enemies and also promised to facilitate the secrecy insisted upon by the Nazis. At first, Hitler's intermediary specified to Schröder that the meeting take place after dark so as to minimize the danger of detection, but it was finally set for midday on Wednesday, January 4, to accommodate Hitler's travel schedule. Upon arriving at Baron von Schröder's palatial townhouse, the two former political foes were closeted for several hours. Their host sat in on much of their conversation but took no part, while Hitler's three companions waited elsewhere in the house.

According to Schröder's later account, Hitler at once took the offensive by raising a number of old grievances. With particular bitterness he upbraided Papen for having led President von Hindenburg to deny him the chancellorship despite his party's triumph in the Reichstag election of the previous July. Reversing the facts, Papen responded that Schleicher, not he, had been responsible for blocking Hitler's appointment, whereas he had favored it. As Hitler disclosed to Goebbels a few days later, Papen revealed an implacable hostility toward Schleicher. "He wants to bring about his fall and get rid of him completely," Goebbels noted in his diary. Papen also informed Hitler that the president had reservations about Schleicher and had not yet provided him with a decree authorizing him to dissolve the Reichstag. Most importantly, Papen gave Hitler to understand that he himself still exercised influence over Hindenburg. As Goebbels put it after hearing Hitler's report: "He has the old man's ear."

When Papen and Hitler turned to the future, they identified a broad area of accord. They quickly established that they were of one mind about the need to replace the Schleicher cabinet with one based on an alliance of Nazis and nationalistic conservatives that would suppress the leftist parties once and for all. Since Papen was a man without a party who could muster at most the same small bloc of rightist Reichstag deputies who had supported his own ill-fated cabinet, no parliamentary majority was in sight for such an alliance, so that it would be feasible only as a presidential cabinet. On that count, Papen assured Hitler that he was confident of gaining the president's consent for such an arrangement.

The two could not, however, resolve the question of who should preside over such a cabinet as chancellor. Invoking President von Hindenburg's well-known resistance to appointing Hitler, Papen urged the Nazi leader to abandon his demand for the chancellorship and delegate some of his trusted lieutenants to represent him in a cabinet headed by Papen as chancellor. As enticement, he gave Hitler to understand that he would accept Nazi ministers of defense and the interior. Since those two ministries exercised command over the armed forces and federal law enforcement, control over them would place the Nazis in a formidable position. Nevertheless, Hitler stubbornly insisted that his party's mass backing entitled him to the chancellorship. After some discussion of a "duumvirate" formula whereby Hitler and Papen would share power, the two politicians ended their exchange inconclusively when Schröder announced that lunch awaited them. Before they parted, Papen and the Nazi leader agreed to continue their consultation, although without setting a specific date.

The Hitler-Papen meeting in Cologne had momentous consequences, for it ended Hitler's political isolation. With one stroke, his flagging fortunes received an enormous boost. He had been on the downslope, the leader of a party that had risen meteorically but seemed to have missed its opportunity for a share of power, with divisive and debilitating effects on its ranks. He had seemed without prospects for attaining his goal of total power. He had shown no readiness to consider any strategy beyond dogged adherence to his demand for the chancellorship on his own terms, an arrangement that the president had already twice emphatically rejected. Now, however, he emerged from the meeting with Papen a major factor in a drastically altered political constellation. He had at last breached the protective ring of advisers that had previously shielded the ultimate arbiter of power—President von Hindenburg—from him. He now had an offer of alliance from a former chancellor whose policies in office had won him the admiration of influential conservative circles and the affection of the head of state.

Hitler gained much important information in his conversation with Papen on January 4. He now knew that the ex-chancellor, despite their differences in the past, was prepared to collaborate with him. He learned as well that Papen hated his erstwhile patron, Chancellor von Schleicher, and hoped to destroy him politically. In future dealings with Papen, Hitler could expect to rely on the ancient adage according to which the enemy of one's enemy is one's friend. He now also had grounds to believe that Schleicher's position might not be as impregnable as it appeared. Indeed, if Papen's information should prove correct, the chancellor was on very shaky ground. For if Hindenburg had in fact not provided Schleicher with a decree authorizing him to dissolve the Reichstag, the chancellor would be in grave jeopardy in the event of a vote of no confidence when the chamber reconvened. Most important of all, Papen's boast of influence over Hindenburg gave Hitler hope for the first time of a channel through which the president's objections to him might be overcome. The chancellorship, the goal that had grown ever more elusive during the previous months, once again seemed within Adolf Hitler's reach.

The Cologne meeting also revived the political fortunes of Franz von Papen. He had come to Baron Schröder's house a failed former chancellor whose brief term in office had left him with a few admirers but with many more political enemies, while costing him the support of his own party. He emerged from the meeting with hopes of using the country's most dynamic mass political movement to exact revenge against the man who had elevated him to power only to strip him of it. To be sure, Hitler's continuing unwillingness to forgo the chancellorship posed an obstacle to Papen's ambition to regain that office. But on that count he could hope that the Nazi leader would eventually back down in the face of President von Hindenburg's repeatedly demonstrated unwillingness to appoint him. As to his own reappointment, Papen foresaw no difficulty, in light of the personal hold he enjoyed over the president. In hopes of keeping him in office, after all, Hindenburg had the year before twice agreed to violate the constitution by dissolving the Reichstag without scheduling a new election within the required sixty days. The president had also urged him, after his fall, to turn down Schleicher's offer of the ambassadorship to France, requesting that he instead remain in Berlin and make himself available as an adviser. Papen thus did not lack grounds for believing that Hindenburg could be persuaded to recall him to the powerful office he longed to regain.

The Cologne meeting was not a complete success, since the efforts to keep it secret failed. The day before, a Berlin newspaper predicted that Hitler and Papen were about to confer. Papen at once issued a flat denial, as did Goebbels' tabloid newspaper in Berlin, *Der Angriff.* When the former chancellor stepped out of a taxi in front of Baron Schröder's house on January 4, he was therefore unpleasantly surprised to find a photographer aiming a camera at him. Papen assumed that military intelligence had found out about the meeting by tapping his telephone at Schleicher's direction. In actuality, however, the photographer had been sent to Cologne by a politically well-connected Berlin dentist whose practice included such diverse patients as former chancellor Heinrich Brüning, Gregor Strasser, and Schleicher.

The dentist had caught wind of plans for the meeting beforehand, probably from Brüning, who later reported learning of it at the end of December from Gregor Strasser, who was presumably alerted by one of his allies within the party. In hopes of aiding both Strasser and Schleicher, the dentist arranged for one of Strasser's loyalists to follow and photograph Papen. Upon receiving confirmation that the former chancellor had met with Hitler, the dentist at once relayed the news to the *Tägliche Rundschau,* a Berlin newspaper sympathetic to Schleicher. He also sent a copy of the photograph of Papen to the chancellor. When the report reached the newspaper, the presses were halted partway through the run of the edition for January 5 and the story inserted at the top of the front page under a large headline, "Hitler and Papen against Schleicher."

News of the Cologne meeting dropped like a bomb into what had been a brief holiday calm in German politics. Articles about it commanded front-page attention in newspapers all across the country for several days. In response, the conspirators sought to put a harmless face on what had taken place. On January 5 Papen issued a statement dismissing as "fabricated" charges that the meeting had been directed against Schleicher. He and Hitler had merely discussed a question he had been working on for the previous half year: how to bring the Nazis into a broad rightist cabinet. On January 6 Baron von Schröder announced that he alone bore responsibility for bringing the two politicians together. The aim of the meeting, he claimed, had been to explore ways to achieve an understanding among all nationalist—that is, rightist—forces. Also on January 6, Hitler and Papen made public a joint declaration in which they claimed to have discussed only "the possibility of a broad nationalist political unity front." They explicitly denied having exchanged views about the Schleicher cabinet. The same day, Goebbels' *Der Angriff* stated that there was nothing unusual about such exchanges of information between politicians. But after having on January 6 initially characterized the meeting as a "casual conversation about the political events of the past weeks," the Nazis' national newspaper, the *Völkischer Beobachter,* the next day attributed the meeting to Papen's desire to share with Hitler "interesting details" about his fall as chancellor and about Schleicher's appointment to replace him.

These clumsy efforts at obfuscation failed to receive the searching public scrutiny they deserved because of failings on the part of the news media. In seeking to explain the Cologne meeting, much of the press fell victim to the anticapitalist sentiment then in vogue among German intellectuals. By that time, the myth that the Nazis had been bankrolled by Germany's capitalists had already become a firm article of faith in many circles. Now, since Hitler and Papen converged at the house of a banker, Communist and Social Democratic journalists, as well as some who wrote for liberal papers and even the maverick conservative daily that broke the story, the *Tägliche Rundschau,* immediately assumed that a capitalist conspiracy must be behind it. A headline in *Vorwärts,* the national newspaper of the Social Democrats, encapsulated its interpretation: "Caught In Flagrante!" Readers of *Rote Fahne,* the Communist paper, learned that "Since Hitler has been heavily financed by many groups within Rhenish-Westphalian industry and since such subventions are customarily channelled through private banking houses, the background of this meeting becomes clear."

In the following days, imaginative though wholly unsubstantiated allegations of behind-the-scenes machinations by sinister and politically powerful business interests abounded in the press. In those speculations, Hitler and Papen shrank to secondary importance as mere pawns of purportedly mightier economic forces. Still other versions added to the confusion. Some journalists accepted the denials of the participants at face value, while others speculated that Papen must have been acting with Schleicher's knowledge in an effort to persuade Hitler to support the incumbent cabinet. Only a minority recognized that the simplest explanation was the most likely: namely that two politicians with grounds for hostility to Chancellor Kurt von Schleicher had come together to conspire against him under a cloak of attempted secrecy.

Among those who failed to grasp the obvious was Schleicher himself. Surprised by the news from Cologne, he was greatly annoyed at Papen's presumptuousness and complained to President von Hindenburg, asking him to order Papen to desist from such independent ventures in the future. But Schleicher did not take Papen seriously enough to impute sinister motives to him. His low opinion of the former chancellor was reflected in a remark of his chief aide, Erwin Planck, on the occasion of Papen's speech to the Gentlemen's Club in mid-December. When a member of the audience sought to warn Planck that Papen had revealed hostile intentions toward Schleicher and posed a danger because of his ties to Hindenburg, Planck responded: "Let him talk, he's completely insignificant. No one takes him seriously. Herr von Papen is a pompous ass. This speech is the swan song of a bad loser."

Instead of recognizing the dangers revealed by the Cologne meeting, Schleicher assumed that Papen had, in hopes of restoring himself to favor, ill-advisedly taken it upon himself to attempt a reconciliation between Hitler and the Schleicher cabinet. This became apparent when the chancellor confided his views on the matter to Ambassador François-Poncet over tea late on the afternoon of January 6. He and the ambassador enjoyed cordial relations, in part because Schleicher adhered to the view that France should be conciliated in the hope of gaining its acquiescence in an eventual revision of the eastern boundaries imposed upon Germany by the Versailles Treaty. In seeking to explain the Cologne meeting to François-Poncet, the chancellor told him that Papen had made a grave error in meeting with Hitler. But, he added, the former chancellor had not intended to do him any harm. "He is frivolous," Schleicher told the ambassador. "He imagined that he was going to pull off a master stroke and serve up Hitler to us on a platter. As if Hitler had not shown many times that he cannot be trusted! Now Papen is embarrassed. He fears our reproaches. I won't scold him. I'll just say to him: 'my Fränzchen, you've committed another blunder!'."

On Monday, January 9, Papen arrived back in Berlin and called on Schleicher. He later depicted the meeting as a cordial reunion of old friends that completely cleared up any misapprehensions on the chancellor's part about his meeting with Hitler. In support of that contention, Papen quoted the communiqué he and Schleicher jointly issued to the press afterward, which branded reports of differences between the two as "completely groundless."

For his part, Schleicher left no record of his talk with Papen on January 9, but remarks he made four days later, while speaking off the record to a small group of journalists who were his guests for dinner, provide clues about what Papen said. Papen had informed him, the chancellor told the journalists on January 13, that Hitler had insisted he must personally become both minister of defense and interior minister. This was very different from what Hitler had told Goebbels, who recorded in his diary that Papen had offered to make those two ministries available to Nazis of Hitler's choice if he deferred to Papen's reappointment as chancellor. Schleicher did not specify to the journalists who, according to Papen, had been foreseen as chancellor of the cabinet in which Hitler had purportedly sought the two ministries for himself. But it would hardly have been plausible for Hitler to demand for himself the chancellorship as well as the two key ministries. On the other hand, Papen would surely not have confessed to Schleicher his discussion with Hitler about the possibility of a second Papen cabinet. The only remaining possibility was the Schleicher cabinet. On January 9, that is, Franz von Papen related to Kurt von Schleicher the same mendacious version of the Cologne meeting he was to repeat many times after the collapse of the Third Reich: namely, that he had merely been seeking to bring Hitler to support Schleicher's cabinet. What is more, as Schleicher later conceded, after Papen took his hand, looked him straight in the eye, invoked their old friendship, and gave him his word of honor, "I was fool enough to believe him."

Following his conversation with Schleicher on January 9, Papen called on President von Hindenburg and gave him still another version of what had been said in Cologne. Otto Meissner, the chief of the presidential staff, recalled in his memoirs that, according to Hindenburg, Papen had indicated that Hitler was no longer demanding the chancellorship of a presidential cabinet with access to emergency powers. Instead, Hindenburg had heard from Papen that the Nazi leader was now ready to allow his party to join with conservative forces in a coalition cabinet. From this, Hindenburg concluded that he would have to find another chancellor, since Hitler could not be expected to back the Schleicher cabinet. The man for that role, he gave Meissner to understand, would be Papen. The president also disclosed to Meissner that he had given his consent for Papen to remain in contact with Hitler on a personal and strictly confidential basis.

According to Papen's memoirs, Hindenburg told him on January 9 that Schleicher had denounced his meeting with Hitler as a breach of loyalty and asked the president not to receive him again. But after he had explained the meeting to the president, Papen claimed, Hindenburg responded that he had known all along that Schleicher's version could not be correct. The Cologne meeting would not, Papen recalled the president's assuring him, affect their relations with one another in the least. Only three days earlier, Chancellor von Schleicher had informed ambassador François-Poncet that the president had been "acutely offended" by Papen's unauthorized meeting with Hitler. But now one conversation with Papen sufficed to dispel Hindenburg's misgivings. According to Meissner, on January 9 the president instructed him not to tell Schleicher that Papen had been authorized by Hindenburg to remain in contact with Hitler. The head of state, the supreme arbiter of power who held sole authority to appoint chancellors and endow them with emergency powers, thereby became, perhaps unwittingly, an accessory to a conspiracy aimed at deposing the man he had named to that office just five weeks earlier.

3

Hitler Scores
a Dubious Triumph
amid a Nazi Crisis

A FTER HIS MEETING with Papen on January 4, Hitler
plunged directly into the campaign for the legislative election in the small state of Lippe, which was scheduled for
January 15. Wintry road conditions on the 120-mile drive from Cologne made him two hours late in arriving at the country town where
his first speech was scheduled that evening. A capacity audience,
sheltered from the cold only by a tent, waited patiently and greeted
him exuberantly when he finally appeared at ten in the evening. After
speaking for over an hour to his eager listeners, Hitler moved on to the
state capital, where at midnight he received a similarly enthusiastic
reception from an audience that had also waited for hours to hear him.
During the next eleven days he would deliver fifteen additional
speeches, for the most part in the small, remote towns of Lippe.
Elsewhere in the state, a dozen other nationally known Nazis spoke
during the same period at twenty-three more rallies as part of a
campaign of unprecedented intensity.

Realizing that yet another setback at the polls, coming after those
of late 1932, would confirm the growing popular belief that National

Socialism was in decline, Hitler had decided to gamble for high stakes in Lippe. Since it was one of the seventeen federal states, success there would not go unnoticed. If Hitler's personal involvement and that of the other prominent Nazis engaged in the campaign produced gains in the balloting, the party would be seen as still growing in strength. Success would also provide a much needed boost to his followers' sagging morale. But considerable risk was involved. If the Nazis failed to make a strong showing despite the all-out effort on the part of their top-rank leadership, the damaging effects would be enormously magnified. Here, as so often in his career, Adolf Hitler showed himself to be a politician who habitually went for broke, heedless of the consequences of failure.

It was one of the numerous strokes of good luck in Hitler's career that just when he desperately needed a chance to demonstrate that his movement had not lost its momentum, an election came due in Lippe. For his purposes, the state offered a host of advantages. In both area and population, it amounted to only slightly more than a quarter of one percent of Germany as a whole. This enabled the Nazis to blanket the state with rallies and propaganda to an extent that would have been possible in only a few other corners of the country. Lippe was also just the sort of area where the Nazis fared best with voters. The population was almost 95 percent Protestant, with over 60 percent living in the countryside or in rural villages, twice the national average. The Nazis usually did poorly in highly industrialized regions, where blue-collar workers voted heavily for Social Democrats and Communists, and on that count, too, Lippe offered favorable prospects. The state had no significant mines and considerably less manufacturing than the national average. Small factories producing meerschaum pipes and furniture were more typical there than the sort of huge industrial complexes that abounded not far away to the west, in the Ruhr district. In placing his wager on the Lippe election, Hitler had the odds on his side.

Lippe's location also favored Hitler's party. Since the state was surrounded by more populous regions, the Nazis could easily supplement their local forces by bringing in reinforcements. As observant journalists noticed, a sizable proportion of the audiences at the party's rallies consisted of groups from elsewhere. Since these outsiders were party members, their presence not only swelled the crowds but also guaranteed enthusiastic responses. On the day of Hitler's first two rallies, no fewer than six special trains as well as numerous busses and trucks brought visitors to Lippe, a region not renowned as a winter vacation mecca. Even before that, between six and seven hundred Nazi stormtroopers had arrived, many by bicycle, to augment local units during the campaign. These imported stormtroopers found shelter in many cases in unheated barns or warehouses, where they slept on straw. It struck neither them nor other Nazi loyalists as anomalous that Hitler, famous for his denunciations of class distinctions, lived luxuriously throughout the campaign in a castle as the guest of a baron.

The political situation in Lippe virtually guaranteed the Nazis the appearance of success in the election. The last previous statewide balloting had taken place in 1929, just before the economic depression sent millions of voters flocking to the Nazis. They entered the election campaign with only one of twenty-one seats in the state legislature, which meant that they could count on a dramatic increase in representation. Still another advantage they enjoyed was weak competition. Chancellor von Schleicher could not bring the resources of the national government to bear on the campaign, since none of the contending parties was firmly aligned with his cabinet. The liberals, who had once been a factor in Lippe's politics, had by 1933 been reduced to insignificance by massive losses in national elections. The Catholic Center Party, one of the pillars of the republic, had never played a significant role in the predominantly Protestant state.

The reactionary German-Nationals, the Nazis' chief rivals for the votes of the conservative farmers and small-town residents who predominated in Lippe, operated under a handicap in the January campaign. In hopes of ending the feud that had kept the two rightist parties at each other's throats for more than a year, that party's leader, Alfred Hugenberg, refrained from attacks on the Nazis and similarly moderated the editorials of his party's major newspaper in Lippe. The only other campaign that came close to challenging that of the Nazis in intensity was mounted by the Social Democrats. That party's close identification with organized labor gave it little chance, however, of significantly expanding its base of support in a state where industrial workers were in limited supply.

As had been the case for years all over Germany, those who attended a Nazi rally in Lippe during January 1933 could count on more of a show than any other party provided. Recognizing that the austere style of republican politics fell flat with the many Germans who missed the colorful pageantry of the Empire, the Nazis turned their rallies into theatrical performances. Starting an hour or so before the scheduled beginning of the event, bands made up of uniformed storm-troopers attracted attention by playing stirring martial music as they either marched through the town or performed at the rally site. The meeting places themselves were conspicuously guarded by formations of stormtroopers whose reputation for dealing with hostile hecklers in summary, often violent, fashion was well known. After preliminary speakers had warmed up the audience and anticipation had mounted, the stormtroopers formed two lines, creating an aisle for the entry, to another blast of martial music, of the featured speaker. As the British ambassador observed, in comparison with the stodgy performances of the other parties, the Nazis exerted "the magnetic attraction of a jazz band."

The Nazi campaign speeches in Lippe followed a general pattern. After attributing Germany's woes to a republican "system" allegedly dominated by Jews and Marxists, the party's speakers held out the promise of a racially pure, proud and powerful Nazified Germany. The election was portrayed as a crucial battle for the nation's future between Nazi patriots and traitorous Marxists. Relatively little atten-tion was paid to the local concerns of Lippe's voters. The incumbent state government had been headed ever since the revolution by a minister-president from the republican Social Democratic Party, which had consistently tallied more votes than any other party in previous state elections. Throughout the '20s, the minister-president had collaborated with the moderate non-socialist parties, having won their respect and trust. Nevertheless, in keeping with their long-standing practice, the Nazi campaigners sought to discredit him and his party by denouncing them as unpatriotic Marxist internationalists and lumping them together with the Social Democrats' archenemies, the Communists, who had negligible strength in Lippe.

The Nazis sought as well to identify themselves during the election campaign with Herman the Cherusker, the Teutonic chieftain who, according to legend, had defeated a Roman army in Lippe's Teutoburg Forest in the year A.D. 77. But as the republican *Vossische Zeitung* of Berlin pointed out, an unassuming Social Democrat minister-president hardly fit the role of a Roman general. And as a paper in nearby Bielefeld observed, the Nazis, with their regimented stormtrooper squads and their right arms raised in salutes of Roman origin, more closely resembled the other side in the legendary battle.

While conforming to this general line, Hitler used his appearances in Lippe to defend his all-or-nothing strategy. His first speech on the evening of January 4 contained most of the themes he would repeat over the next ten days. As was his practice, he omitted any mention of having spurned President von Hindenburg's offer the previous November to appoint him chancellor if he could assemble a parliamentary majority. Instead, he referred only to the offers of the post of vice chancellor extended to him by Papen and Schleicher. He had declined that post, he explained, because he was unwilling to trade his good name and that of the Nazi movement for "a title without power." He rejected the view that he should have accepted the vice chancellorship and used it to gain power thorough the back door. "I can only say," he added, "that I have not learned this behind-the-scenes game and also do not want to learn it." Coming as it did just hours after Hitler's clandestine rendezvous with Franz von Papen, this disclaimer provides a clue to what must have been very much on his mind that evening.

ALTHOUGH local circumstances in Lippe favored the Nazis, the election there came at a time when Hitler's strategy of seeking power legally through the ballot box seemed to many Nazis to have reached a dead end. His failure to gain the chancellorship after his party's electoral triumph of the previous July, coupled with the heavy losses suffered in November, had given rise to growing disillusionment and frustration in the Nazi ranks. Those who had joined the party in the expectation of sharing quickly in the spoils of victory began to despair. So did many who had followed Hitler in the hope that he would provide a panacea for their economic plight. As a consequence, widespread demoralization set in among the rank and file. At the end of December the republican political police charged with exercising surveillance over the Nazi Party in Munich, its birthplace and stronghold, noted signs of disintegration: "Numerous resignations occur every day, dues arrive irregularly and expulsions because of arrears become more and more frequent. . . . All sections of the party . . . give the impression of being run down." As to morale, the police report added: "The view that the peak has been passed and favorable prospects probably missed is commonly held among many National Socialists."

This crisis plunged the Nazi movement into grave financial difficulties. With its coffers already badly depleted during 1932 by the expenses of the two rounds of the presidential election, two Reichstag elections and a parliamentary election in the largest state, Prussia, the party now experienced a contraction of its income. Previously, Nazism had been a largely self-supporting operation, with the monthly dues required for membership in good standing serving as the principal source of funds for the national organization. As the party ranks swelled rapidly during the depression years, money had flooded in abundantly at a time when falling prices made that rising income ever more valuable. Now, however, the influx of new members dwindled to a trickle and defections multiplied. Many of those who nominally remained members ceased paying their dues promptly. With hopes of victory receding, members who had in the past made donations in excess of their regular membership dues now proved less responsive to appeals for funds. So did sympathizing non-members who had formerly contributed to the coffers of a party that seemed on its way to power. A major source of income at the local level, admission fees charged at party rallies plummeted as attendance fell off during late 1932, despite sharply reduced ticket prices, as public interest in the party waned.

By the turn of the year money had become an acute problem for the Nazis. Since equipment and supplies for election campaigns had frequently been obtained on credit, local party officials found themselves dunned by merchants demanding that they personally pay outstanding debts incurred for the party. Obtaining new credit to meet those debts became increasingly difficult or impossible. So did meeting the party's own bloated payrolls. During the heady years when income had constantly mounted, thousands of Nazis had become full-time party functionaries with salaries that were handsome by depression standards. The staff of the national headquarters alone grew from 56 in 1930 to 275 in 1932. With party funds contracting while salaries and other expenses remained high, accusations of misappropriation of funds and other forms of corruption now poisoned the atmosphere. Friction developed between components of the movement as dwindling resources led party and stormtrooper units to compete with each other for scarce donations. The Nazis' financial distress became conspicuously visible to the public, as bands of uniformed stormtroopers accosted passersby on sidewalks all across Germany, rattling cans to solicit coins. In some places, party units conducted lotteries in order to raise money, with members pressured to buy tickets.

Under such straitened financial circumstances, it would have been exceedingly difficult to conduct an elaborate, intense campaign anywhere other than in a small, compact territory like Lippe. Transportation costs were minimal there, and accommodations and meeting facilities were relatively inexpensive. Almost all the labor was donated by party members, as were the vehicles that toured the countryside, announcing rallies by loudspeaker. Volunteer door-to-door canvassers swarmed over the state, approaching voters at home to seek their support. To economize, posters left over from the November Reichstag election were recycled by pasting fresh information over the old. To supplement these, members produced homemade placards. Since most rallies featured nationally known Nazi leaders, admission prices that were quite substantial by depression standards found takers. The overhead for the rallies was low. Most of the prominent Nazis brought in as speakers were either salaried party officials or parliamentarians with railway passes, so that no honoraria or travel costs needed to be paid. Where tavern keepers or owners of meeting halls could not be persuaded to accept modest rental fees, three rented tents provided economical shelter for rallies.

Even under the favorable conditions offered by Lippe, the need for money dogged the Nazis throughout the January election campaign there. In a marked departure from past practice, Hitler had to dip into the royalties from his book *Mein Kampf* that were his principal source of personal income in order to augment the dwindling resources of the local party. At one point, one of his aides desperately approached his press secretary Otto Dietrich with a request for a substantial personal loan, explaining that not enough money was on hand to pay the fee demanded in advance for rental of the hall where the party leader was scheduled to speak the next day. On another occasion, a bailiff sequestered the box-office receipts from a party rally to meet the claims of impatient local creditors.

The Nazi election campaign in Lippe labored not only under these financial difficulties but also under a cloud of uncertainty about the intentions of Gregor Strasser, the former head of the party's bureaucracy. Since Strasser remained out of public view following his resignation in early December, Hitler and confidants like Joseph Goebbels were left to worry about persistent rumors in the press to the effect that he was scheming behind the scenes to split the party and join Schleicher's cabinet. Their anxiety was not wholly unfounded.

Some of Strasser's admirers, among them Reichstag deputies and gauleiters—regional party chieftains—refused to give up on him. After his resignation, they set up informal networks to perpetuate what they saw as his heritage of taking seriously the socialistic aspects of National Socialism. By January, dissident Nazi newsletters were circulating in several parts of Germany. One of the Strasser loyalists, the gauleiter of Hesse-Darmstadt, who was also a Reichstag deputy, either resigned his party post or was expelled in mid-December. During the following weeks he sought to rally support for Strasser through articles in one of the dissident newsletters. He and others publicized Strasser's warning that Hitler's all-or-nothing strategy was inviting a dissolution of the Reichstag elected in November and another election that would cost the party still more votes.

In a pattern endemic to Nazism throughout its existence, the dissidents placed the blame for Strasser's resignation not on Hitler himself but rather on "paladins" such as Goebbels and Göring, who allegedly shielded the party leader from reality and misled him with bad advice. Initially, the dissidents claimed to seek merely a reconciliation that would bring Strasser back to Hitler's side. But as frustration with Strasser's inactivity increased during January, their pronouncements began to display increasing defiance toward the course the party was following under Hitler.

The question of Strasser's role worried Hitler and Goebbels greatly during the Lippe campaign. On January 10 disturbing reports reached them that pro-Strasser sentiment was undermining the loyalty of Nazis in the country's second largest city, Hamburg. The local leader there was reputed to sympathize covertly with the renegade. "Strasser wants to fight under the slogan: Against Göring and Goebbels," the latter noted in his diary. When news that Strasser had met with President Hindenburg the previous week reached Lippe on January 12, the worst fears of Hitler's retinue seemed confirmed. Goebbels confided in his diary: "Strasser is plotting. He was with Hindenburg. . . . That's what I call a traitor. I always saw through him. Hitler is badly shaken."

On that same day, January 12, embarrassing evidence of dissension in the Nazi ranks in Lippe itself became public. A local newspaper published an angry letter of resignation by a physician who had been a veteran Nazi and leader of the party in his district of the state. The physician branded Hitler's strategy of seeking power through the ballot box as a failure and denounced the low quality of the party's officials. Too many "little political charlatans . . . sorcerer's apprentices, [and] hot-air merchants" had, he wrote, risen to high party posts solely because of their rabble-rousing talents. He charged that their "rampant Byzantinism" was alienating loyal party members and warned: "With the souls of slaves, one cannot conduct a struggle for freedom." In repeated public declarations, Nazi spokesmen in Lippe gave assurance that the physician was a lone malcontent. In fact, no additional defections followed. Nevertheless, the specter of rebellion marred the last days of the Nazi election campaign.

In addition to having to contend with demoralization within the party proper, Hitler faced growing dissension in the ranks of the party's 400,000-man stormtrooper auxiliary, the SA. Relations had often been strained between the political leadership and the paramilitary SA, only some of whose members also belonged to the party. Some SA leaders had always been skeptical about Hitler's decision to seek power through legal means, preferring instead to prepare for a forcible overthrow of the republican state by their army of stormtroopers. Friction between SA and party mounted sharply when Hitler failed to attain power during 1932 and the number of party members began to dwindle, curtailing the share of monthly dues that had previously underwritten the SA. The doubts of some SA commanders about the party's political course seemed confirmed. As frustration mounted during the summer and autumn of 1932, violent, often murderous terrorist attacks by stormtroopers on political opponents increased dramatically. In some instances, these attacks were ordered by local SA commanders; in others they resulted from a breakdown of discipline. Where acts of terrorism by the SA had been particularly numerous and flagrant, party officials angrily attributed the Nazis' heavy losses in the November

Reichstag election in part to public indignation at the stormtroopers' crimes. Party officials in many places also complained of inadequate participation by stormtroopers in the campaign leading up to the election. By the end of 1932 relations between the party and the SA were noticeably deteriorating. Early in January, a high SA commander took the extraordinary step of publishing in a nonparty newspaper an article denouncing Hitler's pursuit of power by legal means and calling upon him to adopt more direct methods.

In the midst of the Lippe campaign, there was a major outbreak of stormtrooper insubordination. The trouble spot was central Franconia, a predominantly Protestant region in northern Bavaria that had long been one of Nazism's strongholds. During the latter half of 1932 an increasingly bitter quarrel developed between the commander of the SA in Franconia, Wilhelm Stegmann, and the gauleiter of central Franconia, Julius Streicher. A veteran Nazi and Reichstag deputy whose SA rank was equivalent to that of an army general, Stegmann, like Strasser, stressed the adjective "socialist" in the party's name. He repeatedly clashed with the autocratic and venal Streicher, who had gained notoriety as publisher of *Der Stürmer,* a pornographic anti-Semitic magazine. The quarrel escalated in late 1932 when Stegmann charged the gauleiter with reneging on a commitment to reimburse the local SA for heavy election campaign expenses. Streicher retaliated by accusing Stegmann of embezzlement and prevailed upon the national headquarters of the SA to strip him of his command. Stegmann was able to defy that order, however, by retaining the loyalty of his stormtroopers.

The dispute in Franconia burst into the headlines during the second week of January. One of Stegmann's aides broke into the SA headquarters in Nuremberg, locked up a stormtrooper loyal to Gauleiter Streicher and removed official files. A bloody brawl ensued between Stegmann's followers and supporters of the gauleiter at the party headquarters. Hitler responded by stripping Stegmann of all authority. Then, on the last day before the balloting in Lippe, Stegmann was summoned there to meet with Hitler. Surrounded by the leader's henchmen, he was subjected to one of the lengthy, angry harangues Hitler routinely employed to intimidate others. At its close, Stegmann signed a statement of abject submission to the party leader that was at once released to the press. Staged for election campaign purposes, this much publicized reconciliation would prove short-lived. But it achieved its purpose at the time, as the voters of Lippe went to the polls under the impression that unity again prevailed in the Nazi ranks.

The outcome of the balloting in Lippe on Sunday, January 15— the last fully free election in Germany before the Third Reich—has usually been depicted as a victory for Hitler and his party. At first sight, the numbers seem to bear this out. With 39.5 percent of the votes, the Nazis finished first among the nine parties on the ballot and emerged with more deputies than any other party—nine—in the twenty-one-seat legislature. This amounted to a nearly 70 percent increase in votes over the last state election. The results looked quite different, however, when measured against the Nazis' performances in Lippe at the time of the two national elections of 1932. Out of just under 100,000 votes cast, they received slightly more than 39,000, some 5,000 more than in the November Reichstag election. But they fell short by some 3,500 votes of equaling the level they had attained in Lippe in the July Reichstag election. They gained no ground on the leftist parties they had attacked so vigorously in the campaign. Indeed, the Social Democrats tallied 3,000 more votes than in November. Aside from attracting previous non-voters, the Nazis profited mainly at the expense of the German-Nationals, who lost nearly 4,000 of their November votes. The balance between the parties of the Right and Left thus remained essentially unchanged, despite Nazi promises to vanquish Marxism from Lippe.

In view of the high-powered campaign unleashed by the Nazis on the voters of Lippe and the multiple advantages they enjoyed there, the result proved less than imposing. In objective terms, Hitler's party could be said to have halted its decline, but it had not managed fully to make good its losses of November. In any case, Lippe's lilliputian size and atypical characteristics rendered dubious any claim that the addition of five thousand Nazi votes there somehow reflected a trend among the more than thirty-five million Germans who had cast ballots in each of the two national elections of 1932. A Catholic newspaper in nearby Paderborn dismissed Nazi attempts to portray the Lippe results as indicative of public opinion in general: "Why? Because no party in Germany possesses or can obtain or create or put to use a) so much money, b) so many campaign speakers, c) so many tents, autos, motor-cycles, or loudspeakers as to repeat the [Nazis'] procedure in Lippe in order to subject every electoral district to the same sort of high pressure that was used to secure the outcome of Lippe." Ambassador François-Poncet concluded on similar grounds that "the result has something artificial about it." Theodor Wolff, the sagacious editor of the republican newspaper *Berliner Tageblatt,* made the same point more colorfully: "In truth, Hitler has brought home from his heroic struggle in Lippe only a fly impaled on the tip of his sword."

Such clear-sighted observations did not deter the Nazis from claiming a great victory in Lippe with momentous implications for Germany as a whole. The party's national newspaper, the *Völkischer Beobachter,* proclaimed that the outcome "cannot be assessed too highly in its political significance as a measure of the general mood of the people. It not only refutes in convincing fashion our opponents' claim that the National Socialist movement is receding but also serves as incontrovertible proof that the stagnation of the party has been completely surmounted and that a new upward development has now begun. The National Socialist wave is rising again. . . . This is less the time than ever for weak-kneed compromises."

In his tabloid, *Der Angriff,* Goebbels conceded that Lippe was something less than a major theater of political action, but otherwise substituted typical Nazi rhetoric for analysis: "From this little sector of the trenches the offensive against the [republican] system has been re-sumed. The avalanche of the people's upheaval has once more come into motion, and we shall see to it that it never again stops." The out-come of the balloting, Goebbels claimed, had vindicated Hitler's re-peated rejection of proposals for Nazi participation in government that fell short of his all-or-nothing terms. Without mentioning his arch-enemy Strasser by name, Goebbels invoked the Nazis' gains to ridicule "know-it-alls on the fringes of our own party" who had concluded that Nazism had ceased to grow and should therefore settle for compromises in order to hold on to what it had gained. "The Lippe election has taught these party defeatists a hard lesson," Goebbels contended. "Insofar as they are not incurable, they will now beat their breasts repentantly and begin to realize that the people never falter if their leaders remain strong." With his customary bravado, the future propaganda minister boasted that the Nazis' renewed show of strength at the polls in Lippe meant that Chancellor Schleicher could no longer assume that a dissolution of the Reichstag would lead to new Nazi losses.

Despite the dubious aspects of the Nazis' self-proclaimed triumph in Lippe, it unquestionably amounted to an important plus for Hitler. The election success came just in time to revive flagging hopes in the Nazi ranks that his uncompromising stance would lead to total power and to cast doubt upon those who dissented from that view. Hitler did not wait long to exploit this. Unshakably confident, as always, that his wager on victory in Lippe would succeed, he had redoubled it by summoning, in advance of the balloting, Nazi functionaries from all over the country to a conclave in the city of Weimar, beginning on the afternoon of January 15. If the election had produced disappointing results, he would have faced, in very embarrassing circumstances, the men without whose backing he could not hope to retain absolute control of the party. Among them, as he well knew, were admirers of Gregor Strasser who still harbored doubts about his all-or-nothing approach. On the afternoon of January 15, before the results of the balloting in Lippe became known, Hitler greeted the arriving participants in Weimar by confidently predicting that the election would show Nazism to be once again on the rise.

Bolstered by the fulfillment of his prophecy regarding the outcome in Lippe, Hitler addressed a closed-door gathering of gauleiters, the regional chieftains of the party, on Monday, January 16. Enjoying extensive autonomy over party affairs in their regions, the gauleiters formed the backbone of the national organization. Without their loyalty, Hitler could not hope to cope with the mounting unrest in the party. It was therefore essential that he win over his audience. In keeping with Nazi practice, no formal discussion would follow the leader's speech, and no vote would be taken. Success depended on his listeners' reaction on the spot to his words. Hitler began his three-hour tirade before the gauleiters on a note described by Goebbels as "brusque intransigence," which left no doubt about his determination to hold to his demand for the chancellorship on his own terms. Then he played his trump card. With his hand now strengthened by the freshly arrived news of 'victory' in Lippe, he was at last ready for a final reckoning with his longtime confederate Gregor Strasser. He had prepared the ground for that move the previous week by summoning to Lippe the leaders of a Nazi labor organization built up by Strasser, and holding out to them the prospect of a major role in his future plans. Now, unleashing the full fury of his anger against Strasser, he reviled the renegade as a traitor and accused him of numerous offenses going back many years.

By implying that anyone who expressed doubts about his own strategy was a confederate of the disgraced Strasser, the party leader adeptly stifled dissent among the gauleiters. Only days earlier, Goebbels had expressed in his diary the fear that Strasser would betray the movement by accepting a post in the Schleicher cabinet. Now he exultantly recorded the reaction of the gauleiters to Hitler's diatribe: "At the end, everyone went wild. Hitler has pulled off a total victory. The Strasser case is all over. . . . Poor Gregor! His best friends have turned against him. . . . Everybody has deserted Strasser." In marked departure from the usual Nazi practice of trumpeting Hitler's every utterance, the party press left unreported Hitler's Weimar speech. By seeking to keep his denunciation of Strasser secret, Hitler obviously hoped to shield the party from political damage resulting from public disclosure of a breach in its ranks. Within days, however, word of Hitler's final break with Strasser reached Chancellor von Schleicher.

Goebbels' jubilation proved well founded, for Strasser was

indeed finished. Hitler's Weimar speech put an end to the possibility of reconciliation. In all likelihood, Strasser had abandoned any thought of challenging Hitler much earlier, if indeed he had ever seriously considered such a course. The phlegmatic former pharmacist from a small provincial town in Bavaria lacked the ego and lust for power that would have been necessary to defy the Nazi leader. He also suffered under the paralyzing handicap of recognizing Hitler's indispensability for National Socialism. Still a believer in the Nazi cause, Strasser could not bring himself to turn against the man who was at once its prophet and its messiah. Late in the third week of January he meekly approached Göring and agreed to abstain from political activity for two years. After Hitler gained power, Strasser withdrew from politics altogether and took a job with a pharmaceutical firm in Berlin. But although he remained a party member and never ceased to profess loyalty to its leader, Strasser was a marked man. At the time of the bloody Nazi purge at the end of June 1934 that became known as "the night of the long knives," he was murdered by thugs in the service of the dictator he had helped lift from obscurity.

BUOYED by the successes of Lippe and Weimar, Hitler moved on to Berlin, intent upon quickly exploiting the improvement in his political prospects. On Tuesday, January 17, he met with Alfred Hugenberg, leader of the German-Nationals, in hopes of gaining that conservative party's support for a Hitler cabinet. The two men had a troubled relationship. Hugenberg regarded the Nazis as little better than rabble, with dangerously radical social and economic notions. But he recognized that they were far more successful than his party in mobilizing mass support and hoped to harness their movement to destroy the republic and establish a rightist authoritarian regime. For Hitler, Hugenberg and his party were hopeless reactionaries who wanted merely to turn the clock back, unable to comprehend the need for a radical transformation of German society. Hitler saw, however, that the German-Nationals could be useful to him because of the respect they commanded in influential conservative circles.

In 1929 Hugenberg had given Hitler a major boost, lending him respectability by enlisting him for a rightist committee that sponsored an unsuccessful national plebiscite against a government-approved plan to revise the terms for German reparation payments to the victorious powers. Even though the Nazis' election gains soon stripped the German-Nationals of millions of former voters, Hugenberg continued to court Hitler. In the fall of 1931 the two joined in a much publicized antirepublican rally in the town of Bad Harzburg. Prorepublican observers feared that a 'Harzburg Front' of united rightist forces had coalesced, but the Nazis and Nationalists soon quarreled. At the time of the presidential election of 1932 Hugenberg's refusal to support Hitler's candidacy widened the breach. That summer Hitler denounced Hugenberg and the German-Nationals for supporting the Papen cabinet. In the July Reichstag election, the Nazis inflicted heavy losses on Hugenberg's party. But in the November election the German-Nationals succeeded in recapturing a sizable portion of the votes earlier lost to the Nazis by attacking them as irresponsible radicals. In hopes that the Nazis' setback would make Hitler more tractable, Hugenberg set out to seek a reconciliation while Nazism was still a major force. In December the two met secretly, and during the Lippe election campaign Hugenberg refrained from attacking the Nazis.

Four days prior to his meeting with Hitler on January 17, Hugenberg had conferred with Chancellor von Schleicher, and although their talk ended inconclusively, Hugenberg came away with hopes for an arrangement that would make him a member of the cabinet with control over national economic policy. Hugenberg therefore proved unresponsive to Hitler's offer of a cabinet post in return for his support for the Nazi leader's appointment as chancellor. Instead, he proposed to Hitler that they both enter Schleicher's cabinet and cooperate to block any relapse into parliamentary rule. For his part, Hitler refused to budge from his demand for the chancellorship, although he did concede that he would be willing to accept Schleicher as defense minister if the Nazis were allowed to use vigilante methods to crush

"Marxism," that is, the Social Democrats and Communists. When Hugenberg pointed out that President von Hindenburg's opposition ruled out Hitler's attainment of the chancellorship, the Nazi leader scornfully dismissed the president as "a phonograph record" with a "political vocabulary consisting of eighty sentences." Afterward, Hitler told Goebbels that in response to Hugenberg's contention that he had no hope of becoming chancellor, he had replied: "Rubbish! [Hindenburg's] handlers are the ones who are opposed." The meeting between Hitler and Hugenburg had ended with the two rightist leaders still far apart.

Hitler continued his quest for support by seeking another meeting with former chancellor Franz von Papen. As an intermediary he relied upon a champagne salesman who would later become his foreign minister, Joachim von Ribbentrop. A former army officer, Ribbentrop was an avid social climber with political ambitions, but little in the way of ability aside from a suave manner. He had, as Goebbels once caustically observed, bought his name and married his money, prevailing upon an impoverished but noble relative to adopt him in return for a pension so that he could add the coveted 'von' to his name, and then taking as his wife the daughter of a wealthy Rhenish champagne bottler. In the summer of 1932 Ribbentrop had approached Hitler with an offer to serve as intermediary with then chancellor Franz von Papen, with whom he had become acquainted in Turkey during World War I. Hitler made no use of Ribbentrop's services then, but Ribbentrop joined the Nazi Party and let it be known he was at its leader's disposal.

When Hitler's staff asked Ribbentrop in January to arrange a confidential meeting with Papen, he eagerly accepted. Papen proved ready to resume negotiations as early as January 10, when Hitler used a gap in his campaign schedule in Lippe to spend a day in Berlin. But Hitler instructed Ribbentrop to wait until the results of the Lippe election were in. The meeting was therefore postponed a week. At noon on January 18, accompanied by the stormtroop commanders Heinrich Himmler and Ernst Röhm, Hitler joined Papen for lunch at Ribbentrop's villa in the fashionable Berlin district of Dahlem.

Over lunch at Ribbentrop's on January 18, Hitler renewed his demand for the chancellorship. On the strength of the Nazis' gains in the Lippe election, he now emphatically ruled out any possibility of his serving as a junior partner in a cabinet headed by Papen. The former chancellor protested that he lacked sufficient influence with Hindenburg to overcome the president's opposition to appointing Hitler chancellor. As in Cologne two weeks earlier, Papen again held out the offer of collaboration against Schleicher that would lead to a cabinet headed by him and backed by the Nazis. That was, however, still unacceptable to Hitler. As a result, the luncheon meeting with Papen, like the exchange with Hugenberg the day before, ended without result. The former chancellor and the Nazi leader parted with no firm plans to meet again. The Nazis again sought to keep the meeting secret, leaking a cover story that placed Hitler elsewhere for lunch on January 18 and afterward denying any knowledge of contact between their leader and Papen. Some journalists nevertheless got wind of the meeting and at once published reports of it that were, however, in most cases embellished with inaccurate details.

The inconclusive meetings with Hugenberg and Papen left Hitler ill-equipped to combat the crisis that gripped his party. Acute financial difficulties continued to plague Nazi leaders at all levels. In mid-January the chargé d'affaires at the American embassy in Berlin reported that a "trusted lieutenant" of Hermann Göring had approached him "with regard to the possibility of obtaining a loan for the Nazi Party in the United States." Party newspapers lost subscribers and saw their street sales decline; some went into bankruptcy, and meeting the payrolls of staff writers became a struggle. Throughout the country, Nazi officials found themselves bereft of income and beset by creditors. Accusations of cronyism and financial irregularities became more frequent. In some places the resulting tensions brought local organizations to the verge of breaking up.

These difficulties could to some extent be kept from public view, but that was not the case with a renewed outbreak of rebellion within the SA. Only a week after Hitler had staged a reconciliation with the renegade Wilhelm Stegmann on the eve of the balloting in Lippe, the Franconian SA leader bolted again. Proclaiming his defiance of Gauleiter Streicher, he formed an independent paramilitary organization that most of the six to seven thousand central Franconian stormtroopers joined. Hitler retaliated by expelling Stegmann from the party. In the rare previous incidents of rebellion in the Nazi ranks, which had taken place while the party was gaining strength, Hitler's ban had sufficed to isolate and neutralize the ringleaders. But now, with many Nazis demoralized, Stegmann successfully defied his ban and retained the loyalty of most of his followers among the Franconian stormtroopers. They, too, were publicly denounced and expelled. Nevertheless, the altercation spread still further. Local Nazi organizations sided with either Gauleiter Streicher or Stegmann, so that the party in its former stronghold of central Franconia effectively ceased to function as a unit.

Initially, Stegmann was careful to specify that his quarrel was solely with the gauleiter and not with Hitler. But after his expulsion his public statements revealed that an underlying reason for his revolt had been doubt about the political course followed by Hitler. Like numerous other SA commanders who were war veterans, Stegmann had long looked upon Hitler's policy of seeking power through the ballot box with skepticism. He had trained and equipped the stormtroopers under his command for combat in the expectation that they would see action in a final struggle for power, and he chafed at the inactivity imposed by Hitler's legality course. At a well-attended rally in Nuremberg on January 24, Stegmann denounced that strategy, while still avoiding a personal attack on the party's leader. The "movement's historic moment has been missed," he told his followers, predicting that the party would "lose every future election." The masses who had placed their hopes on the attainment of power by legal means were, he warned, losing faith. The SA must, Stegmann contended, cease being a mere "fire department" or "palace guard" for the party. Instead of pursuing the "mania of legality," the time had come for the struggle for power to be conducted "in a more brutal and revolutionary fashion."

The Stegmann revolt was symptomatic of widespread unrest among Nazi stormtroopers in January 1933 as a consequence of the frustrations of the previous months. Appeals for support sent out by Stegmann following his expulsion from the party received favorable responses from a number of regions. In the state of Hesse, repeated mutinies by stormtroopers led to large-scale defections and expulsions from the SA. As in the Stegmann revolt, the Hessian dissidents established a paramilitary organization of their own after leaving the SA. In mid-January the police in the Hessian city of Kassel had to be called in to fend off dissident stormtroopers who had seized the local SA headquarters there in protest against alleged financial improprieties by local party leaders. Soon thereafter, a hostel and soup kitchen for SA men in Stuttgart had to be closed amid charges that funds had been misappropriated. On January 21, the Munich police reported that the SA there was in rapid decline: "No fewer than thirty-five men were expelled from SA Company 1 in December and fifteen in January because they were no longer attending to duties."

In Berlin, partisans of Gregor Strasser within the SA waited in vain throughout January for a signal from the man they continued to hope would challenge Hitler for party leadership. Some of the frustrations of SA men found vent in the bloody street battles with Communists and Social Democrats that continued unabated throughout the month. SA units also clashed in some places with those of the smaller, more selective security guard, the Schutzstaffel, or SS. The elitist pretensions of the SS and its leaders' practice of enticing particularly zealous stormtroopers to exchange the brown shirts of the SA for its smartly cut black uniforms made it a ready target for the frustrations of the predominantly plebeian SA. The SS itself was not immune to demoralization, as the resignation en bloc of one of its units in the Saxon city of Meissen demonstrated. In various parts of the country disillusioned Nazi stormtroopers defected to the

Communists, who readily enlisted them in their own paramilitary units.

In addition to these signs of deteriorating stormtrooper morale, sober examination of the Nazis' heavy losses in the national election of the previous November fed a growing mood of pessimism about the party's future prospects. In an effort to increase its support from workers, the party had during the autumn conducted a campaign that emphasized social radicalism and denounced the Papen cabinet as a tool of the rich and privileged. The result had been at best minimal gains among workers and the defection of large numbers of middle-class Germans whose earlier votes had contributed importantly to the movement's meteoric rise. The implication was that any move to either right or left in the future could only cost the Nazis votes.

A secret, internal Nazi analysis conducted in the wake of the November electoral debacle concluded that the party had reached the limits of its vote-getting potential. That same analysis revealed wide-spread agreement among Nazi functionaries that those voters who had deserted the party in November had not been true believers in the movement's cause. Opportunists who had previously cast their ballots for the Nazis out of protest against conditions in general or out of hopes for a quick fix of Germany's problems were losing interest or patience or both. In view of these discouraging findings, the internal analysis reached the conclusion that "it must not come to another election." If the Nazis had to face the voters again, "the results could not be imag-ined." Looking to the future, the analysis warned: "Nothing more is to be done with words, placards, and leaflets. Now we must act!" There was no mention, however, as to what action should be taken, aside from an expression of hope that Hitler would somehow "bring about a political transformation" and "appear before the German people as a man of action."

The mounting difficulties of the Nazis did not go unnoticed in governmental circles. On January 19, the permanent undersecretary in the Foreign Ministry, a veteran official with access to a wide range of information, depicted Nazism's predicament in stark terms in a letter to the German ambassador in Washington: "The National Socialists are not doing well at all, the party organization is badly shaken, and the financial situation is pretty much hopeless. Some people are even concerned that the party could under certain circumstances break up too fast, so fast that it would be impossible to reabsorb the voters, so that many would go over to the Communists." A month earlier, the Austrian consul general in Munich characterized Nazism as a movement held together by negation of all aspects of the existing order. He predicted that in the face of decisions about how to engage in practical politics the party would fall apart. At the moment, he observed, those elements seemed to have prevailed that regarded any practical response to Germany's problems as "the beginning of the end."

The full extent of the crisis in the Nazi ranks in January 1933 can probably never be determined. Much discontent in all likelihood went unrecorded, as party officials strove to prevent it from reaching public view. When Hitler suddenly became chancellor at the end of the month, most dissidents presumably rushed to cover their tracks so they could join in the scramble for the spoils of victory. In all probability, then, the surviving evidence understates the ferment within the Nazi movement. Most discontent was directed toward local party leaders. While this shielded Hitler personally, it nevertheless diminished the dynamism of the party. The surviving evidence makes clear, among other things, that the leading dissident Nazis were not impressed by the party's 'victory' in the Lippe election. As seasoned political veterans, they recognized the election there for what it was: a cheap propaganda triumph of no real significance. An expert on the history of the SA has written that "immediately before Hitler's takeover transformed its fortunes literally overnight, the SA was nearing collapse." His findings, together with the other evidence of Nazism's increasing fragility, suggest that only the capture of the chancellorship put an end to mounting dissatisfaction with Hitler's leadership. In the absence of that all-transforming windfall, continuing frustration over failure to attain power would presumably have given rise to still more disillusionment with the party leader's political course.

In an effort to stem the deteriorating morale of his party in the days following his fruitless mid-January meetings with Hugenberg and Papen, Hitler launched into a round of speeches designed to raise the spirits of Nazi functionaries. Clad in the quasi-military brown tunic, tan jodhpurs, and black jackboots that had become his party uniform, he addressed a rally of officials of the party's Berlin regional organization on January 20 at the Sportpalast, the city's indoor sports arena. They must remember, he instructed them, that they were engaged in a struggle that would determine the future of the German people for centuries to come. Just as Prussia had overcome the fragmentation of the country to achieve national unity in the previous century, the Nazi movement would provide the strength needed to surmount the political parties and interest groups that now divided Germans. To Nazism's opponents he issued a message of defiance: "You can strike blows against us but you can never defeat us! We shall always take up the battle again and never desert our flag. My mission is to advance ceaselessly as banner-bearer of the movement. So long as destiny lets me live, so long shall I carry this banner, never striking it, never furling it." The party would triumph, he assured his listeners, if its leaders remained unwaveringly resolute. As always, for Hitler politics was ultimately a matter of willpower.

Despite Hitler's rhetorical bravado, an undertone of defensiveness ran through his speech at the Sportpalast. Conceding that the party had suffered setbacks, he again rejected compromise or, as he put it, the "substitution of tactical dodges for principles." At such critical moments, he admonished his underlings to remember that they were the "embodiment of the nation's conscience" and must remain resolute. They must summon up the "heroic decisiveness" needed to "break the neck of defeatism." Although Hitler avoided mentioning Strasser by name, it was clear that his renegade lieutenant and those Nazis who sympathized with him were the targets of these menacing words. For the movement to succeed, Hitler admonished his listeners, unity was indispensable, and he reminded them what it meant to be a good Nazi: "Party comrades, racial comrades, when you enter here you must merge your will into the will of millions of others, then you must dissolve yourself in that great will, you must become a man and entrust yourself to a single Leader." Even he, the supreme leader, could err, he admitted. But he assured his listeners that what counted in the end was "who makes the fewest mistakes." Their opponents' resistance, he assured them, would only serve to steel Nazi strength, and by surmounting that resistance they would gain justification for their "final victory."

During the days that followed, Hitler carried his appeal for blind trust to still more gatherings of Nazi functionaries. Commenting on his Sportpalast speech in a dispatch to Paris, Ambassador François-Poncet struck a decorous note of skepticism: "It is obviously difficult to discern the extent to which Mr. Hitler thereby expresses a personal conviction or submits to the necessities of propaganda." In the ambassador's judgment, the grave internal crisis of the Nazi Party was far from over, and he suspected that Hitler had decided that the best way to hold his troops in line was to keep them stirred up.

A striking aspect of Hitler's response to his precarious position during the second half of January was the composure he maintained in the face of daunting circumstances. Although his all-or-nothing pursuit of power showed no signs of producing positive results, and although this lack of success imperiled the movement that had become his life's sole purpose, he betrayed no loss of nerve. The unshakable belief in his calling to lead Germany, which inspired blind trust in so many of his followers, did not desert him under stress. Incapable of entertaining the thought of failure, he confidently awaited the power he remained convinced would somehow soon be his. Meanwhile, he continued to lead the self-indulgent, semi-bohemian life which his freedom from the normal constraints of life had permitted him to cultivate throughout his political career. The afternoon coffee hour usually found him presiding over a table full of admirers and retainers. In Berlin those gatherings took place in the ornate café of the fashionable Kaiserhof Hotel, his home in Berlin. His evenings, customarily spent in the company of his closest henchmen and various hangers-on, stretched on into the small hours of the morning.

On the evening of Wednesday, January 18, with his political fate hanging uncertainly in the balance following his inconclusive talks with Hugenberg and Papen, Hitler went to see a new motion picture, *The Rebel,* that had just opened in Berlin. The film's melodramatic depiction of a student's heroic resistance to the Napoleonic occupation of the Austrian province of Tyrol left Hitler "all fired up," as Goebbels, who accompanied him, noted in his diary. Hitler was so excited by the film that he returned to the theater the next evening for a second viewing. He presumably found confirmation for his own struggle in the story of a hero whose intense patriotism and fiery oratory enabled him to rise from humble origins and lead his people's ultimately successful nationalist uprising against foreign oppression. Like Hitler, the protagonist of *The Rebel* rejected compromise. He unhesitatingly committed his life to his cause and manifested an outlook that, as a prominent film critic of the time later observed, "excludes surrender, even though it does not preclude defeat." The ficticious Tyrolean student's fanatical certitude gave him the same kind of hold over others as did Hitler's unwavering belief in his destiny. That *The Rebel* ended with the hero suffering a martyr's death did not diminish Hitler's enthusiasm for the film. For he, too, was prepared for martyrdom. As he explained to his followers at the Berlin Sportpalast on January 20, "I have chosen this task because I had no other choice, because it is self-evident to me that it is my life's work, with which I shall rise or fall."

4

Schleicher Falls Victim to Illusions

WHILE HITLER WAS SAVORING Wagner's *Die Meistersinger* in Munich on the evening of New Year's Day, Chancellor Kurt von Schleicher attended a performance in Berlin of the operetta *La Princesse de Trébizonde* by Jacques Offenbach. When the plot of that lighthearted musical farce, staged in an exotic oriental setting, reached a crisis point, one member of the cast exclaimed despairingly, "What shall we do now?" Departing from the libretto, another responded: "We'll form a new cabinet and dissolve the Reichstag." This timely improvisation drew a burst of laughter from the audience and elicited from the chancellor a mischievous grimace, suggesting awareness on his part that the political situation was less than stable.

The continuing turbulence in the country was mirrored by that day's press reports of numerous acts of political violence that had marred New Year's Eve celebrations despite a holiday political truce. In Berlin alone, bloody clashes between Communists and Nazis of the sort that had turned the streets of Germany into battlefields during the previous three years left dozens wounded and some sixty combatants under arrest. A seamstress, walking home late in the evening in a workers' district of the capital, died after being shot by a Nazi storm-trooper she had never seen before. The murderer, who shouted "Heil Hitler!" as he rode away on his bicycle, later testified that he had mistaken the victim for a Communist. Elsewhere in the city that same night, another Nazi stabbed a nineteen-year-old Communist to death, while a sixteen-year-old member of the Hitler Youth organization succumbed to stab wounds inflicted by unknown assailants presumed to be Communists. In other parts of the country, too, the political mayhem continued unabated, casting a dark shadow over the optimism that greeted the new year in republican circles.

Underlying this atmosphere of political violence was the wide-spread privation resulting from three years of dire economic depression. The signs of improvement registered by the stock and bond markets as well as by other indices since the middle of 1932 had brought no immediate relief to the over six million unemployed workers and their families. By the beginning of 1933 more than half of the jobless in Berlin had exhausted their eligibility for government unemployment insurance benefits and become dependent on the meager municipal dole, which was barely sufficient for subsistence survival. An American journalist calculated that a family of three living on the dole had to survive on a daily diet consisting of six small potatoes, five slices of bread, one small cabbage, a cubic inch of margarine, and a half liter of milk for the child. No meat reached their table. On Sundays their budget allowed for one herring each. Malnutrition, especially among children, had become an acute prob-lem. Forced to choose between food and rental payments, many had lost their homes and become dependent on charitable soup kitchens for their food and flophouses or municipal warming halls for shelter from the winter weather. Those who still had jobs had to fear joining the ranks of those who peddled apples and pencils on the streets or walked about bearing signs soliciting work. The depression might at last be waning, but its effects were still very much present.

In a radio address to the nation in mid-December Chancellor von

Schleicher had addressed the plight of the unemployed by promising that his program would consist of two words: "Create Work!" Breaking with Papen's policy of seeking to stimulate employment indirectly by granting easements to businesses, the new chancellor committed himself to government financing of projects that would directly generate new jobs. He pledged as well a major effort to accelerate and expand the efforts of previous cabinets to settle some of the urban unemployed on rural homesteads in the underpopulated northeastern regions of the country. In response to protests by organized labor, he announced repeal of a Papen cabinet decree that had allowed employers to reduce wages below levels set by collective bargaining contracts. Similarly, he rejected Papen's imposition of a means test for unemployment compensation and called for a restoration of benefits for the jobless as a social insurance entitlement. Proclaiming himself a proponent of neither capitalism nor socialism, the new chancellor promised a pragmatic approach to the country's economic problems. Lest there be any doubt about his populistic intentions, he informed his listeners that he had no objection to being called a "social general," a label he contended was wholly consistent with the army's tradition of solidarity between officers and troops.

Schleicher also used his radio address to reassure defenders of the republic about his political intentions. He had accepted appointment as head of government only with great reservations, he announced, in part because a defense minister as chancellor "smells of military dictatorship." But in his case, he assured his listeners, such fears were unwarranted. "I have said before and repeat today: One does not sit well on the points of bayonets, that is, one cannot govern over the long run without broad public support." Conspicuously missing from his talk was any mention of the plans for revising the constitution that Papen had proposed. By way of defining his chancellorship, Schleicher asked to be regarded not merely as a soldier but rather as the "nonpartisan steward of the interests of all sections of the population for what will hopefully prove only a short period of emergency." He had come, he added, "not to bring the sword but rather peace." As to how he proposed to govern, the chancellor expressed the hope that the Reichstag, "to which I grant a strong dose of distrust, will give the cabinet a chance to carry out its program without interfering and without the all-too-well-known parliamentary methods."

Out of public view, Schleicher was less conciliatory toward the Reichstag. In order to achieve his aims, he thought he would need at least two years free of parliamentary trammels. During that time he envisioned the Reichstag's meeting every few months to let off steam, but without affecting the work of his cabinet. By focusing public attention on national security, he hoped to relegate to secondary status the domestic disputes that had so deeply divided the country during the economic crisis. Shortly after he had taken office, the victorious powers of World War I had, after lengthy negotiations, conceded in principle Germany's right to equality in arms. Rather than complying with the Versailles Treaty's provisions for general disarmament, the victors were now inclined to allow the Germans to rearm to a level that would assure them military parity within a security system still to be devised. Although exactly what that concession would mean in practical terms remained uncertain, it cleared the way, in Schleicher's view, for formation of a compulsory militia that would serve as the first step to a resumption of universal conscription. He planned, that is, to commit his cabinet to the cause of rearmament and reap the political credit for ending Germany's military impotence.

By the first week of January, after a month in office, Schleicher had made little progress toward these goals. His repudiation of the most unpopular policies of the Papen cabinet had enabled him to dispel the danger of a civil war that had loomed at the end of Papen's chancellorship. But with the Reichstag scheduled to reconvene on January 24, he faced the problem of how to avert a massive no-confidence vote in the legislature similar to that which had begun Papen's downfall. Whereas Papen had enjoyed the support of at least the German-Nationals, Schleicher still had no firm parliamentary backing aside from that of the two small and politically insignificant liberal parties.

Schleicher's conciliatory gestures to organized labor had, to be sure, gained him some credit. The leaders of the Christian Unions, closely linked to the Catholic Center Party, showed guarded signs of receptivity to his overtures. The leaders of the country's largest labor organization, the Free Unions, also looked with favor upon his promise of government-financed measures to create jobs, hoping for relief of the widespread unemployment among their members. But the attitude of the Free Unions was of limited political value to Schleicher, since the closely affiliated Social Democratic Party remained resolutely cold toward the new chancellor, whose cabinet it condemned as a mere continuation of the despised Papen regime. The Social Democrats regarded Schleicher as implicated in the Papen cabinet's deposition of the government of Prussia, which had been their party's prime source of patronage. As a consequence, the Social Democrats' 121 Reichstag deputies stood in implacable opposition, along with the 100 deputies of the Communists, whose hostility toward the Social Democrats ruled out any cooperation beyond negation of the Schleicher cabinet.

In the interests of keeping Hitler from power, one prominent Social Democrat was ready to defy his colleagues by putting aside past differences with Schleicher. On January 6, Otto Braun, the deposed long-time minister-president of Prussia and one of the most accomplished of Social Democratic politicians, paid the chancellor a visit and proposed a bold bargain. If Schleicher would prevail upon Hindenburg to reinstall his cabinet in Prussia, Braun offered to join with the chancellor in urging the president to dissolve both the Reichstag and the Prussian state legislature without scheduling new elections within the constitutionally required periods. The two would then collaborate to keep the Nazis at bay, governing by means of emergency decrees until the spring.

Hitler's party was already in decline, Braun contended. It would suffer devastating losses if elections were held after several months had passed, especially in view of signs that the economy had bottomed out and was showing signs of improvement. New elections held under such circumstances would, he predicted, yield a Reichstag and a Prussian legislature capable of functioning normally. Braun's proposal drew a negative response from Schleicher, who explained that he had no hope of bringing the president to restore the old friction-ridden relationship between the national and Prussian governments. He neglected to mention that he himself had effectively foreclosed the option of cooperating with the largest republican party when he played a major role the previous summer in persuading Hindenburg to strip Braun and the rest of the Prussian ministers of their authority.

Unlike Braun, Schleicher was not looking for ways to weaken the Nazis. Instead, he planned to use them. He still hoped to make their 196-member Reichstag delegation the basis of a parliamentary majority willing to support his cabinet or at least refrain from opposing it. As he later put it, he thought the prospects good for reaching a "modus vivendi" with the Nazis. Throughout the first half of January, his hopes continued to focus on Gregor Strasser, despite Strasser's resignation from his Nazi Party post and sudden disappearance into Italy a month earlier. As Schleicher had explained to a gathering of generals in mid-December, he sought "the cooperation of the Nazis under Strasser with the messiah's blessing of Hitler." Come January, he told the generals, he would pose to the Nazis the question, "Will you play along?" If they refused, then the moment for combat would have arrived, and the Reichstag would have to be dissolved. In order to retain the moral advantage, he continued, he would have to make every effort to bring the Nazis to accept a share of responsibility for the government. But if it came to a confrontation with them, he would not limit himself to pinpricks. It would be a tough fight, but, he added, it would not be in the interest of the state to destroy Hitler's party. As before, Schleicher overlooked the barbarous aspects of Nazism, saw it as useful for his purposes, and feared its breakup would release energy and talent to the Communists.

At the time, the Nazi leaders assumed that Schleicher had offered a place in his cabinet to Gregor Strasser in hopes of producing a split in the Nazi ranks, a view shared by many observers and accepted by most historians. Such was not the case, however. The chancellor's meeting with Strasser in early December seems to have gone well. The same was apparently true of a visit with Hindenburg on January 6 which Schleicher arranged for Strasser under cover of secrecy. The president reportedly expressed relief at finding nothing radical about Strasser and indicated his readiness to accept him as vice chancellor. But despite the favorable impression that Strasser made, there is no evidence that Schleicher ever actually offered him a cabinet appointment. Nor is there any evidence that the chancellor sought to use Strasser to split the Nazi Party in order to gain the support of a part of its Reichstag delegation for his cabinet, as was widely assumed at the time and has been ever since. The political arithmetic of the situation alone ruled that out. Schleicher himself estimated that, at most, about 60 of the 196 Nazi Reichstag deputies would follow Strasser. But even if Strasser should successfully lead such a secession, the votes of 60 Nazi deputies would not—in combination with those of the middle and right-of-center parties—have sufficed to produce an acquiescent parliamentary majority willing to refrain from opposing the cabinet. The remaining 130-some Nazi deputies could join with the 121 Social Democrats and the 100 Communists to carry a no-confidence motion in the 584-seat chamber.

As Schleicher admitted to his cabinet on January 16, the backing of a Nazi secession led by Strasser would not solve the cabinet's parliamentary problems. Only with Hitler's cooperation, he told the ministers, could a favorable majority in the Reichstag be attained. The chancellor's problem was how to bring the Nazi leader to back down from his repeatedly expressed resolve to oppose any cabinet he did not himself head. In hopes of achieving that, Schleicher was seeking to use Strasser as a lever to move Hitler, not as a wedge for splitting the Nazi Party. For that tactic to work, Hitler had to be led to believe that a secession was a real danger. For the time being, Strasser was more valuable to the chancellor outside the cabinet than in it, since his appointment would undoubtedly lead Hitler to break irretrievably with his former lieutenant, thereby solidifying Nazi opposition to the cabinet. Meanwhile, Schleicher encouraged talk of a split in the Nazi ranks led by Strasser.

Another lever Schleicher used to exert pressure on Hitler was the threat of a new Reichstag election. In view of the Nazis' heavy electoral losses during the last months of 1932 and their obvious financial difficulties, he assumed that the prospect of another costly national campaign and still more lost votes would be daunting for Hitler. Schleicher preferred to avoid such an outcome, lest Nazi losses result in an increase in the Communists' strength. But to exert pressure on Hitler, he had his staff indicate to the press that in the event a no-confidence vote became probable, he would obtain from the president a decree dissolving the Reichstag and scheduling yet another election. To discourage Hitler from stalling in order to avoid the alternatives of cooperating with the cabinet or facing the electorate again under unfavorable circumstances, Schleicher and his aides let it be known that if the Nazis supported an extension of the Reichstag recess or put off a confidence vote, the chancellor would publicly interpret such a maneuver as acquiescence on their part in his cabinet's rule by presidential decree. That would implicate the Nazis in the cabinet's policies and deprive them of the political advantages of remaining untainted by governmental responsibility at a time of great economic hardship. It would also dispel the aura of defiant opposition that Hitler had so successfully cultivated.

Despite Hitler's emphatic public reaffirmations of his all-or-nothing course, Schleicher repeatedly expressed confidence during the first half of January that the Nazi leader would give way. "Hitler's on the verge of desperation," he assured a journalist on January 10, "because he senses his party is falling apart under him without his ever seeing it attain a position of power." At his off-the-record dinner for journalists on the evening of January 13, the chancellor responded to a question about the Nazis with a smile and a dismissive gesture. "I'll take care of them," he assured the journalists. "They'll soon be eating out of my hand." His goal, he explained, was to force the Nazis to abandon their "messianic beliefs" and to so weaken them that they would have to support an authoritarian government headed by him. Asked during the evening about the Lippe election, he rated the Nazis' prospects as dim. Hitler's participation in the campaign there resembled, he scoffed, a "visit to a fortune-teller." Clearly, an observation about Schleicher made by a fellow officer during the war was still valid: "He perhaps inclines to underestimate what is required to surmount difficulties."

The chancellor's confidence in his ability to harness Hitler rested on three crippling illusions. The most obvious of these was his assumption that the Nazi leader would respond in prudent, rational fashion to threats of a Strasser-led rebellion and a new national election. Faced with such risks, most politicians would have given way and compromised in order to cut their losses. But although Schleicher had talked with Hitler at length on several occasions, he had failed to notice that the Nazi leader was not an ordinary politician. It had escaped him that Hitler firmly believed not only that he alone possessed the correct formula for Germany's future but also that he could not fail because destiny was on his side. Unshakably convinced that he would eventually gain total power, Hitler had not the slightest inclination to compromise in order to avert political difficulties of the sort Schleicher sought to exploit. The chancellor's strategy was thus based on fundamentally faulty assumptions about Hitler's mentality.

The second illusion that clouded the chancellor's vision was his assumption that Hitler was still isolated politically. On that point, Schleicher fell victim to his underestimation of Franz von Papen. The chancellor remained incapable of taking seriously the man he had once thought of as a willing tool and still looked upon as a guileless blunderer. Thinking Papen incapable of duplicity, Schleicher had accepted his predecessor's mendacious claim that he had met with Hitler in Cologne merely in an effort to enlist the Nazi leader's support for the Schleicher cabinet. As a consequence, the chancellor remained unaware that a conspiracy had been launched against him by his former friend. Least of all did he suspect that the man who had called him to the chancellorship, President von Hindenburg himself, had become an accessory to that conspiracy. On January 10, just one day after Hindenburg authorized Papen to serve as his secret liaison to Hitler, Schleicher assured a journalist that although the Nazi leader's goal in Cologne had obviously been to establish contact with the president, his hopes had been in vain. "Hitler has almost as bad an effect on Hindenburg as a Communist," he added.

The third and most bizarre of Schleicher's illusions was his belief that Hitler was not actually seeking the chancellorship. In mid-December Schleicher suggested to a gathering of generals that nothing had come of Hindenburg's November offer to appoint Hitler chancellor of a parliamentary cabinet because the Nazi leader did not "at the bottom of his heart" want the office. By January that suspicion had hardened into a firm conviction. The reason lay, once again, with Schleicher's trusting acceptance of the version of the Cologne meeting related to him by Franz von Papen. In Papen's false claim that Hitler had demanded for himself both the ministry of defense and the interior ministry as the price for Nazi support of the Schleicher cabinet, the chancellor saw confirmation of a pattern of behavior on Hitler's part. As he explained in the course of his dinner with journalists on the evening of January 13, the Nazi leader's demands had obviously been meant for Hindenburg's ears, since Hitler knew that anything he told Papen would be promptly relayed to the president. Moreover, in requesting ministries that would give him control over both the army and the police, Hitler had deliberately asked for more than he knew Hindenburg would grant him. This fit a pattern of behavior on his part over the past months: at every crucial juncture Hitler had obviously set terms too high for the president because he wanted them to be rejected. As Schleicher confided to journalists at the off-the-record dinner and then again to his cabinet on January 16—just two weeks before Hitler replaced him as chancellor—the conclusion was inescapable: the future dictator did not really want power.

Neither Schleicher's cabinet ministers nor the journalists he sought to enlighten about Hitler's aversion to high office challenged him on that point. That may well have been because they assumed the chancellor knew more than they, and from better sources. Many well-informed persons in Berlin political circles believed that as defense minister Schleicher presided over a highly developed, pervasive espionage network. Former chancellors Brüning and Papen, Hindenburg's chief of staff Otto Meissner, and at least one member of Schleicher's own cabinet all suspected that their telephones were tapped by his agents. No confirmation of those suspicions has ever come to light, however. Indeed, far from having a wealth of information at his disposal, Schleicher seems to have suffered from a paucity of reliable intelligence on the attitudes and activities of other political figures. His knowledge about what was going on in the Nazi Party was particularly deficient. On that count, he paid particularly close attention to letters forwarded to him by former German crown prince Wilhelm, who had received them from a sixty-five-year-old retired general who held a peripheral post in the Nazi stormtroop administration in Munich. A Strasser loyalist, the crown prince's informant could provide only minimal information, often mixed with misleading rumors, especially after Strasser broke with Hitler in December. From all indications, the chancellor knew little during January 1933 about the activities and intentions of the man who would soon succeed him or about the crisis that gripped the Nazi Party.

When Schleicher's efforts to win Hitler's cooperation by means of intimidation yielded no results, he intensified his efforts. On January 10 he and his press secretary planted reports in the press of plans to secure a political "underpinning" for his cabinet through the appointment of three new ministers. Gregor Strasser was identified as the proposed vice chancellor and interior minister in the national cabinet as well as minister-president of Prussia. Adam Stegerwald, a prominent Catholic Center Party parliamentarian and Christian Trade Union leader, was designated as labor minister. Two ministries, agriculture and economics, were earmarked for Alfred Hugenberg, leader of the German-National Party. Even after this realignment, Schleicher specified in briefing one journalist, his cabinet would continue to be presidential rather than parliamentary, since it would remain free of formal ties to the parties of the three new ministers. But he also indicated that he expected their inclusion would result in a cooperative attitude on the part of their parties, which together commanded a comfortable majority in the Reichstag.

In leaking these reports to the press, Schleicher was bluffing. He had made no offer to Hugenberg, much less obtained that cantankerous politician's agreement to join the cabinet. Nor had he sounded out Stegerwald about a cabinet post. He also still held back from bringing his negotiations with Strasser to culmination. The target of his bluff was obviously Hitler, and its purpose was to heighten the pressure on him. Schleicher was trying to bully the Nazi leader into dropping his opposition to the cabinet by threatening that, unless Hitler came to terms quickly, his former lieutenant would assume a prominent place in a broad-based national cabinet and take over as head of the patronage-rich Prussian state government. Equipped with the spoils that would come with those posts, Strasser would be in a position to hold out handsome rewards to Nazis who deserted Hitler to follow him.

To ratchet up the pressure on Hitler, Schleicher's press secretary disclosed to the press on January 10 the news of Strasser's secretive meeting with Hindenburg the previous week. The chancellor also let it be known through journalists that while he did not intend to initiate a meeting with Hitler, his door was always open to him. Once again, however, Schleicher had miscalculated in expecting Hitler to respond in a prudent manner to threatened political perils. Although the news of Strasser's visit to the president momentarily stunned the Nazi leaders when it broke in the midst of the Lippe campaign, Hitler made no request for a meeting with the chancellor. To do so, he undoubtedly realized, would cast him in the role of a supplicant and thus place him at a severe disadvantage.

Within a week, Schleicher's bluff lost all plausibility. Informed political observers immediately responded with skepticism to his formula for providing his cabinet with a parliamentary underpinning. Quite aside from the difficulty of integrating even a relatively reasonable Nazi like Strasser into the government, the wide political gap that separated the republican trade unionist Stegerwald from the German-National Hugenberg, an antidemocratic arch-foe of organized labor, made cooperation between those two seem highly improbable. That quickly proved to be the case. Meeting with Hugenberg on Friday, January 13, Schleicher offered him the ministries of agriculture and economics. Hugenberg specified, however, that he would be willing to enter the cabinet only if the chancellor agreed to establish a thoroughgoing authoritarian regime that would, for at least a year, take no notice of the Reichstag—a step totally unacceptable for Stegerwald's Center Party. On the following Monday morning, January 16, the newspaper of the Christian Unions announced in no uncertain terms that there was no possibility of Stegerwald's serving in a cabinet alongside Hugenberg. That same morning, the leader of the Catholic Center Party, Monsignor Ludwig Kaas, visited the chancellor to deliver the same message. Later in the day, Hitler made his break with Gregor Strasser permanent with his speech to the Nazi gauleiters in Weimar.

Schleicher received news of the latter development only days later, but by mid-morning of January 16 the incompatibility of Hugenberg and Stegerwald as well as the Nazis' gains in the Lippe election had become public knowledge. It was therefore indicative either of an appalling lack of information or a loss of touch with reality that at a cabinet meeting late that same morning the chancellor made no reference to the outcome of the balloting in Lippe and confidently unveiled his already defunct scheme for gaining a parliamentary underpinning. His sole concession to reality was to omit mention of Stegerwald and speak only of "a representative of the Center party" as the third element in combination with Strasser and Hugenberg.

During the week following the cabinet meeting of January 16 any lingering hopes Schleicher had of bringing even the right-wing German-Nationals behind his cabinet vanished. Having failed to exact from the chancellor his conditions for entry into the cabinet, Hugenberg came under increasing pressure from his party's extremist elements to embark upon a course of all-out opposition to Schleicher. On Friday, January 20, he agreed to a strongly worded party resolution that called for replacement of the cabinet. It accused Schleicher of "a policy of vacillation and delaying tactics" that threatened to undermine the authoritarian course initiated by President von Hindenburg at the time of Papen's appointment as chancellor. Alluding to the chancellor's endorsement of the breakup of bankrupt rural estates into settlers' parcels, the resolution detected in Schleicher's policies "a backsliding into socialist-internationalist patterns of thought" that posed "the danger of rural Bolshevism." The text of this inflammatory document was not published until January 24, but a copy was personally delivered to the chancellor by a prominent German-National deputy on January 21. From that point on, there could be no doubt that Schleicher faced only unabating hostility from Hugenberg and his party. By the 21st the chancellor was himself disclaiming any intention to revamp his cabinet.

Even before his underpinning scheme collapsed, Schleicher had unnecessarily complicated his position by spreading confusion about his intentions. During his dinner session with journalists on January 13, he reacted angrily to rightist charges that he was accommodating labor unions and other republican groups in an effort to cultivate parliamentary support. His aim, he insisted, was a strong, authoritarian regime, free of dependency on the Reichstag. That was, however, difficult to reconcile with the plans he had made known just a few days earlier to revamp his cabinet in order to gain parliamentary backing. At that same dinner session, Schleicher also undercut his threat to schedule a new election in the event that the prospect of a no-confidence vote led him to dissolve the Reichstag. The previous November, he told the journalists present, everyone had wanted another round of balloting, but now the mood of the country had changed. Neither the parties nor the voters nor the business community nor labor would object if a new election were postponed beyond the constitutionally mandated sixty days in the event of a Reichstag dissolution. Three days later, on January 16, Schleicher said essentially the same thing to his cabinet. As a result, the possibility of such a violation of the constitution by the chancellor became a topic of discussion in the press.

In broaching the possibility of avoiding a new election, Schleicher was reviving a plan he had twice endorsed during Papen's chancellorship but had finally rejected. He had presumably come to the realization by mid-January that while another round of national balloting would cost the Nazis votes, there was no likelihood of a significant shift of parliamentary strength in his favor. For some time, he had toyed with the idea of establishing a new "presidential party" that would provide voters with a means to support a cabinet that answered only to Hindenburg, but he had taken no steps to implement that idea. Whatever his motives, however, Schleicher made a tactical mistake in revealing his fallback position in the event that his efforts to gain the Nazis' parliamentary cooperation should fail. Although reports that the chancellor might block a new election scarcely sufficed to determine Hitler's intransigent stance, they may have stiffened his resolve by suggesting a lack of confidence on Schleicher's part that the Nazis would suffer heavy losses if the country voted again. If Hitler was looking for indications as to whether Schleicher was really resolved to beat the Nazis with the stick of a new election, such signals could only have provided him with hope that this was not the case.

Press reports that Schleicher might prevent a new election greatly alarmed defenders of the republic. Apprehension about such a breach of the constitution was particularly strong among the leaders of one of the key parties whose support Schleicher hoped to gain, the Catholic Center. As spokesmen of a religious minority that had experienced persecution under the Empire's first chancellor, Bismarck, the Centrists were particularly vigilant guardians of the letter of the republican constitution. The possibility that Schleicher might be considering a flagrant violation of one of its articles therefore heightened their wariness toward the chancellor. For the Social Democrats, that possibility only confirmed their profound misgivings about Schleicher. By contrast, anti-republican conservatives greeted the reports as a welcome sign of resolve on the chancellor's part to break openly with the hated Weimar constitution and parliamentary democracy. When, only days later, the Chancellery issued a denial of any intention to postpone a new election unconstitutionally, everyone was left confused, and mistrust of Schleicher mounted. Through his own careless words, it now became obvious, he had added to the political isolation he was striving to escape.

That isolation extended even into the cabinet. Rather than select a new panel of ministers loyal to him at the time of his appointment, Schleicher had retained all but two members of Papen's cabinet of conservative, nonpolitical experts. When a young aide in the defense ministry pointed to the danger that this arrangement would transfer the unpopularity of his predecessor's cabinet to his own, Schleicher replied: "Yes, sonny boy [*Kerlchen*], you're completely right; but I can't do without these people at the moment, because I have no one else." From the outset, Schleicher regarded his cabinet as merely provisional and made no secret of his readiness to replace incumbent ministers with men who would provide additional political backing. He therefore chose not to rely on the cabinet for guidance in charting his political strategy and tactics. The increasingly infrequent cabinet meetings dealt almost exclusively with routine business. On the rare occasions when Schleicher addressed the political situation, he allowed the ministers only glimpses of his intentions. As a consequence, some of them arrived at quite erroneous views of what he sought.

Unsurprisingly, morale in Schleicher's cabinet was low. His secretive, overbearing manner at cabinet meetings contributed to this. So did his refusal to immerse himself in the details of government. Members of the cabinet who sought his assistance in dealing with knotty problems met with little or no cooperation. That was the experience even of Günther Gereke, an energetic, conservative advocate of activist government added by Schleicher to the cabinet as a special commissioner to oversee the programs for job creation and rural resettlement the chancellor had promised would be his top priorities. Gereke's assignment was to accelerate the mobilization of government resources to reduce the high level of unemployment that remained the country's most pressing domestic problem. He was therefore profoundly disappointed when, early in January, Schleicher turned down a request on his part for intervention by the chancellor to clear away bureaucratic roadblocks that were obstructing progress on those projects.

Schleicher also sidestepped the thorny issue of trade policy. The ministers for agriculture and economics he inherited from Papen had long been at loggerheads on that count. With food prices at all-time lows, farming interests pressed for government intercession on behalf of producers of foodstuffs. In particular, the spokesmen of agriculture demanded higher tariffs and other barriers to reduce competition from imported foodstuffs. Industrial interests responded by warning against such protectionist measures, lest food-exporting countries retaliate by erecting barriers against German manufacturing exports. The minister of agriculture sided with the agrarians, the ministers of economics with the industrialists. Refusing to involve himself in the details of the dispute, the chancellor instructed the two ministers to reach a compromise on what they regarded as irreconcilable differences. While maintaining a pretense of accord in public, they continued to checkmate each other behind the scenes, issuing threats of resignation to back up their positions and accomplishing little. The minister for agriculture later characterized his experiences in the Schleicher cabinet as "true torture."

FAR more damaging than the alienation of cabinet ministers was a growing estrangement between Schleicher and the ultimate arbiter of power, President von Hindenburg. Almost from the outset, reports of coolness on the president's side circulated in Berlin. By the second week of January the chancellor and his staff were openly conceding to journalists that Schleicher enjoyed less cordial relations with Hindenburg than had Papen, although they denied that this posed a problem.

The causes of this deterioration of relations between the two men will probably never be fully known. It seems likely, however, that one factor was a not unwarranted suspicion on the president's part that intrigue by Schleicher had caused the downfall of his favorite, Franz von Papen. That view was widely held in the capital's political circles despite efforts by the chancellor and his staff to counter it.

At the onset of his chancellorship, Schleicher was given to understand by Hindenburg that he would be expected to defend his predecessor's record, but he soon proved negligent in that regard. By January he was making caustic comments about Papen's performance as chancellor to journalists, including some who had covert lines of communication to Papen, who was unlikely to have withheld reports of such indiscretions from the president. Another of Hindenburg's sources of information was the disaffected commissioner for job creation, Gereke. Having managed the finances of the president's reelection campaign the previous year, Gereke had become an intimate of the Hindenburg family. He enjoyed particularly close relations with the old field marshal's son and military adjutant, Colonel Oskar von Hindenburg. Given Gereke's increasingly jaundiced view of Schleicher, the Hindenburgs presumably heard little that was positive about the chancellor from him.

Papen undoubtedly contributed in a major way to the deterioration of Schleicher's relations with Hindenburg. Secretly resentful and longing for revenge, the former chancellor continued to enjoy privileged access to the president. At Hindenburg's request, he stayed on in the apartment in the Interior Ministry building on Wilhelmstrasse where he had lived as chancellor. Only the Foreign Ministry stood between that building and the Chancellery, where Hindenburg had, in the spring of 1932, taken over the apartment normally occupied by the chancellor, having been forced to vacate the presidential palace three doors away when extensive repairs became urgently necessary there. By exiting through the rear of the Interior Ministry and passing through the gates that separated the secluded gardens behind the official buildings along Wilhelmstrasse, Papen could enter the Chancellery from the rear and visit the president without attracting notice. Free of all responsibilities, he was in an ideal position to intrigue full-time against the man who had taken his place as chancellor.

In contrast to Papen's easy access to the president, Schleicher seems to have had limited personal contact with the head of state. Both Hindenburg and Schleicher conducted business in the Chancellery, but the president's office in the older part of that large, sprawling building was some distance from Schleicher's, which was located in an annex added on the Wilhelmstrasse side in the late '20s. Moreover, unlike Papen, Schleicher did not reside in the Wilhelmstrasse complex of official buildings. Instead, he chose to stay on in the private dwelling some distance away into which he and his wife of a year had recently moved. Schleicher also spent many of his working hours at the Defense Ministry, over a mile away from the Chancellery, where he continued to rely heavily on his military staff, even on matters that fell within the purview of the chancellorship.

Although Schleicher had for years served as one of Hindenburg's closest advisers, the personal chemistry between the two suffered from their interaction as head of state and head of government. By contrast, Papen had ingratiated himself with the old field marshal while chancellor, in no small measure because of a personal solicitude that verged on obsequiousness. Having grown accustomed to Papen's servile displays of devotion, Hindenburg found the brusk and self-centered Schleicher insufficiently attentive to his sensibilities.

In a conversation with an Austrian diplomat a week after Hitler became chancellor, Oskar von Hindenburg provided a revealing glimpse of the strained relations between Schleicher and his father. Praising Papen's "qualities of character," Oskar contrasted his conduct as chancellor favorably with that of "another gentleman," a circumlocution the diplomat immediately recognized as a reference to Schleicher. The younger Hindenburg then went on to relate how, on a recent occasion, his father had, upon hearing of a planned governmental measure, exclaimed apprehensively, "They'll jump all over me for that." The reply of "the other gentleman" had been: "*Jawohl,* there's no way to avoid that." Not long before, according to the president's son, Papen had, as chancellor, responded to a similar expression of concern on the part of his father with the reassuring words: "How so? That's what I'm here for." In the younger Hindenburg's neofeudal frame of reference, and presumably that of his father, Papen's fawning words constituted "knightly fealty," a virtue he found deficient in Schleicher. In reporting this conversation to Vienna, the Austrian diplomat observed: "Many things that seem politically inexplicable become comprehensible in human terms if one looks behind the scenes."

During January additional friction developed between the chancellor and the president over a matter close to the president's heart. Like many other conservative Germans of his generation, Hindenburg accorded agriculture a position of primacy. It was for him not merely one sector of the economy but rather the foundation of national life, the source of wholesome traditions and values. He was therefore upset when the leaders of the principal farm lobby, the Agrarian League, complained to him on January 11 that the Schleicher cabinet had not made good on promises to continue Papen's policy of erecting protectionist barriers to shield German farm products from the competition of cheaper foreign foodstuffs. The League's spokesmen also demanded renewal of a Papen decree that Schleicher had allowed to lapse at the end of December, which accorded bankrupt farmers a grace period by shielding them from loss of their land through foreclosure.

Exceeding his constitutional authority, Hindenburg responded to these complaints by peremptorily summoning the chancellor, as well as the ministers of agriculture and economics, to meet with the Agrarian League's leaders in his presence later that same day. At that session, Schleicher and the two cabinet ministers succeeded in mollifying the agrarian spokesmen with regard to trade barriers by informing them that plans were underway for future measures. But when Schleicher balked at committing himself to a renewal of foreclosure protection because of the hardships that would impose on those owed money by bankrupt farmers, Hindenburg intervened to put him on notice that he found the cabinet's position unsatisfactory and expected to be informed the next day about plans to deal with the matter.

Although Schleicher submitted to this presidential browbeating in the presence of the Agrarian League's spokesmen on the afternoon of January 11, his patience with that organization ran out minutes after the meeting ended. As the chancellor recognized, the League had long since ceased to be a normal economic pressure group and become a political tool of Adolf Hitler's party. By winning the allegiance of large numbers of Protestant farmers, the Nazis had infiltrated the League at the grassroots and gained strong representation at all levels of its organization. For the Nazis in the leadership ranks of the League, it was not enough to extract economic concessions from Schleicher. They wanted to bring him down so as to clear the way for Hitler. At their urging, the League's executive body had therefore adopted and released to the press on the morning of January 11 a harshly worded resolution that amounted to a broadside attack on the chancellor. It characterized his cabinet as a tool of "the almighty money-bag interests of internationally oriented export industry and its satellites" and accused it of displaying "an indifference to the impoverishment of agriculture beyond the capacity of even a purely Marxist regime." The League's spokesmen made no mention of this resolution while meeting with the president and chancellor that afternoon, and Schleicher learned of it only at the close of the session, when one of their number handed him a copy. Furious both because of the resolution's demagogic content and because it had been withheld during the meeting, he responded by having the Chancellery immediately release to the press a statement denouncing the League for a breach of good faith and proclaiming that the cabinet would engage in no further negotiations with its leaders.

Whereas Schleicher angrily broke with the Agrarian League, having seen through the Nazis' manipulation of it, the president responded in a manner that left no doubt that he still viewed the organization favorably. In him, the League's leaders had found a sympathetic listener. As they well knew, Hindenburg was a descendant of a venerable

East Prussian family who prided himself on his ties to the Junker aristocracy that dominated the agriculture of eastern Germany. His career as a professional military man had, to be sure, allowed him limited exposure to rural life and no direct experience with agriculture. But late in life he became a landowner through no effort of his own. On his eightieth birthday in 1927 he received as a gift—paid for mainly by contributions from industrial interests—his family's ancestral estate in East Prussia. It soon became his favorite refuge, where he relished assuming the role of country squire whenever he could escape the round of official duties in the capital.

Hindenburg found congenial the company of Junker neighbors at his rural retreat, who traditionally looked to the Agrarian League for defense of their economic interests. The League in turn came to regard him as an ally. After Schleicher broke with the League on January 11, the president received letters and telegrams of protest from its regional branches. In all likelihood, he heard much the same from his Junker neighbors. On January 12 the League's leaders appealed to Hindenburg for support in an open letter in which they rejected the chancellor's charges of bad faith and claimed to be motivated solely by concern for suffering farmers. These entreaties were not in vain. On January 17, a day after Schleicher had acquiesced in his cabinet's compliance with Hindenburg's insistence upon a new measure to protect bankrupt farmers from foreclosure, the president addressed a cordial letter to the leaders of the organization with which the chancellor had publicly broken relations less than a week earlier.

On January 18, events took a turn that widened the growing breach between Schleicher and Hindenburg. At a session of the Reichstag's budget committee a deputy of the Catholic Center Party leveled sweeping charges of fraud at Junker beneficiaries of what was known as the eastern aid program. Implemented several years earlier to rescue from bankruptcy heavily indebted agricultural proprietors in the economically backward eastern parts of Prussia, the program had distributed millions of marks of government funds. Drawing on detailed financial records of undisclosed origin, the Center Party deputy and other republicans accused a number of prominent Junkers, among them friends and relatives of the president, of misappropriating the taxpayers' money granted them under the program. Instead of using the funds to pay off mortgages and invest in equipment to make their estates viable, they had, it was alleged, expended the grants to buy additional land, racehorses, and expensive automobiles or to pay for lavish vacations at such resort areas as the French Riviera at a time when millions were suffering grave privation.

For a week, the budget committee's inquiry generated sensational front-page reports in newspapers all across Germany on what became known as the eastern aid scandal. There is no evidence that Schleicher had anything to do with the charges raised in the budget committee; a month earlier he had contemptuously dismissed the continuation of Reichstag committee meetings during the chamber's recess as a "fool's game." Nevertheless, his reputation for behind-the-scenes intrigue lent plausibility in the eyes of some to rumors that he had arranged to have damaging information leaked to the committee as revenge for the Agrarian League's attacks on his cabinet. In view of Hindenburg's close relations with some of those accused of fraud, it is unlikely that either those rumors or his Junker friends' resentment of the chancellor's failure to obstruct the inquiry escaped the president's attention, especially with Franz von Papen frequently at his side.

The mounting signs of coolness toward Schleicher on Hindenburg's part gave rise to doubts in political circles about whether the chancellor had in hand, like Papen the previous September, a presidential decree that would enable him to dissolve the Reichstag at his bidding. Questioned about the matter by a journalist on January 10, the Chancellery press spokesman conceded that Schleicher's relations with the president were less cordial than Papen's had been. He insisted, however, that it was "absolutely certain" that the chancellor would receive a dissolution decree, thereby revealing that Schleicher had yet to obtain the official paper. Yet at his dinner with journalists on January 13, Schleicher spoke with such confidence about his plans to dissolve the parliament if he faced a hostile majority that most of those who dined with him concluded that he must already have the necessary document in hand.

Some of the journalists present on the evening of January 13 came away with a very different impression. The table at which they had been seated was presided over by Günther Gereke, who revealed during the dinner that Oskar von Hindenburg had the day before confided to him that Schleicher did not have a dissolution decree and would not get one from his father. The younger Hindenburg, once a friend of Schleicher's, now intensely despised him, Gereke added. Struck by the discrepancy between Gereke's words and the chancellor's self-assurance, one of the journalists asked the Chancellery press spokesman for clarification after the dinner. He received a flat assurance: Hindenburg had already granted Schleicher a dissolution decree. When the journalists compared their impressions afterward, they found themselves hopelessly baffled about the crucial question of the president's willingness to support the chancellor if he faced a hostile parliament.

Despite all signs to the contrary, Schleicher remained confident that he would obtain a dissolution decree. The matter was simple, he explained to his staff: Hindenburg had promised him at the outset that he stood ready to employ the full range of presidential powers on his behalf, and that was all he needed to know. He held stubbornly to that view despite danger signals such as that registered at the cabinet meeting of January 16 by the president's chief of staff, Otto Meissner. Upon hearing the chancellor's announcement of his plan to gain a political underpinning for his cabinet by adding Gregor Strasser, Adam Stegerwald and Alfred Hugenberg to it, Meissner cautioned that such a step would compromise the presidential nature of the cabinet and thus jeopardize Hindenburg's continued support. In typically imperious fashion, Schleicher brushed Meissner's objection aside, asserting that he had thoroughly discussed the matter with the president. Although none of the cabinet members present asked, they must have wondered how, if that were the case, this had escaped the attention of Meissner, who was renowned for his intimate knowledge of Hindenburg's views. A few days later, Schleicher mentioned in passing to one of the cabinet ministers that the president was pressing him to dissolve the parliament. Yet on January 19, one day before the Reichstag's agenda committee was scheduled to meet to determine when the parliament would reconvene, the press office of the Chancellery conceded to journalists that the chancellor had still not received a dissolution decree.

By mid-January Schleicher was rapidly losing the political initiative. He had made no progress toward gaining a political underpinning for his cabinet and had failed to deliver on his promises of bold governmental measures to alleviate unemployment. To the frustration of Gereke, who was charged with expediting job creation and rural settlement, the chancellor's refusal to intervene left those projects still bogged down in committees, where bureaucratic obstruction slowed progress to a crawl. On the politically sensitive issue of trade policy, the cabinet remained divided and incapable of action, while Schleicher temporized by promising agricultural interests protectionist measures while assuring industrial spokesmen of his opposition to such measures.

Finding these problems frustratingly intractable, Schleicher focused his attention increasingly on rearmament, which he hoped would soon relegate domestic issues to the background. At his dinner for journalists on January 13 he spent most of the evening setting forth his strategy for exploiting the victorious powers' recognition, a month earlier, of Germany's right to equality in arms. He planned, he disclosed, to have a compulsory militia functioning by the spring of 1934 and then move toward universal military service. Soon, he boasted, the armed forces would have the heavy weapons denied to Germany by the Versailles Treaty. On January 15 he used a speech to an organization of retired army officers to proclaim publicly his commitment to the goals of armament equality and universal conscription. But what was obviously intended to be a major public relations coup failed to attract much attention amid the news about repeated setbacks for the Schleicher cabinet during the days that followed.

On January 18 Schleicher's illusions about Papen were finally shattered. Despite the efforts of the Nazis to keep secret Hitler's luncheon rendezvous that day with the former chancellor at Ribbentrop's house, news of it appeared that evening in the Berlin press. Asked for comment, the Chancellery press office led journalists to believe that Schleicher had approved the meeting in advance and that Papen had merely sought to bridge the differences between the Nazis and the cabinet by clarifying certain questions. Schleicher, however, knew better. As at the time of Papen's meeting with Hitler in Cologne on January 4, he had no foreknowledge of his discarded protégé's doings. Now, though, in light of the dressing-down he had given Papen after the Cologne episode for meeting with Hitler without first consulting him, he could no longer attribute Papen's flirtations with the Nazi leader to well-intentioned ineptitude. The only remaining explanation was that the man he had once elevated to the chancellorship and then banished from it was conspiring against him.

As events approached a climax at the end of the third week of January, Schleicher clung rigidly to a political strategy the premise of which had proved invalid. By that time, there was abundant evidence of the failure of his efforts to gain Hitler's cooperation by using Gregor Strasser as a cudgel and by threatening the Nazis with the loss of still more votes in a new election. But despite his military training, the chancellor had committed a cardinal strategic error by neglecting to prepare an avenue of retreat in the event that his plans failed to work out. He was still banking on Hitler's flinching and, failing that, on Hindenburg's willingness to back his dissolution of the Reichstag without scheduling a new election. Schleicher thus gave no consideration to adopting a defensive posture that would at least buy him time to consolidate his hold on power. Instead, he pressed ahead with his strategy of offense as though nothing had changed. As a consequence, he lost an opportunity to prolong his chancellorship by staving off a confrontation with the parliament.

That opportunity arose on Friday, January 20, when the agenda committee of the Reichstag met to review its earlier decision to reconvene the chamber on January 24. The outcome would determine when the seemingly inevitable confrontation between the Schleicher cabinet and a hostile parliamentary majority would take place. At the meeting, spokesmen of both the Communists and Social Democrats pressed for holding to the scheduled date and left no doubt about their intention to propose a prompt no-confidence vote. But the Nazi spokesman on the committee, Wilhelm Frick, adopted a much less confrontational stance, despite the defiant clamor in the Nazi press for an early vote of no confidence.

A former civil servant, Frick was, for a Nazi, a cautious man. He shared Gregor Strasser's misgivings about Hitler's all-or-nothing course and had distanced himself from the Nazi renegade only at the last moment in December. Like Strasser, Frick feared that a new election resulting from a dissolution of the Reichstag would bring disastrous Nazi losses. Other Nazi leaders also shrank from a show-down. Goebbels, usually a firebrand, concurred with Frick, writing in his diary on January 20: "We must gain time." After a strategy session with Hitler, Göring and Goebbels the previous evening, Frick proposed to the agenda committee on January 20 that the parliamentary recess be extended until the cabinet could present its budget. Since Schleicher's finance minister had a short time earlier announced that the budget could not possibly be ready before the spring, Frick thus indicated that the Nazis were willing to put off reconvening the chamber until then.

If Frick's proposal had been accepted, subsequent events might have taken a very different course. With the Reichstag in recess until the cabinet was ready to present its budget, the expected confrontation between the cabinet and the hostile majority in the chamber would have been put off until the spring. Had a no-confidence motion been adopted then, a new election could have been delayed, even within the constitutionally mandated sixty days, until late spring or early summer in the event of a dissolution of the Reichstag. And by that time Schleicher's situation might well have improved markedly. He would have been in a position to reap the political benefits of the job-creation program that Gereke was doggedly pushing to completion, despite a lack of help from the chancellor. Credit for the slow but discernible overall improvement in economic conditions that had begun during the second half of 1932 would also have gone to Schleicher. During the Reichstag's prolonged recess, Adolf Hitler would have had no opportunity to raise the morale of his followers through a show of ballot-box strength, as in Lippe, since no more state elections were scheduled until the fall. The crisis within Hitler's party could well have worsened rapidly as frustration continued to mount at the failure of the Nazi leader's attempt to gain power. A new Reichstag election held under such circumstances in late spring or early summer might well have dealt sufficient setbacks to both the Nazis and the Communists to lower the fever pitch of political extremism, thereby still further strengthening the chancellor's hand.

None of this was to be. Although there was enough support among the parties represented on the agenda committee to approve Frick's motion to extend the recess, the cabinet's spokesman at the meeting, Chancellery chief of staff Erwin Planck, summarily rejected it. He announced that the cabinet demanded the earliest possible clarification of the political situation and therefore opposed any lengthy prolongation of the recess. Acceptance of Frick's proposal would, to be sure, have involved a tactical retreat on the chancellor's part. Throughout the previous weeks, Schleicher had, in hopes of browbeating Hitler into cooperation, held to the unyielding position Planck adopted at the agenda committee's meeting. There is, however, no indication that Schleicher ever even considered backing away from that position in order to gain additional time to consolidate his position and await the political benefits of economic improvement. Nor does Planck seem to have had discretionary authority to alter tactics in the event of an unforeseen development such as Frick's proposal. As it was, Planck's rejection killed the Nazi's motion, which died without a vote. With Planck's acquiescence, the Catholic Center Party then gained support from a majority of the agenda committee for its proposal that the recess be extended for one additional week in order to allow further consultations. The crucial date in German politics thus became January 31.

The missed opportunity of January 20 proved a turning point. Although Schleicher could not know it at the time, he had passed up one of his few remaining chances to escape the web of conspiracy Franz von Papen was weaving around him. Papen's goal was to gain Hitler's support, bring Schleicher down by turning President von Hindenburg against him, and then step forward as architect of a rightist cabinet that included the Nazis. A lengthy postponement of the showdown between Schleicher and the Reichstag of the sort proposed by Frick would have made Papen's scheme more difficult. Above all, it would have put off Schleicher's need to test the president's support by requesting authority to dissolve the Reichstag.

By spurning a lengthy Reichstag adjournment, Schleicher brought the question of the president's confidence in him to a head just as the conspiracy against him was gathering momentum. By accepting a one-week extension of the recess, moreover, he gave the conspirators badly needed additional time to reconcile their differences and win over the president. The chancellor's only hope for retaining power now depended completely on his ability to obtain a dissolution decree from Hindenburg at a time when he had little by way of accomplishments to show for his time in office.

Kurt von Schleicher's failure to consider tactical alternatives at the time of the agenda committee's meeting on January 20 was based on what would prove the most costly of his many illusions: his belief that, come what may, he could count upon President von Hindenburg to make good on his promise, at the outset of his chancellorship, to use the full powers of the presidency on his behalf. Disillusionment was not long in coming. Shortly after the agenda committee meeting, a shaken Erwin Planck telephoned former chancellor Brüning and told him: "It's all over." As Planck subsequently explained to Brüning, the stand he had taken at the meeting on behalf of Schleicher had been based on assurances from Oskar von Hindenburg that his father would grant the chancellor a dissolution decree. But since then, Planck reported, Schleicher had learned that the younger Hindenburg had turned against him and that he would therefore not get the decree. Without it, Schleicher would be defenseless against a no-confidence vote when the Reichstag reconvened on January 31. Brüning proposed reconvening the agenda committee at once, but Planck rejected that as futile. Schleicher was, he resignedly stated, "finished." That was not yet necessarily so, but the chancellor's illusions had greatly diminished his prospects for political survival.

5

The Conspiracy Widens
and Schleicher
Relinquishes Power

LATE ON THE BONE-CHILLING, overcast morning of
Sunday, January 22, a squad of uniformed policemen invaded
Karl Liebknecht House, the headquarters of the Communist
Party on Bülowplatz, a major square in a working-class district of
Berlin. They searched the building and expelled most of those at work
there, including an editor of the Communist daily newspaper *Rote
Fahne,* who was escorted out at gunpoint. Outside, truckloads of
policemen arrived and fanned out over the snow-covered square,
ordering pedestrians to leave and sealing off the area to private vehicu-
lar traffic. Armored police trucks and machine-gun squads took up
positions at intersections. Still other police units formed picket lines,
with rifles at the ready, down the centers of the deserted streets that led
into the square. From the roofs of many buildings in the neighborhood, policemen scanned the area with binoculars. Curious residents
who ventured onto the balconies of their apartments or opened windows to see what was afoot were ordered to get inside and keep their
doors and windows closed. Some dwellings in the neighborhood were
searched. At about one o'clock in the afternoon the reason for these

extreme measures became manifest when a column of brown-shirted Nazi stormtroopers approached the square under police protection. As they marched, they chanted, "We shit on freedom! We shit on the Jew republic!"

Altogether, some fifteen thousand stormtroopers had converged on Bülowplatz, shielded from the hostility of the local residents by about the same number of policemen. The ostensible purpose of this government-approved demonstration was the march that ensued to a nearby cemetery, where Hitler dedicated a memorial to Horst Wessel, a notoriously brutal Berlin stormtroop leader who had been shot and killed by Communists three years earlier. But the underlying aim was to raise flagging Nazi morale by staging a defiant show of force on the very doorstep of the Communist Party. The results exceeded all expectations. Not only did the government refuse to permit a Communist counterdemonstration, but in carrying out their orders to prevent violence, the police clashed repeatedly with Communist protesters, shot and wounded two and arrested about seventy of them. The rally thus lent the Nazis an aura of respectability by aligning them with the forces of law and order against the Communists. It also delivered a demoralizing blow to the German Left. During the following days, the Nazi press trumpeted the event as a great victory. In a memoir published three years later, a Berlin stormtrooper recalled it as marking a memorable upward turn in the party's fortunes. Goebbels could hardly contain his elation in his diary entry: "The Commies raging in the side streets . . . Armored vehicles, machine guns. Police preventing anyone from shooting at us from windows . . . SA marching in front of Karl Liebknecht House. A fantastic thing! . . . We have won a battle."

The Nazis' success was a setback for Schleicher, and a self-inflicted one at that. As late as the day before, Goebbels had feared the government would put a stop to the demonstration. The chancellor, he heard, wanted to prohibit it but was prevented from doing so by resistance from within the Defense Ministry. No evidence supports that view, however. As commissar for Prussia under the terms of the national government's takeover of that state the previous July, the chancellor commanded ultimate authority over police power in the capital. He thus had at his disposal the means to ban the march or require the Nazis to stage it in a less provocative location than the site of the Communists' headquarters. But instead of doing that, he permitted arrangements that turned the police into guardians of the same thugs who had for several years been unleashing lethal mayhem on the streets of the capital and other German cities.

The reasons for Schleicher's passivity in the face of what was clearly a Nazi provocation remain unclear. He may have harbored the illusion that Hitler could be cajoled into cooperating with his cabinet. Indeed, some republican observers suspected that the government's acquiescence in the demonstration was intended as a conciliatory gesture. Schleicher may, on the other hand, have been immobilized by the shock of hearing, shortly beforehand, that he could not count on President von Hindenburg's issuing him a dissolution decree, which Schleicher had been led to believe would be his for the asking. A Berlin correspondent for the principal Catholic newspaper in the capital, *Germania,* observed that an "eerie fatalism" seemed to hamper any activity on the part of the government. A correspondent for the *Frankfurter Zeitung* characterized the chancellor's attitude as one of "Olympian detachment." But whatever the explanation, Schleicher had given Hitler a priceless boost in allowing the Nazi demonstration to take place and extending to it the protection—and implicit approval—of the government.

On the evening of that same Sunday, January 22, two men and their wives took seats in a box at the State Opera House on Berlin's famous boulevard, Unter den Linden, where *Das Liebesverbot,* Richard Wagner's youthful operatic version of Shakespeare's *Measure for Measure,* was being performed. During the intermission the two couples mingled with the rest of the audience and greeted acquaintances. At the bell signaling the beginning of the next act they returned to their seats. But after the houselights dimmed and the music resumed, the two men quietly rose and departed. After collecting their coats and hats from the cloakroom they left the opera house through a rear door.

Outside, they crossed Opera Square in a heavy snowfall and hailed a taxi. Only after peering through the cab's rear window to establish that they were not being followed did they instruct the driver to take them to the fashionable district of Dahlem. Upon leaving the taxi there they proceeded on foot toward their destination, which they found only with difficulty because of the snowy conditions. It was the house of Joachim von Ribbentrop, and the two secretive visitors were Oskar von Hindenburg and Otto Meissner, the president's son and chief of staff. Upon their arrival, they found awaiting them former chancellor Franz von Papen and Adolf Hitler, who was accompanied by Hermann Göring and two other prominent Nazis.

This nocturnal rendezvous was the work of Franz von Papen. Having found Hitler more insistent than ever in his demand for the chancellorship at their luncheon meeting at Ribbentrop's on January 18, Papen had reached what turned out to be the most momentous decision of his life: he had decided that the most promising way to return to power lay in conceding the chancellorship to Hitler, but on terms that would enable him to use the Nazi leader for his own purposes. He therefore set out to explore the possibility of a Hitler cabinet in which he, thanks to his close relationship with President von Hindenburg, would hold the actual reins of power. If that effort failed, he was prepared to reassume the chancellorship himself, despite the massive political opposition from both Right and Left that had marked his previous experience in that office. On Friday, January 20, two days before the evening meeting at Ribbentrop's, Papen had set out to widen the conspiracy against Schleicher by unveiling his plan to the president's son and chief of staff. By the evening of January 20, Papen could inform Ribbentrop that Oskar von Hindenburg and Meissner had agreed to join him in meeting with Hitler the coming Sunday evening.

In drawing Oskar von Hindenburg into his scheme, Papen had reached out to a man who stood closer to the elderly president than anyone else and who also shared the former chancellor's hatred of Kurt von Schleicher. A career army officer like his father and grandfather, the younger Hindenburg could claim distinction in nothing except his ancestry. Ambassador François-Poncet found him "thick-featured, churlish and ill-educated, as tall and massive as his father but without his gracious demeanor." With a lackluster military career behind him, the son served officially as the president's military adjutant and unofficially as his closest confidant. No one saw more of the president than he, since he and his wife and children shared the presidential residence with his widowed father. As the elder Hindenburg entered his eighties, the son's influence increased in political importance to the point that he became known among Berlin wits as 'the constitutionally unforeseen son of the president.'

Once a close friend of Schleicher's, Oskar von Hindenburg had become his implacable enemy as a consequence of an incident that occurred at about the time the general became chancellor. Neither man ever publicly disclosed exactly what destroyed their friendship. But all indications are that it can best be explained by a prophecy about Schleicher made by a fellow officer during the war: "I foresee a great future for him if he doesn't make enemies with his cheeky tongue." Something Schleicher said to the younger Hindenburg, that is, apparently wounded his pride beyond all forgiving. Among men who subscribed to the Prussian officers' code of honor, verbal slights were regarded as grave matters; in earlier times, duels to the death could result from perceived indignities of that sort. Whatever the cause, Oskar had developed an intense enmity toward Schleicher. That hostility was fully shared by his wife. A haughty baroness, she referred to Schleicher in conversation with a member of his own cabinet as "our Fouché," a reference to an unscrupulous police chief during the French Revolution whose skill at opportunistic intrigue enabled him to survive and serve both the Napoleonic Empire and the Bourbon restoration.

By adding Otto Meissner to the conspiracy against Schleicher, Papen had tapped the man closest to the president after his son. As chief of the presidential staff, Meissner controlled official access to Hindenburg and sat in on virtually all his important conferences. He was therefore in a position to sway the president's decisions, even if his influence was not as great as those contemporary observers imagined who derisively referred to Hindenburg as a 'Meissner figurine' (an allusion to porcelain statuettes made in the city of Meissen). Ambassador François-Poncet, who encountered Meissner numerous times, disdained him as "an eerie personage" and described him as "florid-faced, puffed-up and pudgy, always a bit too corpulent for his clothes, concealing his glances behind thick-lensed spectacles." A career civil servant who had headed the presidential staff since 1920, Meissner experienced no difficulty in transferring his allegiance from the first president, Social Democrat Friedrich Ebert, to the conservative Hindenburg. Obsequious and devious, he had the mentality of a wily subaltern, including a shrewd sensitivity to shifts in the power relationships among his superiors. At the outset of Schleicher's chancellorship, Meissner had cultivated his favor, just as he had that of previous holders of that office. But by the third week of January he had begun to sense that the chancellor's hold on power was slipping and that it was time to ingratiate himself with those who seemed most likely to be the future wielders of authority.

Upon arriving at the late-evening gathering at Ribbentrop's on January 22, Meissner and Oskar von Hindenburg initially joined with the others in general conversation lubricated by some of their host's champagne. But after a short time Hitler announced that he wished to speak in private with the president's son. The two disappeared into a separate room, where they remained closeted for about an hour. In taking on the younger Hindenburg, Hitler faced someone who had hitherto shown no sympathy for Nazism. Two months earlier, in a remarkably perceptive memorandum, the president's son had sought in vain to alert his father to the dangers of entering into negotiations with Hitler. Recognizing the Nazi leader's unswerving determination to become a presidential chancellor, the younger Hindenburg had accurately predicted that Hitler would seek to blur the distinction between parliamentary and presidential cabinets. He had also warned that Hitler could not be expected to keep any agreements he might make, and that his appointment would inevitably result in a one-party dictatorship.

What passed between Hitler and Oskar von Hindenburg on the evening of January 22 has long been the subject of speculation. It has often been suggested that Hitler threatened to blackmail the younger Hindenburg or his father unless he were named chancellor. That seems improbable, however, because there were no plausible grounds for such blackmail; besides, even Hitler would have realized that such crude methods might well backfire in the case of the Hindenburgs, with their aristocratic hypersensitivity to questions of honor. It is more likely that Oskar von Hindenburg essentially told the truth at his de-Nazification trial after the Second World War. There he recounted how Hitler had subjected him to the same sort of lengthy monologue about his political struggle and his plans to remedy the ills besetting Germany that he habitually employed in an effort to bend others to his will. The younger Hindenburg went on to relate that Hitler concluded by addressing the current political situation and stating his resolve to oppose any cabinet in which he did not participate. At that point, Oskar testified, he protested that politics was not his business and that he had no influence on his father's decision. For his part, Hitler left no record of his conversation with Oskar. But two days later he told Goebbels that he had failed to win over the president's son, describing him as "the personification of stupidity."

While Hitler was haranguing the younger Hindenburg, Hermann Göring engaged Otto Meissner in conversation. As the son of a high colonial official in the old imperial government who had gained national attention as an ace fighter pilot during the war, Göring was the closest approximation in the Nazi leadership ranks to a member of the German upper-class establishment. His presence at Hitler's side lent the upstart Nazi leader respectability in the eyes of prominent and privileged figures such as Meissner and the younger Hindenburg. Socially adept, the rotund and affable Göring could put others at ease and invite open communication, whereas the rambling, visionary monologues of Hitler precluded meaningful two-way exchanges. Rushed in from Dresden at the last minute on the evening of January 22, the future air force minister and field marshal assumed the role of Hitler's chief spokesman, which he would play with great skill during the crucial behind-the-scenes negotiations of the following week.

In his approach to Meissner, Göring adopted a conciliatory stance. If Hitler were made chancellor, he informed the president's chief of staff, the Nazis would settle for only one additional cabinet post. The other ministries could be assigned either to coalition parties or to nonpartisan experts, and the choice of both the defense minister and the foreign minister would be left to the president. Göring also gave Meissner to understand that a Hitler cabinet would eventually move to restore the monarchy, an obvious attempt to curry favor with Hindenburg, who made no secret of remaining a convinced monarchist even while serving as republican head of state.

When Hitler and Oskar von Hindenburg rejoined the others, Ribbentrop invited his guests to partake of a light meal and more champagne. In the ensuing conversation, everyone present agreed on one point: Kurt von Schleicher must go. By the time those present parted company, moreover, a crucial bargain had been implicitly struck. Papen had indicated his readiness to settle for the post of vice chancellor in a Hitler cabinet. Through Göring, Hitler had signaled his willingness to make major concessions with regard to the composition of a cabinet headed by him. Only Meissner and Oskar von Hindenburg remained noncommittal on the subject of Schleicher's successor. As would soon become apparent, the president's chief of staff had in fact been won over to Hitler, while Oskar von Hindenburg continued for several days to favor Papen's restoration to the chancellorship. Nevertheless, Meissner later recalled that during their taxi ride back from Dahlem to the center of Berlin, the younger Hindenburg turned to him after a long period of silence and resignedly told him that since Papen now favored bestowing the chancellorship on Hitler and was willing to settle for the vice chancellorship himself, there would probably be no way around that outcome.

Former Field Marshal Paul von Hindenburg, who as president of Germany's Weimar Republic appointed Adolf Hitler chancellor on January 30, 1933. [BAK]

Colonel Oskar von Hindenburg, the president's son and military adjutant, helped to prevail upon his father to abandon Chancellor Kurt von Schleicher and replace him with Hitler. [LbsB]

Together with his wife and children, Oskar von Hindenburg shared his widowed father's official residence on Berlin's Wilhelmstrasse. [BAK]

President von Hindenburg strolling with his grandchildren in the rear garden of his official residence. [Lbs]

Former General Kurt von Schleicher, Hitler's predecessor as German chancellor, whose ineptitude opened the way for the Third Reich. [UB]

General Kurt von Schleicher (left) with General Kurt von Hammerstein. [BPKb]

Chancellor Kurt von Schleicher and his wife, both murdered in their home by agents of Hitler's regime in June 1934. [LbsB]

General Kurt von Schleicher (second from right) with General Kurt von Hammerstein at a diplomatic reception in Berlin. [BSV]

General Kurt von Schleicher and Franz von Papen (right) as friends, 1932. [BSV]

Franz von Papen, German chancellor June–December 1932, who
during January 1933 successfully conspired to make Hitler chancellor. [BAK]

Chancellor Franz von Papen (right) with Presidential chief of staff Otto Meissner (left), 1932. [BAK]

Franz von Papen, delivering a speech as Hitler's deputy chancellor, 1934. [BPKb]

Chancellor Franz von Papen (left) and Otto Meissner riding in Berlin's Tiergarten, 1932. [DHM]

Joseph Goebbels, Nazi gauleiter of Berlin who in March 1933 was appointed
propaganda minister by Hitler. He encouraged Hitler to hold to his all-or-
nothing strategy in January 1933. [UB]

Nazi Hermann Göring, presiding officer of the Reichstag, September 1932–January 1933, who on January 30, 1933, became minister without portfolio in Hitler's cabinet with authority over the Prussian Interior Ministry. [BPKb]

Ertappt!

Hitler mit Papen unter einer Decke!

"Caught!" Republican ridicule of the failed secrecy surrounding the clandestine Hitler-Papen meeting of January 4, 1933. Caption: "Hitler with Papen under one blanket!" [*Vorwärts*, January 7, 1933 (#12)]

Beim Geldsack

Hitler speiste am Mittwoch mit dem Schwerinaustriellen Fritz Thyssen.

100000

"With the Moneybags," a Social Democratic commentary reflecting the widespread misapprehension that Hitler was financed by German big business. Caption: "Don't leave me in the lurch, lest everyone desert me." The statement below the title, "Hitler dined with heavy industrialist Fritz Thyssen on Wednesday," was erroneous. [*Vorwärts*, January 19, 1933 (#32)]

Schleicher überlegt

a, welcher sticht wohl welchen

"Schleicher Pondering," which depicts the chancellor attempting to decide between two Nazis, Hitler and Gregor Strasser. Caption: "Well now, which one trumps the other?" [*Vorwärts*, January 17, 1933 (#28)]

Franz Seldte (left) and Theodor Düsterberg leading a parade of the Stahlhelm veterans' organization, whose participation was a key element in the plot that brought Hitler to power. [BAK]

Theodor Düsterberg of the Stahlhelm, whose resentment of Nazi attacks on him because of a Jewish grandfather threatened to upset the plot to make Hitler chancellor. [BPKb]

Franz Seldte of the Stehlhelm, who became labor minister in the Hitler cabinet installed on January 30, 1933. [BPKb]

Policemen posted in the working-class district of Berlin where the Schleicher cabinet permitted a Nazi demonstration on January 22, 1933 and extended it official protection. [UB]

Nazi stormtroopers massed in front of Communist Party headquarters in Berlin during the demonstration of January 22, 1933. [DHM]

The German parliament building, the Reichstag, prior to Hitler's regime.
[BPKb]

The Reichstag after the end of the Third Reich. The building was gutted by
fire in February 1933, then bombed and shelled during the Second World
War. [UB]

"Ripe for Attack," a republican depiction of Chancellor von Schleicher being undermined from multiple directions. Caption: "I don't understand. Previously *I* was the expert at laying mines."
[*Vorwärts*, January 16, 1933 (#43)]

"Hugenberg's Driving School" reflected the widespread view that Hitler would be dominated by conservatives in his cabinet. Caption: "Hugenberg to Papen: 'That newcomer up there in front can imagine all he wants that he's steering, but we'll set the economic course!'"
[*Vorwärts*, February 1, 1933 (#53)]

Hitler, Papen, and Hugenberg conferring at the Chancellery on January 30, 1933. On the left, Frick and (back to camera) Otto Wagener. [BPKb]

Hitler leaving the Kaiserhof Hotel to attend the first meeting of his cabinet on the afternoon of January 30, 1933. [UB]

The first photograph of Adolf Hitler as German Chancellor, at his desk in the Chancellery, January 30, 1933. [BPKb]

On the morning of the following day, Monday, January 23, Papen called on Hindenburg and presented his plan. His proposal that Schleicher be replaced encountered no objection, since the president's support for the man he had appointed chancellor seven weeks earlier had eroded badly. But when Papen proposed Hitler as the successor to Schleicher, the president balked. He wanted to restore to that office Papen himself, to whose removal from office he had never become reconciled. Mistrustful and scornful of Hitler, Hindenburg resisted Papen's proposal that the Nazi leader be called to the head of the government. As Hindenburg privately confided to a conservative aristocrat at about the same time, he regarded Hitler as qualified, at best, to head the postal ministry.

When the president called in Meissner and Oskar von Hindenburg to join in the discussion with Papen on the morning of January 23, Meissner seconded the former chancellor's proposal that Hitler be appointed chancellor. A cabinet headed by Hitler, with Papen as vice chancellor, Meissner argued, would offer the best way out of the political crisis. It would attract support from other parties and, by saddling the Nazis with governmental responsibility, put an end to their revolutionary demagogy and set them on an evolutionary path. Meissner thus advocated the same strategy of 'taming' the Nazis as had Schleicher earlier, but now by means of a formula that excluded the latter. Both the elder Hindenburg and his son remained skeptical, however, holding to the view that Papen, rather than Hitler, should be assigned the chancellorship if Schleicher fell from power. As a consequence, Papen left the meeting having made no discernible progress in his scheme to boost Hitler into the chancellorship, even though he personally remained in high favor with the Hindenburgs.

Despite the efforts of the conspirators to keep the meeting at Ribbentrop's on the evening of January 22 secret, news of it quickly reached the chancellor. On the morning of January 23, Meissner received a telephone call from Schleicher, who inquired about what had taken place the previous evening at Ribbentrop's. There is no record of Meissner's reply, but nothing he might have said could conceal the fact that not only Papen and Hitler but also the two men closest to the president were now actively conspiring against the chancellor. Fully aware at last of the precariousness of his position, Schleicher decided to put Hindenburg's loyalty to him to the test. He therefore arranged an appointment with the president for eleven-thirty that same morning.

In initiating what would prove a fateful meeting with Hindenburg on January 23, Schleicher apparently acted on the spur of the moment. The only guidance he is known to have received regarding the political moves available to him came in the form of a memorandum prepared by his staff at the Defense Ministry. It set forth three options for dealing with the hostile Reichstag majority. The first of these involved the same measures that Papen had proposed at the end of his chancellorship: dissolution of the Reichstag and postponement of a new election beyond the constitutionally mandated sixty days. That course of action would, the memorandum warned, result in charges of unconstitutionality from a broad array of political parties and force the Schleicher cabinet onto the defensive. The same warning accompanied the second option, which called for a forced adjournment of the Reichstag, combined with an offer to reconvene the legislature whenever a parliamentary majority could agree on a constructive course.

The third option set forth in the Defense Ministry memorandum addressed a gap in the republic's constitution identified earlier by eminent legal experts. The authors of the constitution, the experts pointed out, had failed to foresee the possibility of a negative parliamentary majority. Yet since the July Reichstag election of 1932 just that had been the case. Holding more than half the seats in the parliament between them, the Communists and Nazis could combine to pass no-confidence measures but were incapable of joining together to support a cabinet. In hopes of remedying this deficiency, some experts urged adoption of a constitutional amendment that would invalidate a vote of no confidence unless those who supported it had, in advance, agreed upon a replacement cabinet that would enjoy a parliamentary majority. A similar provision would, after the collapse of the Third Reich, become a constitutional cornerstone of the postwar German Federal Republic. But under the political circumstances of January 1933, with a negative majority dominating the Reichstag, an amendment to the constitution, which required a two-thirds vote, was clearly out of the question.

The Defense Ministry memorandum endorsed as its third option an interim remedy recommended by other expert critics of the constitutional gap: a cabinet subjected to a no-confidence vote could simply remain in office on a caretaker basis. Since the president had sole authority to appoint the chancellor and the cabinet, those experts argued, he could leave a caretaker chancellor in office indefinitely without violating the constitution. If that displeased the parties that made up a negative parliamentary majority, they could at any time arrive at a remedy by uniting behind a chancellor and cabinet of their own choice.

The authors of the Defense Ministry memorandum clearly favored this last approach. So did the Reichstag deputy of a small conservative party, Wilhelm Simpfendörfer, who proposed the same course in a meeting with Schleicher on January 19. Earlier, the Bavarian envoy in Berlin had made the same proposal to him on the eve of his appointment as chancellor. A precedent had already been set by the republican cabinet in the state of Württemberg, which had in late 1932 refused to heed a no-confidence vote adopted by a negative majority in the state legislature. By addressing an undeniable flaw in the Weimar constitution, this third option offered the appreciable advantage of being the least vulnerable to accusations of unconstitutionality. It also involved far less provocation of the political parties than did either of the other two options. But above all, it necessitated no action on the part of the president aside from passive acquiescence in the continuation in office of a chancellor in whom a Reichstag majority had voted no confidence. Hindenburg's increasing aversion to making major decisions clearly favored this strategy.

The third option also offered Schleicher an opportunity to

broaden his perilously narrow base of political support. The defenders of the republic would predictably join with the Communists and Nazis in attacking him if he violated the constitution by postponing a new election. But they might well react with restraint if he invoked, as justification for defying a no-confidence vote, a flaw in the constitution identified by distinguished experts, including some with republican credentials. Nor was such a course likely to encounter opposition from either organized labor or the business community, both of which feared that the uncertainties arising from another change of cabinets and another national election might derail the fragile economic upswing of the previous months. Backed by such an array of support, Schleicher would be in a position to argue that only the extremists of Right and Left, the Nazis and the Communists, objected to his continuation in office on a caretaker basis. There was, to be sure, no assurance that Hindenburg, given his personal coolness toward the chancellor, would have agreed to allow him to defy a no-confidence vote. But the third option certainly represented Schleicher's best chance to retain the chancellorship. It thus also offered the best chance to thwart Hitler's drive for power long enough to allow the frustration of his followers to deepen the crisis tearing at his party.

Despite the advantages of the plan favored by the Defense Ministry memorandum, Schleicher rejected it. He left no record of his reasons, but a remark he made during his off-the-record dinner for journalists on January 13 provides a clue. A presidential caretaker cabinet might be able to remain in office even after a no-confidence vote, he explained, but a negative Reichstag majority could cripple a cabinet's economic policies by rescinding the emergency decrees with which it enacted legislation. That was indeed a drawback to the plan, and one the Defense Ministry's memorandum neglected to mention. But, as the memorandum pointed out, the third option left open for eventual later recourse the possibility of a Reichstag dissolution and postponement of a new election in the event of continuing conflict with a hostile parliamentary majority. Quite aside from practical considerations, it may well be that Schleicher simply found the third option uncongenial. It would have required him to swallow his pride and back down from his numerous threats to dissolve the Reichstag if it did not cooperate with him. Reneging on such threats and holding on to the chancellorship on a caretaker basis must have smacked of weakness to someone steeped, as Schleicher was, in the Prussian military tradition, with its preference for offensive over defensive combat and its emphasis on personal courage.

There is no evidence that Schleicher's rejection of the memorandum's third option was based on extensive discussion or reasoned analysis. He seems to have sought guidance neither from members of his cabinet nor from the government's constitutional lawyers. Instead, he relied, as usual, on his staff at the Defense Ministry. The only advice he is known to have received came from the lieutenant colonel he had come to rely upon in constitutional matters, Eugen Ott. That officer's recommendation took the form of a handwritten comment on the chancellor's copy of the memorandum. It read, in entirety, "Option 1!"

In line with that laconic recommendation, Schleicher settled upon the first option laid out in the Defense Ministry memorandum. He decided, that is, to ask the president to authorize him to dissolve the Reichstag without scheduling a new election within the constitutionally mandated period. He thus chose the riskiest of the courses open to him. Only a short time earlier, he had received warning that the president's son had turned against him and that he would not receive a dissolution order. But even if that warning should prove unfounded and the president should grant his request, such an overt breach of the constitution invited intense opposition from all across the political spectrum, as the Defense Ministry memorandum warned. Perhaps by way of tactful omission, the memorandum failed to remind the chancellor, moreover, that President von Hindenburg would undoubtedly remember that Chancellor Franz von Papen had proposed precisely the same steps two months earlier. Nor did the memorandum point out that the president was unlikely to have forgotten that Papen's proposal had led to his downfall as a result of objections raised by members of his cabinet, led by Schleicher himself.

From the chancellor's standpoint, to be sure, his objections to a violation of the constitution by Papen at the end of November no longer applied, since the circumstances had changed. He was confident that his abandonment of Papen's project to alter the constitution and his cultivation of organized labor had banished the danger of civil war that had existed at the end of November. Economic conditions had also eased since then, and his job-creation program would soon provide additional relief. But most importantly, Schleicher could point to marked improvements in the capacity of the army to cope with civil disorder. On his orders, the Defense Ministry had during December and January implemented a number of measures designed to rectify shortcomings detected during November by the ministry's critique of the army's incapacity to respond to a simultaneous uprising of Communists and Nazis. In contrast to the situation at the time of Papen's fall, the army now had at its disposal extensive plans for suppressing political strikes as well as greatly expanded supplies of tear gas. Arrangements had been made to bring the Prussian police force, which was nearly half the size of the army, under military command if necessary. As a consequence of the Western powers' recognition in December of Germany's right to armament parity, the army was also now in a better position to augment its ranks through the enlistment of volunteers without provoking recriminations from abroad.

Armed with these arguments, Schleicher met with Hindenburg at eleven-thirty on Monday, January 23. He asked for a decree dissolving the Reichstag, explaining that a majority would in all likelihood approve a no-confidence motion if the chamber reconvened on January 31. Predicting that another election would not appreciably alter the composition of the Reichstag, he also requested that a new round of balloting be postponed beyond the constitutionally mandated sixty days. Although the official record of the meeting, which was apparently written by Meissner, provides only a sketchy account of what was said, Schleicher would almost certainly have sought to defend his requests by pointing to the improvements in the political situation since his appointment as chancellor as well as to the heightened readiness of the army to deal with domestic disorder.

Hindenburg remained unresponsive. His personal estrangement from Schleicher was already far advanced, and there seems to have been little personal contact between them since the meeting with the Agrarian League spokesmen on January 11. Only a short time earlier on the morning of January 23, the president had raised no objections when Papen, Meissner and his son had spoken out in favor of dispensing with the chancellor. Nevertheless, a request on Schleicher's part to ignore a no-confidence measure and remain in office on a caretaker basis might well have forced Hindenburg to reconsider his inclination to discard him, especially if it had been supported by expert opinions about the gap in the constitution. But the chancellor's proposal of exactly the same course of action he himself had opposed less than two months earlier when it had been advocated by Papen, must have awakened painful memories for Hindenburg. It also made it easier for him to rebuff Schleicher. He replied to the request for a dissolution decree by stating that he would take it under advisement but offered no encouragement in that regard. He bluntly rejected the proposal to postpone a new election beyond the stipulated sixty days, however. Such a step would, Hindenburg protested, leave him open on all sides to charges of acting unconstitutionally. It could only be considered, he informed Schleicher, if the leaders of the political parties endorsed the declaration of a state of emergency and agreed not to accuse him of violating the constitution.

As Schleicher well knew, any such agreement among Germany's warring political leaders was out of the question. As he also knew, Hindenburg had earlier twice unconditionally agreed to back plans by Papen to postpone a new election indefinitely, although circumstances had prevented realization of those plans. Clearly, Hindenburg's constitutional scruples functioned in a selective fashion. In an effort to mollify the president's concerns, Schleicher suggested that the leaders of business and labor be asked whether they would accept postponement of a new election, but Hindenburg failed to respond positively to that proposal either. Indicating that he had not expected an immediate decision on his request for a dissolution decree, the chancellor brought what had become a frosty meeting to a close by announcing his intention to take up the matter with the president at a later time.

Hindenburg's rebuff on January 23 dealt Schleicher a severe blow, but it did not seal his fate. There was no announcement to the press about what had occurred, so as far as the public knew, his hold on the chancellorship remained firm. Schleicher was now aware, however, that the president would not agree to rescue him by violating the constitution, so that the first two options set forth in the Defense Ministry memorandum were no longer relevant. Hindenburg had not altogether ruled out a dissolution of the Reichstag, but without postponement of a new election, a dissolution offered no solution, since there was no prospect that a new round of balloting within sixty days would eliminate the hostile majority facing the chancellor. After an election he would still have to reckon with a no-confidence vote.

There remained the third option of invoking the gap in the constitution as grounds for remaining in office on a caretaker basis despite a no-confidence vote by a negative Reichstag majority. Schleicher was still in a position to enlist the expert legal critics of that constitutional flaw in a crash effort to win at least acquiescence to such an arrangement on the part of the republican parties, organized labor and the business community. Time was short, since adoption of a no-confidence motion was expected within days after the Reichstag reconvened on Tuesday, January 31. But if he succeeded in marshaling an array of constitutional experts and powerful interest groups in support of the third option, he could go back to the president with impressive backing for a proposal that involved neither outright violation of the constitution nor dissolution of the parliament.

An adept politician in Schleicher's position would have recognized this possibility for holding on to power and grasped it. As any serious practitioner of that calling knows, power is the prerequisite to accomplishment, and retaining power once it is attained is the ultimate test of one's ability. For serious politicians, whether absolute monarchs or democrats, civilian or military dictators, these are self-evident truths. No one understood this better than Adolf Hitler. He made no secret of his resolve to keep power if he got it. The previous October, in a speech in the city of Königsberg, he had proclaimed: "If we once get power, then we shall, God help us, keep it. We shall not let it be taken away from us." Unfortunately for Germany, Kurt von Schleicher lacked that kind of single-minded focus on retaining power.

Astonishingly, in view of his schooling in military strategy and tactics, Schleicher had, despite the obvious precariousness of his situation, once again failed to prepare a fallback position. As a cadet and junior officer, he had learned that a prudent commander must always think out in advance of any planned action alternative tactics in case the plans should go awry. Yet when he faced the supreme test of his political career, Schleicher made no use of that lesson, despite its obvious applicability to politics. Instead, in a manner that suggests a loss of touch with reality, he clung unrealistically to his plan to postpone a new election after a dissolution of the Reichstag, despite the president's flat rejection of that proposal.. Once again, he proceeded without seeking guidance from either the members of his cabinet or from the veteran permanent officials of the government.

By his unwillingness to abandon his plan to postpone a new election unconstitutionally, Schleicher irretrievably burned his bridges with the defenders of the republic. There might well have been support within the Catholic Center and Social Democratic parties for acquiescence in the third option set forth in the Defense Ministry memorandum if the chancellor had gained the support of pro-republican constitutional experts for such a course. But despite denials by his staff, rumors to the effect that he planned to declare a state of emergency as justification for not holding an election within the constitutionally mandated period brought forth cries of protest from the Centrists and Social Democrats. Schleicher himself gave credence to those rumors when he returned to that plan on January 26 in an unsuccessful effort to enlist support for it during a meeting with trade-union leaders affiliated with the Social Democrats. As a consequence, anti-Schleicher sentiment in the largest republican party became so strong that even Otto Braun, the deposed Social Democratic minister-president of Prussia, now reversed his earlier willingness to join with the chancellor in asking the president to postpone a new election unconstitutionally. In a letter to Schleicher, a copy of which he sent to Hindenburg, Braun branded such a step as "incitement to treason." In the face of this and other expressions of hostility toward Schleicher on the part of leading Social Democrats, even the trade-union leaders aligned with that party who had earlier been inclined to go along with the chancellor as a lesser evil now distanced themselves from him.

As the Social Democrats' behavior revealed, they, too, had lost touch with the political realities of late January 1933. The same was in large measure true of the Catholic Center Party. Having seen the authority of the parliament erode and that of the presidency expand during the previous three years, the leaders of both those parties—with the notable, if temporary, exception of Otto Braun—had become fixated on defending the letter of the constitution. During the crucial month that would determine Germany's fate, the parties that had been the bulwarks of the republic remained preoccupied with what they perceived as the most acute peril: a breach of the constitution by Schleicher or, if he fell, by Papen. So obsessed were they with this concern that they lost sight of the fact that Adolf Hitler posed an immeasurably greater danger. Indeed, by inciting public opinion against Schleicher they may have helped to turn Hindenburg against the chancellor, thereby inadvertently lending assistance to Hitler's ultimately successful quest for power. By acquiescing in a departure from legality on the part of Schleicher the defenders of the republic might possibly have averted that outcome. Yet precisely that course was for them unthinkable.

With the Social Democrats and Centrists firmly aligned against him, Schleicher was now almost completely isolated politically. Only the two small liberal parties still nominally stood behind his cabinet, and their support was less than unconditional. On the Right, he had few, if any, allies left. Ambassador François-Poncet, whose position brought him into frequent social contact with reactionary circles, analyzed the reasons for their rejection of Schleicher in his dispatch to Paris on January 19. Those rightists who had hoped the general might impose military rule found him disappointingly weak, the ambassador reported, and much too civilian in his behavior out of uniform. Instead of cracking down on the Left, he had made concessions to organized labor and consulted with its leaders. Instead of curtailing the pretensions of the Reichstag, he had flirted with the parties in an effort to persuade a parliamentary majority to accept his cabinet. Finally, instead of bringing the Nazis into the government, he had "declared war" on Hitler by aligning himself with the renegade Gregor Strasser.

"In the midst of the crosscurrents besetting Germany," Ambassador François-Poncet informed his government, "the general cannot bring himself to choose; he gives the impression of waiting to see which of those currents will prevail before he commits himself to it." That was regrettable in the ambassador's opinion, "for at the present time Germany needs men who create a current rather than those who follow one." How long, he wondered, would Hindenburg remain loyal to such a chancellor? "All that one can note at present," he concluded, "is how rapidly the general's star has faded and the frivolity of those who are ready to sacrifice—without knowing how they will replace him—a man who is one of the most gifted and prudent in Germany."

Far from aspiring to dictatorship, as the republic's defenders feared and some on the Right had hoped he might, Schleicher simply abandoned hope of retaining the chancellorship. Rather than even attempt a different approach to Hindenburg, he resorted to the political equivalent of that most desperate of military tactics, the *Flucht nach vorn,* in which a hopelessly beleaguered commander orders a charge directly into the enemy's main forces. When the Reichstag agenda committee again met on Thursday, January 27, to review the schedule that called for the chamber to reconvene on January 31, Schleicher made no attempt to stave off a showdown with the hostile parliamentary majority. He had by then already arranged to see the president at noon on Saturday, January 28. He also scheduled a cabinet meeting to begin half an hour before that. As his Chancellery chief of staff, Erwin Planck, informed the minister of finance on January 26, Schleicher intended to ask for a dissolution decree. Since it was unlikely that this request would be granted, Planck added, the cabinet would probably resign on January 28. Schleicher had in effect resolved to end his chancellorship by asking Hindenburg for something he expected him to refuse.

Schleicher left no record of his motives for this politically suicidal course of action, and the surviving evidence provides no simple explanation. It is possible that he cracked under pressure. According to former chancellor Brüning, who knew him well, Schleicher was given to "trepidation in the face of ultimate decisions." If, as suggested by Theodor Wolff, the astute editor of the republican *Berliner Tageblatt,* he had previously regarded himself as an invincible master of political intrigue, the realization that he had been bested at that game by Franz von Papen may have destroyed his trust in his own abilities. Schleicher may also have simply analyzed the situation and concluded that in view of the odds against him he had no chance of retaining the chancellorship. Emotional factors cannot, however, be excluded. The cool rebuff he had received at the hands of Hindenburg on January 23 seems to have left him badly shaken. In his eyes, it amounted to betrayal of the president's assurance, at the outset of his chancellorship, of his full support. For someone who subscribed to the Prussian officers' code of honor, disloyalty on the part of a trusted superior was a searing experience. Coming on top of the discovery that not only Papen but also Oskar von Hindenburg and Otto Meissner were conspiring against him, the realization that his trust in Hindenburg was merely another illusion may well have been too much for the chancellor.

Schleicher's resentment seems not to have been directed primarily at the president himself. When he met with Brüning two weeks later, in mid-February, he still spoke respectfully of the elder Hindenburg. But on that same occasion he displayed great hostility toward Papen and Oskar von Hindenburg. It was these two former friends who in his view had treacherously undermined him. The realization that the younger Hindenburg had turned against him was, from all indications, especially daunting for Schleicher. An aide later recalled his remarking, with regard to the son's influence over the father, "That's how it always is: when people get old, they think only of their family." The knowledge that the House of Hindenburg, which he had long served so loyally, was now aligned against him, may well have sufficed to convince him that it was pointless to attempt to hold on to power.

There are indications that Schleicher was not altogether distressed at the prospect of relinquishing the chancellorship. Although he usually maintained his customary air of confident self-assurance, a number of lapses betrayed discomfort on his part with that office. During his years at the Defense Ministry, he had kept his desk clear by delegating most tasks to his staff. That arrangement left him free to move about the capital, touching political bases and picking up the latest gossip. But as chancellor, he found himself inescapably entangled in a multitude of complicated and intractable issues. Early in January he complained to Ambassador François-Poncet about the burden of dealing with the details of contentious economic conflicts of interest. In his earlier role of behind-the-scenes kingmaker, he had been able to exert influence under a cloak of anonymity. Now he stood in the unrelenting spotlight of public attention.

Harsh press criticism, especially from the conservative Right, stung Schleicher painfully. On several occasions he confessed to feeling out of place in the Chancellery and expressed a desire to withdraw as soon as possible to the more familiar and congenial Defense Ministry. Those expressions of unease, together with the passivity that marked his response to the prospect of losing the chancellorship, reveal that the man who stood between Adolf Hitler and that office lacked the essential ingredient for success in such a high-stakes contest: the appetite for power. Schleicher was apparently not wholly unaware of this. In a scribbled marginal note to an aide at the Defense Ministry in the fall of 1932 he wrote: "Too bad that I have no propensity for megalomania."

Resigned to losing the chancellorship, an embittered Schleicher now turned his attention to preventing that office from falling once more into the hands of Papen, even if that meant helping Hitler to gain it. During the last week of January, rumors to the effect that Hindenburg intended to reappoint Papen were proliferating in political circles and in the press. On the morning of Friday, January 27, the chief of the army command, General Kurt von Hammerstein, called on Schleicher and asked him about the rumors. Schleicher said nothing to reassure him, replying that he no longer had the confidence of the president and expected to fall from power within a day or two. The alarmed Hammerstein then went to Meissner and warned him that the army would look askance at another Papen cabinet that lacked the support of the Nazis.

Later on the morning of January 27, Hammerstein joined the chief of army personnel, General Erich von dem Bussche-Ippenburg, at the latter's weekly conference with Hindenburg. Although the president resisted the generals' efforts to offer political advice, they sought to warn him that Papen's return to the chancellorship would revive the danger of civil war. Either because he misunderstood them or because he wished to avoid denying the rumors about Papen, Hindenburg assured them only that he had no intention of bestowing the chancellorship on Hitler. The news that the president had not ruled out reappointing Papen could only have stiffened Schleicher's resolve to block his former friend's return to power. He was undoubtedly motivated in part by a desire for revenge, but he also knew full well that if his deadly enemy Papen again became chancellor he was sure to be replaced as minister of defense. On the other hand, he could hope that if Hitler became chancellor there was a chance of his remaining in that post and thus retaining control over the military.

When the cabinet assembled late on the morning of Saturday,

January 28, Schleicher informed his ministers that in a few minutes he would go to the president to request a dissolution decree, since otherwise a no-confidence motion was certain to carry when the Reichstag convened on the coming Tuesday. He expected that request to be rejected, however, and in that event planned to submit his resignation as well as that of the cabinet. Having established that there was no dissent from that position among the ministers, Schleicher said that he saw grave dangers ahead, as it seemed likely that Hindenburg intended to appoint a new presidential cabinet headed by Papen and backed only by Hugenberg and his German-National Party. Such a cabinet could, he added, result in a crisis not only of the government but also of the presidency, since it would be rejected by the great majority of the populace. There would be less danger, he added, in a parliamentary cabinet headed by Hitler. The members of the cabinet who spoke agreed about the dangerousness of a Papen-Hugenberg cabinet, and several ministers expressed their readiness to reinforce that point with the president personally.

At twelve-fifteen Schleicher interrupted the cabinet meeting and strode through the Chancellery building to the office used by the president. He began what would prove his last meeting with Hindenburg by laying out the possibilities as he saw them. One would be a Hitler cabinet backed by a majority of the Reichstag, which would be a solution to the situation but one that he thought unlikely. A second possibility would be a presidential cabinet headed by Hitler, which he pointed out would be inconsistent with the president's previous stands. The third possibility, and the one he recommended, called for continuation in office of his own cabinet, backed by the confidence and emergency powers of the president. He strongly warned against a fourth possibility: a cabinet headed by Papen in combination with Hugenberg. Such a cabinet, Schleicher contended, would face the opposition of nine-tenths of the people. The result would be revolutionary outbreaks and a general governmental crisis. To be able to go before the Reichstag on January 31 with his program, Schleicher said in conclusion, he would need a commitment from the president to dissolve the chamber. He made no mention of postponing a new election beyond the constitutionally mandated period.

The president proved no more responsive to Schleicher's proposals than he had been five days previously. The timing was particularly inauspicious. Earlier that morning, Hindenburg had been visited by Papen, who again urged the president to drop the idea of reappointing him and instead replace Schleicher with Hitler. Hindenburg had also been offended by an editorial in that morning's edition of the *Tägliche Rundschau,* the Berlin newspaper that was widely, but mistakenly, reputed to speak for Schleicher. Under the headline "Playing with a Presidential Crisis?" the editorial warned that if Hindenburg reappointed Papen there would be such widespread opposition that the president's own position would be endangered. From Hindenburg's standpoint, this must have sounded like a disrespectful threat. The belief that it stemmed from Schleicher, which Papen undoubtedly encouraged, could only have hardened his resolve to be rid of the chancellor.

After hearing Schleicher out, Hindenburg replied that under the circumstances he could not grant a dissolution decree. He expressed appreciation for Schleicher's attempt to achieve a parliamentary majority by winning the support of the Nazis. Since that effort had failed, however, he would now have to try another possibility. What that would be he left unmentioned. When Schleicher reported that several members of his cabinet wished to present to the president their views of the political situation, Hindenburg evasively replied that he would take that under advisement. Nothing anyone might say, he added, could alter his decision. He thanked the chancellor and his cabinet in perfunctory fashion for their service to the country and issued the routine request that they remain in office until a new cabinet had been formed. The two men then went over the text of the official announcement of the chancellor's resignation, which had obviously been prepared in advance. In parting, Schleicher expressed the hope that in a new cabinet the Defense Ministry not be assigned to a Nazi.

Hindenburg responded that he, too, was absolutely opposed to such an arrangement.

After little more than a quarter of an hour with the president, Schleicher returned to inform the waiting cabinet members about what had been said. He felt as though he had been talking to a wall, he reported. The president had not fully registered his arguments and had responded with stale, well-rehearsed statements. Clearly, the thoroughly dispirited chancellor had come away from the meeting with the president still assuming that his successor would be Franz von Papen. As its last order of business after only fifty-seven days in office, the Schleicher cabinet then proceeded to give final approval to the financial measures needed to implement the job-creation program the chancellor had promised at the outset would be his top priority. It became law later that same day in the form of an emergency decree signed by the president. The program made available a half billion marks for a variety of public works projects designed to provide employment for the jobless and stimulate overall economic activity. When, in the course of the next six months, nearly two million unemployed Germans found jobs, Kurt von Schleicher would receive none of the credit. Instead, the political beneficiary would be Adolf Hitler.

6

Papen Leads
the Plunge
into the Abyss

SHORTLY AFTER Schleicher submitted his resignation to Hindenburg on Saturday, January 28, the president commissioned Franz von Papen to explore the possibilities for a new cabinet. The man who had been instrumental in poisoning the president's mind against Schleicher thus stepped back into the political limelight. Papen more than anyone else would shape the disastrous developments of the next two days. If he had been willing to become chancellor once again, his wish would have been speedily granted, for he was Hindenburg's preferred choice. But Papen held to his plan to install Hitler at the head of a cabinet in which he intended to wield the real power.

Hindenburg's commission to Papen was a mere formality. The former chancellor had already been engaged in intense political intrigue throughout the previous week, and with the knowledge of the president. Thanks to his privileged access, he had known since Hindenburg's rebuff of Schleicher on January 23 that the chancellor was unlikely to receive a dissolution decree that would rescue him from a no-confidence vote when the Reichstag convened on January 31.

Seeing an opportunity to put his plan into operation, Papen conveyed this information to the Nazis and offered to use his influence with Hindenburg to secure the chancellorship for Hitler.

Since Hitler had gone to Munich for several days, his lieutenants Wilhelm Frick and Hermann Göring took up the negotiations with Papen, meeting with him over tea on January 24 at Ribbentrop's house. The three reached agreement that the best hope of overcoming Hindenburg's opposition to Hitler lay in presenting the Nazi leader as the prospective chancellor of a rightist "nationalist front" cabinet in which he would be surrounded by conservatives. During the following two days the conspirators held out the prospect of participation in such a cabinet to the German-National leader Hugenberg and to Franz Seldte, one of the two leaders of the Stahlhelm, a nationalistic veterans' paramilitary organization with more than three hundred thousand uniformed members. In 1931 Seldte and Hugenberg had participated with Hitler in the short-lived Harzburg Front, but both had been at odds with him since then.

Enlistment of Seldte in the plot to form a new rightist cabinet was achieved without difficulty. The Stahlhelm had dabbled in politics for some time, and the previous year Seldte's coleader, Theodor Düsterberg, had entered the presidential race with the backing of Hugenberg's party. A colorless figure with no significant attainments to his credit, Seldte nevertheless harbored political ambitions himself. The prospect of collaborating with Papen to bring down Schleicher was attractive to him, since there was friction between the Stahlhelm's leadership and the Defense Ministry. Schleicher in particular regarded the Stahlhelm's training exercises for its uniformed members as a threat to the considerably smaller army's control over military matters within Germany. He strove to bring the Stahlhelm, along with other paramilitary organizations, under military control by making them dependent on government subsidies, an arrangement resisted by the Stahlhelm's leadership. As chancellor, Schleicher thus represented a threat to the independence of the veterans' organization, whereas Papen had shown himself more sympathetic to its interests. If joining forces with Papen against Schleicher meant accepting the former chancellor's plan for a cabinet headed by Hitler, that was no obstacle for Seldte.

Whereas the malleable Seldte quickly succumbed to the enticement of a cabinet post, Hugenberg proved a more difficult recruit for Papen's scheme. A stodgy, vain man in his sixty-eighth year, he was in many respects a relic of the imperial era who continued during the republic to use the honorific title of privy councillor (*Geheimrat*) awarded him for obedient service to the Prussian crown. His appearance was, as Ambassador François-Poncet observed, deceptive: "His round gold-rim spectacles, his potbelly, his bristly white moustache lend him the reassuring aspect of a worthy country doctor; in reality, he is narrow-minded and hide-bound, sullenly obstinate, a doctrinaire extremist, a ferocious partisan, one of Germany's evil spirits." Unbendingly opposed to democracy and the republican welfare state, he sought a return to thoroughgoing laissez-faire economics and authoritarian rule by a privileged elite.

Hugenberg lacked, however, the qualities necessary to gain political popularity. Anything but a gifted orator, he read turgid texts in a monotone on the rare occasions when he spoke in public. Although his loyal followers referred to him reverentially as 'the silver fox,' his fusty visage, antiquated attire, and stiff manner led less well-disposed contemporaries to deride him as 'the hamster' or 'the crotchety spider.' As one close associate observed late in 1932, "He has no political sex appeal." He nevertheless hungered for the political power that had eluded him throughout his career, and when approached by Papen, he was tempted by the prospect of at last obtaining a cabinet post. He was restrained, however, by his own past experiences with Hitler and by the mistrust of the Nazi leader on the part of other prominent German-Nationals who preferred an authoritarian regime under Papen that would exclude Hitler. Hugenberg therefore hesitated in response to the proposal of participation in a nationalist front cabinet headed by Hitler.

On Friday, January 27, Papen's scheme came perilously close to collapsing. Upon Hitler's return to Berlin, Ribbentrop explained to him the plan to make him chancellor and persuaded him to invite Hugenberg to discuss the matter. Once he had reached agreement with the German-National leader, Ribbentrop proposed, the final terms could be worked out with Papen that evening. That afternoon, Hitler, Frick and Göring met with Hugenberg and a conservative colleague from his party, Otto Schmidt-Hannover. Göring immediately placed Hugenberg at a disadvantage by disclosing that Seldte had already agreed to enter a Hitler cabinet. That step on the part of the Stahlhelm leader would, as the Nazis well knew, increase the pressure on Hugenberg from within his own party to follow suit.

In exploiting this advantage, Hitler overplayed his hand in the meeting with Hugenberg. He demanded not only that he be made chancellor of a presidential cabinet but also that other Nazis be assigned the national and Prussian interior ministries. Of those, the Prussian ministry was the more important, since it exercised authority over the police in by far the largest of the federal states, whereas the national interior ministry had no direct control over police. In the hands of the republicans who had controlled Prussia until the Papen cabinet deposed them the previous July, the state's well-armed fifty-thousand-man police force, which was half the size of the army, had been a potent weapon against the Nazis. Hitler was therefore determined to gain control over it in order to purge it of republicans and staff it with Nazis. Hugenberg balked at that prospect, however, insisting that the Prussian interior ministry be assigned to a non-Nazi. He also proposed that the Chancellery chief of staff and the cabinet's press spokesman be drawn from the ranks of his own party. Furious at being thwarted, Hitler broke off the negotiations, refused to meet with Papen, and threatened to return to Munich. Only with difficulty did Göring and Ribbentrop persuade him to remain in the capital.

Papen managed to rescue his scheme, but at the price of crucial concessions to Hitler. When Ribbentrop informed him on the evening of January 27 of the Nazi leader's angry reaction to Hugenberg's terms, Papen agreed to support Hitler's demands for the two interior ministries as well as for freedom to choose the Chancellery personnel. Hugenberg's wishes, he indicated to Ribbentrop, were of secondary importance. By siding with Hitler against Hugenberg on the issue of control over the Prussian police, Papen revealed that he was ready to pay a heavy price for Hitler's cooperation. That point was not lost on the Nazi leader. To be sure, Papen expected to succeed Schleicher as commissar for Prussia, the office to which the authority of that state's minister-president had been assigned after Papen had, as chancellor, deposed the Prussian cabinet the previous July. That post would make Papen the superior of a Nazi interior minister in Prussia and enable him, he naively assumed, to keep Hitler's party from using the state's large police force for its own political purposes.

On the morning of Saturday, January 28, Papen met with Hindenburg and learned that the president expected Schleicher to resign when the chancellor appeared for his midday appointment. Recognizing the need to accelerate implementation of his scheme, Papen asked Ribbentrop to locate Hitler, fearing that the Nazi leader had left Berlin. His talk with Hindenburg had convinced him that Hitler's appointment as chancellor was now possible. Having determined that Hitler was still at the Kaiserhof Hotel, Ribbentrop pressed him to meet with Papen. But Hitler now raised the stakes by objecting to Papen's claim on the position of commissar for Prussia. In the course of a heated argument, Ribbentrop won Göring's support for the view that Papen had to be conceded that post. But despite the efforts of both Ribbentrop and Göring to persuade Hitler that he should meet with Papen that afternoon, the Nazi leader insisted that he needed more time to think over the Prussian question. Finally, however, he agreed to confer the following morning with Papen. Informed of this, Papen readily agreed to see Hitler but remained concerned that the question of authority over Prussia might derail his scheme.

On the afternoon of January 28, Papen set out to break Hugenberg's resistance. The Nazis, he informed the German-National leader, must have the interior ministries in both the national government and Prussia. By way of conciliating Hugenberg, Papen responded encouragingly to his request for control over the ministries of economics and agriculture in both governments. Still under strong pressure from conservative party colleagues who mistrusted Hitler and favored an authoritarian Papen cabinet, the German-National leader remained troubled at the prospect of the Nazis taking over the Prussian police. But he was unwilling to abandon his first chance at a share of power and so refrained from breaking off the negotiations.

Later that same day, Papen succeeded in weakening the position of conservative opponents of a Hitler cabinet. By indicating that Hindenburg was ready to accept Hitler and that he himself would consider assuming the chancellorship again only if the plan to construct a broad rightist cabinet under Hitler should fail, Papen won endorsement for his scheme from most of the conservative, nonparty ministers who had served in his cabinet and Schleicher's. At the last meeting of the Schleicher cabinet that morning, it had been agreed that the return of Papen to the chancellorship would be a disaster that might eventuate in civil war. Relieved at the prospect of averting that peril, the ministers readily assented to Papen's project for a nationalist front cabinet headed by Hitler.

Also in the course of the afternoon of January 28, still another peril to Papen's scheme arose. It came from the Catholic parties, the Center and the Bavarian People's Party. Their leaders became alarmed when Hindenburg's commission to Papen seemed to confirm rumors that the former chancellor was about to return to office, presumably once more at the head of an unpopular presidential cabinet backed only by Hugenberg's party. The Catholic leaders had never forgiven their ex-colleague Papen for accepting the chancellorship the previous summer without consulting them. But even more importantly, they regarded virtually any solution as preferable to unconstitutional measures of the sort Papen was known to have favored while chancellor.

After consulting with the leadership of the Center Party, the chairman of the Bavarian People's Party, Fritz Schäffer, approached both Hitler and Papen late on the 28th. The Catholic parties, he announced, would be willing to participate in a parliamentary cabinet headed by Hitler. Together with the Nazis and the German-Nationals, the Catholic parties could provide a solid Reichstag majority for such a cabinet. That arrangement would rule out a return to power by Papen and put the Catholic parties in position to exercise restraint on Hitler. If the Nazi leader should, as chancellor, embark upon policies to which the Catholics objected, they could bring him down by withdrawing their support in the Reichstag, thus depriving him of a majority. This was just the sort of possibility that made Hitler intent upon becoming a presidential chancellor, free of parliamentary constraints. He therefore fended off Schäffer's offer by pointing out that he had not been commissioned to form a cabinet and was therefore not in a position to enter into negotiations.

Schäffer met with no greater receptivity from Papen. This was hardly surprising, since acceptance of the Catholic proposal would have gravely imperiled Papen's own very different plans. Having repeatedly pledged not to appoint Hitler chancellor of a presidential cabinet, Hindenburg might seize upon the Catholics' offer and refuse to appoint the Nazi leader unless his cabinet was parliamentary in nature. As Papen well knew, there was no real possibility of a coalition of Nazis, German-Nationals and the Catholic parties. Hugenberg had irreconcilable differences with the Catholics and could be counted upon to block formation of such a coalition. So could Hitler, who had no intention of becoming a parliamentary chancellor, dependent upon other parties for retention of his office. But if coalition negotiations with the Catholics were launched at the behest of Hindenburg, considerable delay might ensue, thereby disrupting Papen's arrangements for a presidential cabinet headed by Hitler. Any such negotiations for a parliamentary cabinet were also unlikely to remain secret. If they broke down in full public view, it might be difficult for Papen to bring the president to violate his earlier pledges by appointing Hitler chancellor of a presidential cabinet.

Having failed to make headway with Papen, Schäffer extracted from him a promise to convey the Catholics' proposal to Hindenburg. Papen, however, kept the matter to himself. For their part, the Catholic leaders refrained from making their position public, in keeping with the usual parliamentary practice of avoiding a prior commitment so as to maximize bargaining leverage in coalition negotiations. Only a day later did their offer come into play, and then it had, thanks to the deviousness of Franz von Papen, an effect quite different from their intent.

THROUGHOUT the 28th, despite Ribbentrop's assurances that Papen could be trusted, Hitler remained dubious about his co-conspirator's motives. That evening, Goebbels found him at the Kaiserhof Hotel, full of suspicion that Papen intended to double-cross him and use the commission he had received from Hindenburg to take the chancellorship for himself. Hitler welcomed the dismissal of Schleicher earlier that day but saw it as another example of Hindenburg's notorious lack of loyalty, which worried him, as did the president's unpredictability. Fired by his mistrust of Papen and Hindenburg, Hitler revealed his deep-seated hostility toward persons of privileged birth by whiling away the rest of the evening in the Kaiserhof's café, regaling his entourage with a monologue consisting of derisive anecdotes about the foibles of various aristocrats.

Like Hitler, many defenders of the republic feared that Hindenburg's commission to Papen meant that the former chancellor was on his way back to power. Most saw that possibility as a far more likely danger than the appointment of Hitler. Responding to rumors, the republican press had, throughout the fourth week of January, issued repeated warnings against another Papen chancellorship. Such a development, it was widely predicted, would result in unconstitutional measures and give rise to the danger of civil war. In most instances, though, pro-republican editorial writers expressed the belief that President von Hindenburg could be relied upon to defend the constitution and refuse to install another cabinet headed by Papen that would, as before, be backed by little more than Hugenberg's party.

As for Hitler, the stand Hindenburg had taken in November was viewed in republican circles as assurance that the president would never appoint the Nazi leader as chancellor of a presidential cabinet. The alternative of a parliamentary cabinet under Hitler, which Hindenburg had held out to the Nazi leader in November, was seen as still theoretically open but highly improbable in view of Hitler's repeated rejection of any such constraining arrangement. It was symptomatic of the political bankruptcy of the republic's defenders that while they voiced opposition to these possibilities, they offered no positive proposals of their own for resolution of the political crisis.

Despite the earlier statements by Hindenburg to which defenders of the republic optimistically clung, his resistance to appointing Hitler had begun to crumble by January 28. For days, everyone around him had been urging that course of action upon him. His preferred candidate, Papen, had withdrawn himself from consideration and insisted that the Nazi leader must be the next chancellor. His chief aide, Otto Meissner, nudged him in the same direction. So did his son Oskar, who had been won over to the idea of a nationalist front cabinet headed by Hitler after returning to Dahlem for a meeting over tea with Ribbentrop on January 25.

A short time earlier, the elder Hindenburg had received similar advice from a prominent visitor, Elard von Oldenburg-Januschau, an elderly Junker neighbor of the president's at his country estate in East Prussia who had played a major role in conservative politics during the Empire and was still an influential figure in eastern landowner circles. Hopeful of relief measures by a Hitler cabinet for the depressed agriculture of the east, the old Junker assured the president that the army and the forces of conservatism would suffice to prevent a one-party Nazi dictatorship. On the 28th, the president received a reassuring message from Göring. The Nazis, Göring solemnly promised, would respect Hindenburg's authority as president and had no intention of violating the constitution or subjecting the military to political influence. Coming from a fellow officer and decorated war hero, such pledges could hardly fail to impress the old field marshal.

Late on the evening of the 28th, Papen called on Hindenburg and sought to overcome his remaining reservations. Omitting mention of the differences that still separated Hitler from Hugenberg and himself, he portrayed the Nazi leader's position as one of moderation. Reassuring in that regard was his report that Hitler wanted only a minimal number of places in the cabinet for his party and was ready to see the other ministries assigned to nonparty experts acceptable to the president. Also encouraging was Papen's report that most of the conservative ministers who had served in his and Schleicher's cabinets had expressed readiness to continue under Hitler. Despite his dislike for Hugenberg, the president indicated his willingness to grant the German-National leader's wish for personal control over both the national and Prussian ministries of agriculture and economics.

For the two ministries Hindenburg regarded as the most sensitive, defense and foreign affairs, he wanted men of his own choice. He was therefore especially pleased to hear from Papen that the aristocratic professional diplomat who had headed the Foreign Ministry under both Papen and Schleicher, Baron Konstantin von Neurath, would be willing to stay on under Hitler. As for the Defense Ministry, over which Schleicher had presided while chancellor, the president agreed with Papen that a change was needed. For that post Hindenburg passed over a general proposed by Papen in favor of a candidate of his own, General Werner von Blomberg, currently a member of the German delegation at the ongoing disarmament conference in Switzerland. At the close of their meeting, Papen later recalled, the president extracted from him a promise to serve as vice chancellor in a Hitler cabinet. If Hindenburg had not yet fully committed himself to Papen's scheme, he had gone a long way toward doing so by the time they parted.

Sunday, January 29, proved the decisive day. In a dizzying whirl of developments, the contours of a cabinet headed by Adolf Hitler took final shape. In the morning, President von Hindenburg took a major step in that direction by instructing his son to telephone General von Blomberg and summon him to return to Berlin so that he would be available as successor to Schleicher at the Defense Ministry. The tall, socially adept general had made a favorable impression on the president in the course of courtesy calls he paid to the president's country estate in his capacity as army commander in East Prussia. Earlier in January, moreover, he had visited Hindenburg in Berlin. On that occasion, Blomberg, who over the years had clashed repeatedly with Schleicher on a number of issues regarding military affairs, reportedly expressed disapproval of the chancellor's policies and indicated a readiness to see Hitler entrusted with the chancellorship. Although Hindenburg apparently assumed that Blomberg was an unpolitical, professional officer, he had chosen a man highly susceptible to the allures of Nazism. While stationed in East Prussia, Blomberg had come under the influence of pro-Nazi elements in the army, including the chief Protestant chaplain there, who would during the Third Reich become Nazi bishop of the Protestant church. Blomberg's selection by Hindenburg would therefore prove a fortuitous boon to Hitler.

That same Sunday morning, Hitler, accompanied by Göring, kept his appointment at Papen's apartment in the Interior Ministry building on the Wilhelmstrasse, two doors away from the president's residence in the Chancellery. Papen raised no objections when Hitler named Wilhelm Frick as his choice for interior minister in the national cabinet and Hermann Göring as his candidate to take over the Prussian Interior Ministry. Hitler in turn gave in to Hindenburg's insistence that Papen be named both vice chancellor and commissar for Prussia. Hitler then introduced a new demand by announcing that he wanted the Reichstag dissolved so that a new election could be held. As chancellor, he explained, he would need from the Reichstag an enabling act that would transfer legislative authority to the cabinet.

There were precedents for an enabling act of the sort Hitler had in mind. A decade earlier, republican cabinets had obtained such powers from the Reichstag several times in order to cope with crises. Since such a measure amounted to a temporary alteration of the constitution, a two-thirds majority was necessary for passage. Because that was an impossibility in the current Reichstag, Hitler wanted a new election into which he could lead his party as the chancellor chosen by President von Hindenburg. By exploiting that status and the resources of the national government, he hoped to achieve a greatly increased representation in the parliament for his party. If the results of the balloting made an enabling act possible, his cabinet would be able to decree laws without regard to the Reichstag and without reliance on the president's emergency powers. Anxious to move ahead swiftly with his scheme, Papen raised no objections to Hitler's important new demand for a new national election.

On the afternoon of the 29th Papen set out to complete the enlistment of the German-National Party and the Stahlhelm for the projected Hitler cabinet. He summoned to his apartment Hugenberg and the coleaders of the veterans' organization, Franz Seldte and Theodor Düsterberg, and informed them of the readiness of incumbent conservative cabinet members to serve under Hitler and of Hindenburg's intention to appoint General von Blomberg as defense minister. Seldte, Papen indicated, was foreseen as labor minister in the new cabinet. As for Hugenberg, Papen announced that the president wanted him to assume the ministries of agriculture and economics in both the national and Prussian governments.

The prospect of personal command over those four ministries was a powerful enticement for the German-National leader. It would fulfill his long-standing ambition to gain control of the key agencies for economic policy so as to undo what he regarded as the "socialism" of the republic. Hugenberg was especially flattered by Papen's report that Hindenburg, who had previously made no secret of his dislike for him, now particularly wanted him in the cabinet. In keeping with his usual deviousness, Papen refrained from mentioning Hitler's demand for a new election. As he was well aware, Hugenberg would recoil from the prospect of a campaign in which the Nazis would, as the party of the man newly chosen by Hindenburg as chancellor, have a decided advantage over his own German-National Party.

Eager for a share of power, Hugenberg was inclined to accept

Papen's terms, but the Stahlhelm leader Düsterberg and several prominent conservative figures in his party who had gathered at Papen's apartment on the afternoon of the 29th vehemently opposed that step. They recognized Hitler as an unscrupulous fanatic and were appalled at the thought of their party's helping to boost him into power. In an effort to stave off such a step, they implored Hugenberg not to agree to a Hitler cabinet. But as opponents of democracy and parliamentary government, they were not seeking to rescue the republic. Instead, they proposed another Papen presidential cabinet, excluding the Nazis, that would dissolve the Reichstag without scheduling a new election and then rule in authoritarian fashion by means of presidential emergency decrees.

Since even Papen himself now shied away from a course of action that involved bypassing the constitution, Hugenberg rejected that proposal. His expectation that control over the four economic-policy ministries would assure him of a powerful voice in a Hitler cabinet impelled him in that direction. So did his fear that if his party did not enter into alliance with Hitler, the Catholic Center Party, which he despised, might do so, leaving the German-Nationals once more without influence on government policy. Hugenberg therefore agreed to let Papen's scheme go forward. Later on the afternoon of the 29th Papen informed the Nazis that the last obstacles to his plan had been removed, even though he had yet to secure Hindenburg's final approval.

Just how frivolously Hugenberg and Papen underestimated Hitler is revealed by their responses to the conservatives who tried to dissuade them from installing the Nazi leader as chancellor. To the protestations of Stahlhelm leader Düsterberg on the 29th, Hugenberg replied: "We'll box Hitler in." When Ewald von Kleist-Schmenzin, a conservative Prussian Junker aristocrat who would later lose his life for opposing Hitler's dictatorship, protested against Papen's scheme that same day, the latter's rejoinder was: "What do you want? I have the confidence of Hindenburg. In two months we'll have pushed Hitler so far into a corner that he'll squeal." When another conservative warned that Hitler sought a dictatorship, Papen reportedly replied, "You're mistaken. We've hired him!"

WHILE Papen was busy lining up personnel for a Hitler cabinet on Sunday, January 29, Kurt von Schleicher bestirred himself politically. In so doing, he unwittingly facilitated Papen's scheme. Hindenburg's commission to Papen of the previous day had heightened Schleicher's concern that his predecessor might become his successor. He, like most of the leaders of the military, preferred Hitler to the discredited Papen as chancellor. Knowing that if Papen returned he would have no hope of remaining as minister of defense, Schleicher saw Hitler's appointment as his only chance to retain authority over the army. If he could achieve that, he believed he would be able to control Hitler. "If Hitler wants to establish a dictatorship," Meissner later recalled his saying on one occasion, "the army will be a dictatorship within the dictatorship."

On the morning of January 29 Schleicher discussed the situation with a group of generals at the Defense Ministry. At least one general proposed a resort to force to prevent a Papen cabinet, but Schleicher rejected any thought of defying the president. As he had reportedly explained the day before in response to a similar suggestion, his military training ruled out any such insubordination: "I am a general, Hindenburg is field marshal. I have been taught obedience."

In hopes of winning favor with Hitler, and not knowing the advanced state of Papen's machinations, Schleicher decided on the 29th to sound out the Nazi leader about the possibility of cooperation. At his behest, one of his confidants, General Kurt von Hammerstein, the chief of the army command, met secretly with Hitler that afternoon at the Berlin residence of a wealthy Nazi sympathizer. Hammerstein asked Hitler whether those acting on behalf of the president—by which he meant Papen—were negotiating with him seriously for the chancellorship or were behaving deviously. If the latter should be the case and Papen should be seeking the chancellorship for himself, the general offered to try to bring the influence of the military to bear on behalf of the Nazi leader's candidacy. The general also inquired whether Hitler would be willing to retain Schleicher as defense minister if he became chancellor. Keeping his options open even though he was aware that Papen's plans left no place for Schleicher, Hitler responded affirmatively to the latter question. As to the negotiations for a new cabinet, he indicated that he could not yet determine their seriousness but agreed to advise Hammerstein when he knew more.

On the evening of January 29, Hammerstein went to Schleicher's residence to report on his meeting with Hitler and to inquire about new developments. When the two generals were joined by Werner von Alvensleben, a gadabout in conservative circles with entrée to the Nazi leadership, they sent him to Goebbels' apartment, where Hitler and Göring were dining, to inquire about the state of cabinet negotiations. After Alvensleben returned without a clear answer, Hammerstein telephoned Hitler to express his concern that they might be confronted with a fait accompli the next day, by which he meant a Papen cabinet that would exclude the Nazis. Hitler remained evasive, even though he had been assured by Papen that he would soon be named chancellor.

Hitler, Goebbels and Göring had, however, been alarmed by remarks made by Alvensleben during his call at Goebbels' apartment. In the course of his visit, Alvensleben had boasted that the army command stood ready to intervene with force if the formation of a new cabinet did not conform with its wishes. His remarks left the Nazi leaders fearful of a military putsch aimed at thwarting Hitler's appointment as chancellor. Especially alarmed, Hitler placed the Berlin SA on alert and sent notification to a pro-Nazi police officer in the capital to be prepared for such an eventuality. Meanwhile, Göring notified Papen and Meissner of this new development.

Talk of a putsch quickly gave rise to a totally unfounded but rapidly escalating rumor that enabled Papen to speed up efforts to put his scheme into effect. By the time the rumor reached the presidential residence via Meissner and Papen, Schleicher was alleged to be mobilizing troops with the aim of deposing Hindenburg and taking over the presidency himself. Outraged, Oskar von Hindenburg denounced Schleicher as a traitor. His wife reportedly believed Schleicher had ordered the arrest of the president and planned to transport him in a sealed train to his country residence for detention there. So inclined were the president's family and entourage to suspect the worst of Schleicher that no one took the trouble to investigate whether there was any truth to the rumored plans for a military putsch.

Taking advantage of this atmosphere of crisis, Papen secured Hindenburg's agreement on the evening of the 29th to swear in a new cabinet headed by Hitler the next morning. He also obtained the president's approval of a list of ministers. Four nonpolitical members of Schleicher's cabinet, the ministers for foreign affairs, finance, and postal and transport service, as well as the commissar for job creation, Gereke, were to be held over. Hugenberg was designated as minister for agriculture and economics in both the national and Prussian governments. General von Blomberg was to replace Schleicher as defense minister, and Seldte of the Stahlhelm was to become labor minister. The third Nazi, in addition to Hitler as chancellor and Frick as interior minister, was Göring. He was to be minister without portfolio and commissar for air traffic. Göring was also assigned the Prussian Interior Ministry, including command over its large police force. Papen himself was designated as commissar for Prussia and deputy chancellor—rather than merely vice chancellor—a change in terminology that did nothing to alter the fact that the constitution bestowed no authority whatever on a bearer of either of those titles. By way of ensuring that he would have a voice in all vital matters, Papen secured Hindenburg's agreement that he be present at all meetings between the president and Chancellor Hitler.

As the list of ministers approved by Hindenburg on the evening of the 29th and implemented the next day reveals, Papen had resorted to a ruse designed to deceive the president about the kind of cabinet Hitler would head. Knowing that Hindenburg had repeatedly refused to make Hitler chancellor of a presidential cabinet, Papen had avoided disclosing to him that he had given in to Hitler on that point. Now, in the midst of the furor set off by the rumors of a putsch, Papen saw an opportunity to guard against the possibility that the president might again balk at appointing Hitler a presidential chancellor. With the new cabinet scheduled to be hurriedly sworn in the next morning, Papen realized that there would be no time for further coalition negotiations. He therefore played the Catholic card he had been holding since his conversation with the emissary of the Bavarian People's Party, Fritz Schäffer, the previous day. By leaving vacant the post of justice minister in the list of cabinet members, he sought to create the impression that it was being reserved for a Catholic, pending final coalition negotiations. Added to the votes in the Reichstag of the Nazis and German-Nationals, those of the Catholics would provide a comfortable majority and make the Hitler cabinet parliamentary rather than presidential.

This was at least what the omission of a justice minister from Papen's list of ministers was designed to lead Hindenburg to believe. In actuality, neither Papen nor Hitler nor Hugenberg had the slightest intention of forming a coalition with the Catholics or making the new cabinet dependent upon their parliamentary support. Nevertheless, Papen deceitfully gave the president to understand on the evening of January 29 that negotiations were under way with the Catholics aimed at producing a parliamentary, rather than a presidential, cabinet headed by Hitler. Once the new cabinet was sworn in the next morning, Papen knew it would be a simple matter to ensure that talks with the Catholics quickly broke down. But by then, having installed the Hitler cabinet with great fanfare, Hindenburg would find it next to impossible to deny the new chancellor use of the emergency powers he had placed at the disposal of his three predecessors, especially if the president's trusted confidant, Franz von Papen, supported such a step. At what point Papen revealed this ruse to Hitler and Hugenberg remains uncertain. But their acceptance, the following morning, of the vacancy at the justice ministry and the pretense that coalition negotiations with the Catholics were pending leaves no doubt of their complicity. The same was the case with Hindenburg's chief of staff, Meissner, whose cooperation was essential if the deception were to succeed.

On the evening of Sunday, January 29, political circles in Berlin were abuzz with conflicting rumors. Ambassador François-Poncet heard that Papen had abandoned his effort to put together a new cabinet. Similar reports reached the nonparty minister of finance in the Papen and Schleicher cabinets, Count Schwerin von Krosigk, who earlier in the day had been told by Papen that arrangements were on track for a Hitler cabinet that would include him. One of the count's informants reported that Hugenberg was again pressing for Papen's return to the chancellorship. Still another informant told Schwerin von Krosigk that Schleicher was about to use the military against Hindenburg on the grounds that the president was no longer mentally competent. Among those who were the targets of rumors was Otto Meissner, who was awakened at 2:00 A.M. by a telephone call warning him that Schleicher was about to arrest him, along with the president and Oskar von Hindenburg.

On the morning of Monday, January 30, the political situation remained murky. British Ambassador Sir Horace Rumbold indicated to his government that it appeared likely that Franz von Papen would be the new chancellor. Also that morning, Schleicher's Chancellery chief of staff, Erwin Planck, telephoned Count Schwerin von Krosigk to inform him that Hitler had broken off negotiations and had probably already left Berlin. Papen, Planck reported to the count, had been summoned to the president at eleven o'clock that morning and would be sworn in as chancellor at that time.

Shortly after speaking with Planck, Count Schwerin von Krosigk received a call from the president's office, instructing him to appear at the Chancellery at eleven to be sworn in again as finance minister, but without any indication of who would head the new cabinet. Concerned lest he find himself conscripted for another narrowly based Papen cabinet, the bewildered count called Foreign Minister von Neurath, who also rejected such an arrangement and reported receiving a similarly uninformative summons to appear at the Chancellery at eleven. When Count Schwerin von Krosigk thereupon called Papen, he was curtly informed to ignore rumors; the Hitler cabinet, Papen assured him, was a certainty. This only increased the count's bafflement, and he went to the Chancellery later in the morning still uncertain about who was to be sworn in as chancellor.

Early on the morning of the 30th, General von Blomberg arrived in Berlin by train, having traveled overnight from Switzerland after receiving Hindenburg's summons the previous day. When he stepped onto the railway station platform, Blomberg found two military officers awaiting him. One was a major sent by the chief of the army command, General von Hammerstein, who had by chance learned of Blomberg's return to Berlin. The major's orders were to escort Blomberg to the Defense Ministry, where he would meet with Schleicher and Hammerstein, both of whom wanted to deter him from accepting the post of minister of defense in a Papen cabinet. The other officer awaiting Blomberg was Colonel Oskar von Hindenburg, who had come to take the general to the Chancellery, where his father intended to enlist him as defense minister in a cabinet headed by Hitler. Forced to choose between the two awaiting officers, Blomberg went with the younger Hindenburg, who not only outranked the major but also represented the supreme commander in chief of the armed forces.

When Blomberg and Oskar von Hindenburg arrived at the president's office in the Chancellery, the news that an officer from the Defense Ministry had met the general's train and sought to take him to Schleicher lent credence to the rumors of an imminent military putsch. The sense of danger and of urgent need for a speedy resolution of the political situation escalated. As a preemptive measure, Blomberg was sworn in by the president as minister of defense shortly after nine o'clock, thereby stripping Schleicher of all authority over the military.

Upon learning that Blomberg had gone to the president, Schleicher telephoned Meissner and protested that his authority as defense minister had been unconstitutionally violated. Even more clearly illegal, though, was Hindenburg's bestowal of that post on

Blomberg. The constitution specified that cabinet ministers could be appointed by the president only upon nomination by the chancellor, and at the time Blomberg was sworn in on the morning of January 30, Schleicher still occupied that office on a caretaker basis. Schleicher's concern about Blomberg's appointment was, however, only partially justified. Whereas he feared Blomberg would be installed in a Papen cabinet, the general's appointment actually anticipated the formation of what Schleicher himself had come to favor, namely a cabinet headed by Hitler. To be sure, Schleicher had failed to allow for the possibility that his archenemy Papen would play a conspicuous role in a Hitler cabinet or that he himself would be replaced as minister of defense.

Between nine and ten o'clock on the 30th, Hugenberg arrived at Papen's apartment in the Interior Ministry, as did Otto Schmidt-Hannover, a prominent Reichstag deputy of the German-National Party, and the coleaders of the Stahlhelm, Seldte and Düsterberg. There they found an agitated Papen, who warned those assembled that unless the new cabinet was promptly sworn in, a putsch would result in a military dictatorship under Schleicher. There was no time for quibbling, Papen insisted. "If the new cabinet is not installed by eleven o'clock," Düsterberg later recalled his warning, "the army will march. We're threatened with a military dictatorship under Schleicher and Hammerstein."

Hugenberg's colleague Schmidt-Hannover and the Stahlhelm's Düsterberg still had grave reservations about seeing Hitler installed as chancellor. At a minimum, they wanted to slow the rush toward installation of the new cabinet long enough to circumscribe Hitler's authority by withholding from the Nazis the Prussian Interior Ministry, with its control over the police in three-fifths of Germany. After failing to enlist the support of Hugenberg and Seldte, Düsterberg and Schmidt-Hannover went to the Chancellery in hopes of presenting their concerns to Hindenburg. Denied access to the president, they encountered instead Oskar von Hindenburg, who railed against the alleged treachery of Schleicher and showed no interest in their pleas for precautions regarding Hitler.

Upon returning to Papen's apartment, Düsterberg found that Hitler and Göring had arrived there. Düsterberg, whose consent would be required if his colleague Seldte were to enter the cabinet as spokesperson of the Stahlhelm, nursed a personal grievance against the Nazis. Several months earlier, he had belatedly discovered that one of his grandfathers had been born Jewish although he had later been baptized a Christian. That information soon reached the Nazi press, which, in line with the efforts of Hitler's party to entice Stahlhelm members into its own ranks, denounced Düsterberg as the descendant of a Jew and the Stahlhelm as a tool of Jewish interests. The Nazi attacks were a source of consternation for Düsterberg, who himself belonged to the anti-Semitic wing of the Stahlhelm, and his resentment was one of the reasons for his coolness toward Hitler's candidacy for the chancellorship.

When Düsterberg ostentatiously avoided greeting Hitler and Göring when they arrived at Papen's apartment on the morning of the 30th, it seemed very possible that he might refuse to approve Seldte's participation in a Hitler cabinet. Hitler noticed this, however, and acted to dispel the Stahlhelm leader's resentment. After a hurried consultation, he and Göring rose from their chairs and approached Düsterberg in friendly fashion. Speaking in the deep voice he reserved for solemn occasions, Hitler assured Düsterberg that he had neither ordered the Nazi press attacks on him nor approved of them. Disarmed by this gesture, which Hitler accompanied with a show of sincere emotion, including moist eyes, Düsterberg let his objections drop, and the last obstacle to the Stahlhelm's support was removed.

Papen then led Hitler, Hugenberg, Düsterberg and Seldte on foot along the route he had so often taken during the previous months, out the rear entrance of the Interior Ministry into its garden, through the gate in the wall that led to the garden of the Foreign Ministry, then through the gate into the garden of the Chancellery. Entering from the rear, they reached Meissner's ground-floor office in the Chancellery shortly before eleven. The other ministers-designate came separately. Only after arriving did Count Schwerin von Krosigk finally learn that Hitler rather than Papen was to be the new chancellor. With the scheduled swearing in of the cabinet only minutes away, a loose end that Papen had left unresolved threatened to unravel his scheme and block Hitler's appointment. Knowing that Hugenberg would fear losses for his own party in an election held with Hitler in the chancellorship, Papen had refrained from revealing to the German-National leader Hitler's demand for a dissolution of the Reichstag. But now, with the time set for the swearing-in ceremony only minutes off, Hitler announced that he must have a commitment on that point before he could agree to head the new cabinet. Just as categorically, Hugenberg refused to accept Hitler's demand.

With two of the key figures in the planned cabinet at loggerheads, Papen's scheme seemed on the verge of collapse. Since there could be no new cabinet until the issue was settled, heated discussion continued past the appointed hour of eleven. In an effort to mollify Hugenberg, Hitler gave his word of honor that regardless of the outcome of the election, the composition of the cabinet would remain unaltered. When this assurance failed to shake Hugenberg's resistance, Papen accused the German-National leader of endangering a laboriously constructed alliance of patriotic forces at a critical moment. Referring to Hitler's promise that the election would have no effect on the composition of the cabinet, Papen told Hugenberg it was unthinkable for him to doubt the ceremoniously tendered word of honor of a German man. Nevertheless, Hugenberg remained opposed to a new election.

Just as the whole project seemed about to collapse, Otto Meissner broke the deadlock in Hitler's favor. Entering the room with watch in hand, he pointed out that it was eleven-fifteen and that the president had been expecting them since eleven. He could not be kept waiting any longer, Meissner announced. Finding himself the sole obstacle to compliance with Hindenburg's wishes, Hugenberg gave way and acceded to Hitler's demand for a new election. The assembled group then climbed the stairs to the president's second-floor office. There Hindenburg received them, and Papen read the proposed list of cabinet members, still minus a minister of justice. Even then, yet another last-minute snag threatened to derail the rush to swear in the new cabinet. Finance Minister Count Schwerin von Krosigk approached Papen and reminded him that he had agreed to accept reappointment only if he could be sure that sound fiscal and monetary policies would be followed. Papen at once introduced the count to Hitler, whom he had never before seen. The Nazi leader responded vaguely but reassuringly to the minister's hurried queries. In such perfunctory fashion, the negotiations for Germany's new government were finally completed.

At about half past eleven on Monday, January 30, President Paul von Hindenburg administered the oath of office to Adolf Hitler, making him German chancellor. In what was by any objective standard an act of perjury, the Nazi chieftain swore to defend and uphold the constitution and laws of the republic he had so long vowed to destroy. To maintain the ruse devised by Papen to circumvent Hindenburg's unwillingness to accept Hitler as a presidential chancellor, the official announcement was phrased so as to suggest that the new cabinet was intended to be parliamentary in nature. This was achieved by pointedly emphasizing that no minister of justice had yet been appointed and that Chancellor Hitler would immediately enter into negotiations with the Catholic parties.

ALTHOUGH the arch-enemy of democracy had been installed as head of government, the defenders of the republic made no attempt to resist or even to demonstrate against the Nazi leader's elevation to the chancellorship. Having long expected a resort to force by the Nazis, they were caught off guard when no more than the usual amount of political violence marked the day. The leaders of the Catholic Center Party responded defensively to the official announcement of the cabinet's formation, denying any commitment to participate in it and warning against constitutional experiments. The Social Democrats found themselves without a plan for responding to what had seemed the unlikely possibility that Hitler would get power legally. Their stunned leaders reacted by admonishing the party's million-some members and the hundreds of thousands of men who belonged to the Reichsbanner, the paramilitary organization associated with the party, to refrain from any action. An attempt on the part of the new cabinet to violate the constitution would be met, the party's leadership announced, with the most resolute possible resistance on the part of the working class. In the meantime, undisciplined actions could only do harm, since all the forces at the disposal of the movement must be kept in readiness for the final showdown. As events would soon demonstrate, the showdown had already taken place, and the republican cause was lost.

Some republicans recognized that something dire had happened but clung to the vain hope that Hindenburg might still somehow save them. In its evening issue of the 30th, Berlin's *Vossische Zeitung* quoted the words with which the president had expressed his refusal to turn the government over to Hitler in August and November of 1932; what Hindenburg had said then about the Nazis remained just as valid, the paper plaintively pointed out. The Social Democrats' newspaper *Vorwärts* also appealed to Hindenburg in its evening issue: "With the appointment of this cabinet, the president has assumed the most dreadful responsibility ever taken on by a statesman. It is up to him to see that this cabinet does not depart from the constitution and that it immediately resigns if it does not attain a majority in the Reichstag."

Numerous political observers found reassurance in the numerical preponderance of conservative ministers over the three Nazis in the cabinet. Others assumed real power lay not with Hitler but with Papen or Hugenberg. Still others were fooled about the nature of the new cabinet by the calculated ambiguity arising from the vacancy at the Justice Ministry and official assurances that negotiations would proceed with the Catholic parties regarding their participation. From those misleading indications, quite a few veteran political analysts initially assumed that Hitler had been appointed as a parliamentary, rather than a presidential, chancellor. They expected his cabinet would not have access to the president's emergency powers but would instead depend for its survival on a majority in the Reichstag made possible by either the participation or the acquiescence of the Catholics. If the new cabinet lost that majority, predicted Theodor Wolff, the usually perspicacious editor of the republican *Berliner Tageblatt,* it would, like any other parliamentary cabinet, have to resign or face the voters.

The initial response to Hitler's appointment on the part of Germans outside political circles was marked, in view of the momentous importance of what had just happened, by a remarkable degree of indifference. The replacement of one chancellor by another had by then become such a common occurence that much of the public had obviously lost interest. In a newsreel widely shown in movie theaters throughout the country, the installation of the new cabinet was the last of six events depicted, coming after, among others, reports on a ski jump, a horse race, and a horse show. A young Jewish copy editor for a Berlin tabloid later remembered correcting, on the evening of the 30th, the text of a report on what had happened "without the slightest feeling, without any concern that it might affect me." "Most people had no idea what had befallen them," Friedrich Stampfer, the editor of *Vorwärts,* recalled.

Foreign reactions were generally restrained. A Czech diplomat stationed in Berlin saw nothing significant in the new cabinet's installation. "No Nazi government," he noted in his diary, "not even a revolutionary one, even though it carries Hitler's name. No third Reich, hardly even a second-and-a-half." British Ambassador Sir Horace Rumbold informed his government that appointment of the Hitler cabinet marked the end of the experiment with presidential government. But in view of the hostility of Hitler and Hugenberg to the parliamentary system, Rumbold found it "difficult to see how they are to achieve a modification of the . . . system except by unconstitutional means." A British observer of German affairs asked in the

Sunday Times of London: "Have President von Hindenburg and his 'comrade,' Herr von Papen, got Hitler into a cage before they wring his neck, or are *they* in the cage?"

In a dispatch to Paris on the evening of the 30th, the usually self-assured Ambassador François-Poncet betrayed bewilderment about what had happened. Pointing out that the Catholics had not yet committed themselves to the new cabinet, he wondered whether Hitler would seek to govern by means of a parliamentary majority. He also wondered whether Hindenburg would back the Nazi leader if the latter failed to obtain majority backing. Altogether, Hitler's appointment struck François-Poncet as akin to admitting a wolf to the sheepfold in hopes of imprisoning him. One of the few foreign observers who immediately assessed the new situation correctly was a Swiss journalist who laconically pointed out: "A bear is still a bear, even if you put a ring in its nose and lead it by a leash."

O N the evening of the 30th, Chancellor Adolf Hitler stood for hours at an open window of his new office, acknowledging the jubilant salutes of tens of thousands of Nazi stormtroopers who were now joined by Stahlhelm men as they marched down Wilhelmstrasse, bearing torches and singing nationalistic songs. A few yards away, President von Hindenburg viewed the demonstration from a window in the older part of the Chancellery. It was a triumphant conclusion to a remarkable political comeback. A mere month earlier, Hitler had appeared finished. His party had suffered a staggering setback in the last national election, as two of three voters rejected it, and even heavier losses had followed in state and local elections. Dissension and rebellion had broken out among his disappointed followers. Signs of improvement in the economy threatened to deprive him of one of the issues he had so successfully exploited since the onset of the depression. Yet now, only thirty days later, the president who had repeatedly rebuffed him had duly appointed him head of the government. Upon attaining his goal, Hitler himself reportedly marveled at how, as so often before, he had been rescued just as all seemed lost.

This astonishing turnabout left a lasting mark on Germany's new ruler. It confirmed his belief that he was a man of destiny, certain to succeed with his plans to dominate Germany totally, purify it ethnically, expand its boundaries by conquest, and make it the dominant power in Europe for all time to come. It also vindicated in his eyes the all-or-nothing strategy he had followed in pursuit of power. What came to be known as the 'seizure of power' thus contributed to the sense of invincibility and the readiness to run daring risks that would enable Hitler to achieve the extraordinary foreign-policy and military triumphs that ended only ten years later when his luck ran out at the battle of Stalingrad. But as with so much in the mythology of his Third Reich, the belief that January 30th, 1933, marked a seizure of power was spurious. In reality, Hitler had not seized power; it had been handed to him by the men who at that moment controlled Germany's destiny.

7

Determinacy, Contingency, and Responsibility

O N J A N U A R Y 3 0 , 1 9 3 3 , Hitler attained a large measure of power through his appointment as chancellor, but he was still far short of the absolute authority he sought. How he achieved that is a story in its own right, but its highlights can be summarized. By sabotaging coalition negotiations with the Catholics on January 31 in such manner as to make them appear responsible for the impasse, Hitler ended the pretense that he sought to become a parliamentary chancellor, backed by a majority in the existing Reichstag. On February 1 the parliament was dissolved and a new election set for early March. The vacancy at the Justice Ministry was quickly filled that same day by re-appointment of the minister who had held that post under both Papen and Schleicher. On February 4, President von Hindenburg allowed the new chancellor to use presidential emergency powers to decree a law restricting freedom of the press and assembly. The ruse devised by Papen to deceive the president about the nature of the Hitler cabinet thus succeeded brilliantly. Hitler had got what Hindenburg had previously vowed not to grant him: he was now de facto a presidential chancellor.

During the months that followed, Hitler rapidly expanded his authority. A mysterious fire that gutted the Reichstag building in late February enabled him to take a giant step in that direction. On the contrived pretext that the fire signaled a Communist uprising, he prevailed upon the president to grant him a sweeping emergency decree that indefinitely suspended numerous civil rights and greatly expanded the authority of the cabinet. As the campaign for the Reichstag election approached its climax, tens of thousands of Nazi storm-troopers, deputized as auxiliary police in Prussia by his henchman Hermann Göring, subjected political opponents to harassment, intimidation, and arrest. In their quest for votes, the Nazis exploited both the red scare resulting from the Reichstag fire and Hitler's newly gained prestige as Hindenburg's choice for the chancellorship. Nevertheless, they failed to achieve a majority in the less-than-free March election, tallying 43.9 percent of the ballots.

Only by banning the Communist deputies and by resorting to intimidation and mendacity did Hitler secure on March 23 the necessary two-thirds vote in the new Reichstag for an enabling act that transferred legislative authority to his cabinet, ostensibly for four years. A wave of Nazi purges followed, as one institution after another was subjugated. Arbitrary rule replaced government by law in what has aptly been termed a "coup d'état by installments." By summer, all parties except the Nazis had been dissolved, Hugenberg had been forced out of the cabinet, and Hitler had relegated Papen to insignificance by winning the trust of the president. Even earlier, Göring had wrested from Papen control over the government of the largest state, Prussia. Well before the Nazi leader assumed the powers of the presidency upon the death of Hindenburg in August 1934 he had become dictator of Germany.

FOR all these developments, as well as for the appalling consequences that would follow, Hitler's appointment as chancellor was the indispensable prerequisite. As long as Hindenburg occupied the presidency, only the chancellorship offered him a route to power. As he recognized, moreover, if he were to attain the dictatorial authority he would need to pursue his far-reaching goals, he would have, as chancellor, to remain free from dependency on the vagaries of a parliamentary majority based on a coalition of parties. He therefore stubbornly held out for those terms and emerged victorious against heavy odds. Having assumed the chancellorship with only a minority of the German public behind him, he would go on to gain great popularity by presiding over an economic recovery that was already under way when he took office and by scoring one peaceful foreign policy triumph after another.

The events of the first thirty days of January 1933 do not suffice to explain why Hitler got power. For a full understanding of what happened, broader scrutiny of the German past would be required. It would be necessary to refer back at least to the failed attempt at a democratic revolution in 1848 and to the political Right's capture of the cause of nationalism in the course of the country's unification under Prussian leadership. The dominance of a semi-feudal elite over the Empire would have to be taken into account. So would the economic conditions and social tensions that gave rise to a militant working-class political movement and, eventually, to its split into bitterly opposed factions. The weakness and fragmentation of German liberalism, the strength of militarism, and the susceptibility of a part of the public to pseudo-scientific theories of race all played a part in what was to come. So did the shock of defeat in a war the Germans had been led to believe they were winning, the draconian Versailles Treaty, the hyper-inflation that destroyed the value of the country's money, and the crushing impact of the Great Depression.

Versions of Hitler's rise to power that focus on such historical antecedents have an unfortunate tendency to become deterministic. They give the impression that what happened was the inexorable product of great impersonal forces, that it was bound to happen, that there were no alternatives. Yet although such factors may in many cases have been necessary to the outcome, they were not sufficient. They can help to understand how the Third Reich became a possibility, but they cannot explain how it became a reality.

An examination of the events of January 1933 undercuts notions of determinacy by revealing the strong elements of contingency in the chain of events that brought Hitler to power. The Third Reich was unquestionably a product of German history, but it was not the only possibility open to that country at that time. Until the moment Hitler was handed the chancellorship, other political solutions were available. The Nazi leader's success came not as the culmination of a triumphant drive for power but occurred instead at a time when his fortunes had sunk to a low ebb. Just thirty days before he was sworn in as chancellor, seasoned, well-informed observers were busy composing his political obituary. After a meteoric rise from obscurity, his party had lost its momentum and seemed on the verge of disintegration. Far from shaping the events that resulted in his success, the future dictator was rescued from failure only by a series of unpredictable developments over which he had no control.

Decisive in the improbable reversal of Hitler's fortunes that swept him to power were the actions of other persons, for although impersonal forces may make events possible, people make events happen. This was strikingly so in Germany during January 1933, when the fate of a great nation was contingent upon the actions of a handful of individuals. It was one of those frequent junctures in human affairs when the fates of many rested with a very few. Of these, three held Germany's future in their hands: President Paul von Hindenburg, Chancellor Kurt von Schleicher, and former chancellor Franz von Papen. Three others—Oskar von Hindenburg, Otto Meissner, and Alfred Hugenberg—had lesser but also significant parts in what happened. Compared with the roles of these men, Hitler's was essentially reactive. He played the hand they dealt him with great cunning, but the cards were theirs, not his, to deal.

An understanding of Germany's previous development is, of course, essential for an explanation of how men like Hindenburg,

Schleicher, and Papen came to play such crucial political roles. Without the prestige that accrued to the aristocracy because of its prominent part in the unification of Germany and its privileged position in the imperial regime, men with names graced by 'von' would scarcely have continued to seem plausible candidates for high office even after a republican revolution. Similarly, in the absence of the strong element of militarism in Germany's traditions, a defeated field marshal of no demonstrated political ability was unlikely to be elected president of the republic at age seventy-seven and reelected at eighty-four. Nor, but for the failure of the republicans to subject the military to effective civilian control, would a career officer such as Kurt von Schleicher have become a major factor in Germany's politics. Without the breakdown of parliamentary democracy, which had causes reaching far back into German history, the means to determine that country's fate would not have become concentrated in the hands of such men. These and other factors of a suprapersonal sort serve to explain how these individuals came to wield such great influence over the course of events. But those factors do not account for how they used that influence.

It has been alleged that the men whose actions bestowed power on Hitler were merely the pawns of powerful behind-the-scenes vested interests, but a half century of research has yielded no credible support for that contention. This is not to say that those men were immune to any and all influences. Hindenburg made no secret of his solicitude for the economically hard-pressed Junker landowners of eastern Prussia who had acclaimed him as one of them. Junker opposition to Schleicher or sympathy for Hitler may very well have swayed the president's judgment. But to the extent that this was the case, it was a matter of sentiment on Hindenburg's part, not of constraining interest. Schleicher acted on behalf of no one except himself and his conception of the army's interests. To be sure, his commitment to rearmament and his hopes for enlisting the hundreds of thousands of Nazi stormtroopers in an expanded military contributed to his blindness to the danger Hitler posed. But that was the result of defects in Schleicher's judgment, not of compelling constraints. Although Papen sought the financial and political backing of capitalists and tended to favor their economic interests, he charted his ruinous political course very much on his own. The headstrong Hugenberg was notoriously resistant to pressure from any quarter that conflicted with his own views and purposes. Oskar von Hindenburg accorded allegiance only to his father, Otto Meissner only to himself. In short, all these men were free to make political decisions according to their own predilections.

Nothing more strikingly reveals the high degree of contingency in what happened during January 1933 than the weighty effects of shifts in the relationships among the key individuals involved. The elderly president's growing affection for Papen and his estrangement from Schleicher loom large as causes of what happened. So does the hostility toward Schleicher that replaced friendship on the part of Papen and Oskar von Hindenburg. At a moment when the disposition of power in a great nation rested with this small circle of individuals, some of the most elementary of human sentiments—personal affinities and aversions, injured feelings, soured friendships, and desire for revenge—had profound political effects.

Luck—that most capricious of contingencies—was clearly on Hitler's side. He was rescued from isolation by the chance encounter between Papen and Baron von Schröder at the Gentlemen's Club that paved the way for the Cologne meeting and the ensuing conspiracy against Schleicher. The state election in Lippe happened by chance to be scheduled ideally for him, and in a well-nigh perfect place, just when he desperately needed even a minor success to rally the flagging morale of his frustrated followers. The false rumor, two weeks later, of an impending putsch on the part of Schleicher arose at just the right moment to enable Papen to surmount the lingering misgivings of President von Hindenburg and persuade him to appoint Hitler hastily under the misapprehension that the new cabinet would be parliamentary, not presidential, in nature.

In his struggle to maintain control over his increasingly demoralized party, Hitler was also lucky that the only Nazi leader to break with him over his rigid adherence to an all-or-nothing strategy was Gregor Strasser. That renegade proved to be very different from his brother, Otto Strasser, a Nazi until he defected in 1930 over what he saw as the party leader's indifference to the socialistic aspirations of many National Socialists. Fiercely combative, Otto Strasser launched a rival organization, the Black Front, and sought to win over Hitler's followers by relentlessly attacking him as a traitor to the ideals of the movement. Otto's efforts were in vain, however, since his defection coincided with the onset of the phenomenal succession of Nazi electoral successes that made Hitler a major figure in national politics. A schismatic movement led by Gregor Strasser, who commanded a far greater following within the party than had his brother, might well have set off a devastating secession in December 1932 or January 1933, when the party's declining fortunes were leading increasing numbers of Nazis to doubt their leader's judgment. But, to Hitler's good fortune, Gregor Strasser, unlike his brother, proved not to be a fighter.

Hitler's greatest stroke of luck lay in the personality quirks and other limitations of Kurt von Schleicher, the man who occupied the office he sought as January 1933 opened. Schleicher was in a position to thwart the Nazi leader's ambitions, but instead his failure paved the way for the Third Reich. Many of the general's setbacks were self-inflicted. Through his brusque manner, Schleicher offended the elderly Hindenburg, whose confidence he had to have in order to govern. His sharp tongue compounded that liability by irreparably alienating an old friend, the president's hypersensitive son and closest confidant. He elevated another friend, the shallow and devious Franz von Papen, to high office, then turned him into an enemy by bringing about his fall. Despite his renown as a master of intrigue, Schleicher disastrously underrated Papen's skill at that craft and allowed himself to be seriously misled by the latter's mendacity.

As chancellor, Schleicher reached, so to speak, his level of incompetence. Previously, as a behind-the-scenes manipulator, he had gained a reputation for political shrewdness. But upon assuming responsibility himself, he displayed a woeful lack of judgment and a hobbling propensity to self-delusion. Despite his reputation for political agility, he locked himself into the unrealistic strategy of seeking to bluff Hitler into cooperating with him. Long after the futility of that course had become obvious, Schleicher clung to it, having failed to devise a fallback position. Passing up opportunities to prolong his hold on the chancellorship by means of tactical retreats, he revealed a lack of both resourcefulness and appetite for power. Mistrustful of civilians and inclined to secretiveness, Schleicher confided in no one except his military aides, on whom he relied for advice even about high matters of state. Increasingly isolated, he lost touch with political realities. At the end of his brief term of office, he struck his colors and withdrew from the fray, creating the opening Hitler was to fill, while hoping vainly that he would be allowed to retain control over the military.

Had Schleicher been more politically adept and more bent upon retaining power, Hitler need never have had a chance at the chancellorship. It has frequently been argued that the Nazi leader's acquisition of power was unavoidable under the circumstances, since no other solution could provide a mass backing for a government of the Right, the only sort President von Hindenburg was willing to accept. Without such popular support, that argument goes, it would have been impossible for rightists to govern. This view overlooks, however, the very real possibility of a military regime. Hitler realized that danger and feared it. He had but to look at what was happening elsewhere to know that it was an obvious alternative. Germany was by no means the only country where democracy had faltered. In over a dozen countries in interwar Europe, experiments with elected governments had failed or were about to fail. In quite a few cases, the result was the assumption of power by military or quasi-military regimes. As the record reveals, this was a far more likely consequence of a breakdown of democracy than was acquisition of power by a fascist movement. In only two cases, Italy and Germany, did regimes of that sort originate in peacetime.

At the time of Schleicher's chancellorship, no insuperable obstacles stood in the way of military rule by an ambitious and able general.

The army of the republic was small, but it consisted of tightly disciplined professional soldiers who had volunteered for long terms of service. There were Nazi sympathizers among the officers, but they were unorganized and outnumbered in the top echelons by men loyal to the chain of command as long as it had the backing of the revered Hindenburg. As the result of improvements effected by Schleicher, the army was by January 1933 better prepared to deal with domestic disorder than it had been at the end of Papen's chancellorship. The potential sources of mass opposition were, in any case, politically fragmented, with Nazis, Communists, and Social Democrats all irreconcilably opposed to one another. By gaining credit for the economic upswing that sharply reduced the number of unemployed by the summer of 1933, a military regime would have been in a position to defuse much of the discontent that had embroiled German politics since the onset of the depression.

No overt coup d'état of the kind likely to galvanize popular resistance would have been necessary to circumvent the constitution and establish military rule in early 1933. Government by presidential emergency decree during the previous three years provided an ideal political device for gradual transition to an out-and-out authoritarian regime. President von Hindenburg had no principled objection to departing from legality, as he demonstrated during Papen's chancellorship by twice agreeing not to schedule a new election as mandated by the constitution. Initially, to be sure, a military ruler would have had to defer to Hindenburg. But the end of the elderly president's life was in sight, and his death in 1934 would have cleared the way for a general in the chancellorship to assume full authority over the state. Unconstitutional government under military auspices is scarcely desirable, but compared with the Third Reich, a conservative regime of that sort would have been by far a lesser evil. It was Germany's misfortune that at the moment when military rule offered the best available alternative to Hitler's acquisition of power, the general who stood at the head of the government lacked both the ability and the will to grasp the opportunity.

What would have been the effect on Hitler if a military regime riding a tide of improving economic conditions had emerged in early 1933? All indications are that the crisis in his movement would have continued to worsen under such circumstances. Throughout January unrest had festered among frustrated Nazis despite his electoral success in Lippe and his banishment of Gregor Strasser. Just two days before his appointment as chancellor, a gauleiter in the heavily Nazi region of Franconia publicly warned of an "invisible front" of malcontents in the party. If the establishment of a military regime had left Hitler without prospects for gaining control over the state, his movement would in all probability have rapidly shrunk into the sort of sectarian fringe group it had been prior to the depression. Having risen to the very brink of power, he himself could never have become reconciled to a lesser political role or a place in civilian life. In all likelihood, he would have responded to failure just as he often threatened to do and as he eventually did when his war of conquest ended in total defeat: by committing suicide. Had events taken a different turn in January 1933, Adolf Hitler would merit, at most, passing mention in histories of the twentieth century instead of bulking large as one of its principal movers and shakers.

H O W much difference would it have made if the Weimar Republic had been succeeded not by the Third Reich but by a military regime? Even a modicum of reflection quickly yields the emphatic answer: a very great deal indeed. Military rule would not have inflicted on Germany and much of the rest of Europe wounds as deep or extensive as did Hitler's Third Reich. Such a regime would have been fundamentally conservative, free of the fanatical radicalism unleashed by the Nazis. It would have been authoritarian, but not totalitarian; nationalistic, but not racist; distasteful, but not demonic. It might have sought to repress public expression of views regarded as subversive, but it would not have sought to force Germans to affirm and conform to an ideology dictated by the government. It might have suspended or curtailed political and civil rights, but it would not have abolished those rights altogether. It might have filled prisons with political opponents, but it would not have populated an archipelago of concentration camps and staffed them with sadists. It would not have made anti-Semitism a matter of government policy or embarked upon a systematic program of genocide. Like all military regimes in countries that have experienced popular sovereignty, it would have had difficulty in laying claim to legitimacy, and it would very likely not have long survived its dominant personality. Sooner or later, the generals would have fallen out among themselves and Germany's republicans would have reasserted control over the state.

In addition to sparing humanity the shame of the Holocaust, a military regime in Germany would have averted the carnage and destruction of the Second World War. That catastrophe bore the indelible imprint of Hitler's boundless ambition and his racist, social Darwinist fixations. As dictator of a powerful nation, he was to come frighteningly close to imposing his will on Europe. But eventually he overreached himself in pursuit of his paramount goal of acquiring what he dreamed of as *Lebensraum*—living space—for future generations of Germans on the soil of the Soviet Union. Hitler was also instrumental in setting in motion the Asian theater of the Second World War. The Japanese military regime had already embarked on its campaign of aggression against China before he attained power. But the warlords in Tokyo refrained from attacking the Western colonial powers until Hitler had defeated the Dutch and the French, greatly weakened the British, and forced the Soviet Union to concentrate its forces in Europe to resist his invasion. Only then did the Japanese militarists become sufficiently emboldened to strike out against the Western powers, including the United States. The first truly global war, the most destructive in history, was very much the work of Adolf Hitler.

Even in the event of a German military regime, to be sure, there would very likely have been another war. The leading generals shared Hitler's resolve to achieve rearmament and would have seized the earliest opportunity to do so. But their territorial aims were modest in comparison with his. Although they did not admit it in public, the military leaders in Berlin did not aspire to recover Alsace and Lorraine, the provinces that Germany had seized from France in 1871 and that the French had reclaimed in 1919. The Alsatians and Lorrainers had made very poor Germans and were not missed. Nor did the military leadership believe, as did Hitler, that ethnicity dictated the incorporation into Germany of Austria and the German-inhabited areas of Czechoslovakia known as the Sudetenland.

The Polish corridor was another matter. The cession of that swath of territory to the resurrected Polish state in 1919 had not only severed East Prussia from the rest of the country but had also wrought havoc with Germany's eastern defenses. The military leadership in Berlin was determined to recover as much as possible of that territory. Since the Poles were just as determined not to surrender the corridor, war was likely to follow upon German rearmament. Given the disparities in manpower and resources, such a conflict could only have ended in a swift German victory.

A German war of territorial revision conducted against Poland by a military regime would have differed greatly from the ideological war Hitler was to launch with his attack on that country in 1939. For Hitler, war against Poland was only the first step in an essentially unlimited campaign for the conquest and subjugation of other nations. Whereas his onslaught on Poland in 1939 led Britain and France to declare war on Germany, a conservative military regime in Berlin would have striven to avoid conflict with the Western powers. That was well within the range of the possible. A great deal of prior provocation on Hitler's part was required to bring the hesitant and reluctant politicians in London and Paris to issue the guarantees to Warsaw that brought them to declare war on Germany when Hitler's forces invaded Poland. By holding to limited territorial demands and invoking the Wilsonian principle of national self-determination in defense of the German minority in the corridor against alleged Polish repression, a military regime in Berlin could very likely have averted Western intervention. In such a conflict, the Germans could have counted on the acquiescence of the Soviets in return for a share of Polish territory in the east, although German regard for Western opinion would in all likelihood have ruled out a thoroughgoing partition of that country such as that carried out jointly by Hitler and Stalin.

However regrettable, such a brief German-Polish conflict would have been a minor mishap compared with the global conflagration of the Second World War. A German victory under conservative military auspices could have gone a long way toward clearing the international atmosphere in Europe. With Germany's wounded pride assuaged and everyone except a shrunken Poland reconciled to the results, the storm cloud that had hung over the continent ever since Versailles might have been largely dispelled. There would have been no German invasion of the Soviet Union, since the military leadership in Berlin, unlike Hitler, had no dreams of *Lebensraum* and harbored no hostility toward the USSR. Since the 1920s German generals had clandestinely collaborated quite happily with their counterparts in the Red Army to circumvent the disarmament clauses of the Versailles Treaty by jointly training troops and developing weapons at Soviet military bases.

With no major sources of international conflict remaining after a successful revision of Germany's eastern border, Europe might well have settled down after years of tension. The Second World War and the horrors it brought—including the atom bomb, which was produced out of fear that Hitler might be the first to obtain it—was no more inevitable than his rise to power. In the absence of the latter development, in fact, that global conflict, with whose aftereffects much of humanity still struggles, could not have taken place.

Without Hitler's Third Reich and the war he unleashed on the world, many aspects of human affairs since January 1933 would have been quite different. In the absence of the previously unimaginable horror encapsulated in the name 'Auschwitz,' humanity would be more innocent and optimistic than has been possible since the name of that hitherto obscure town took on its now all-too-familiar sinister significance. The same is true of a second place-name that has become synonymous with horror, 'Hiroshima.' Another concept that would be missing from common usage is 'Cold War.' It was Hitler's successes that forced the United States and the Soviet Union together as unlikely allies, and it was his defeat that threw them into friction-ridden contention in postwar Europe. Otherwise, there was little if any likelihood of an armed clash between those two countries, despite their ideological differences. Only under the pressures of the Cold War was the United States later drawn into wars in Korea and Vietnam that involved no vital American national interests.

In short, if one traces many chains of causation that have shaken the world since January 1933 back to their origins, it becomes apparent that a great deal of what has happened since then was contingent on the turn taken by German politics during that month. Like Paris in the summer of 1789, at the onset of the French Revolution, Berlin became for a moment the hinge of fate for a large part of humanity. What happened there at midday on January 30 was nothing less than an event of world-historical proportions. Power over an advanced, industrial nation was bestowed upon a man bent on overturning the civilized order of the world. His use of that power would result in great suffering for a considerable part of humanity, violent death for tens of millions, and unprecedented material destruction in many parts of the world. His regime would reveal that centuries of civilization had not diminished the capacity of Homo sapiens for profound evil and that modern technology and bureaucratic structures make possible unspeakable crimes of hitherto unimagined magnitude.

T O explain Hitler's acquisition of power in deterministic terms is to rule out the question of responsibility for that disastrous development or its far-reaching consequences. If his appointment as chancellor was the inexorable result of impersonal forces beyond the control of the individuals involved, then it would obviously be unjust to hold any of them responsible. Some of the participants in the events of January 1933 sought to defend themselves after the catastrophe of the Third Reich on just those grounds. Hitler's rise to power had been inevitable, they contended, and nothing could have stopped him. If, however, determinism is rejected, the question of responsibility must be addressed. In this instance, the record is sufficiently clear to permit an allocation of culpability, which in the cases of some of those involved can only be termed guilt.

One level of responsibility—that of omission rather than commission—must be assigned to the defenders of the Weimar Republic. Without intending to do so, they helped to pave the way for Hitler's triumph. It was the unwillingness of republican politicians to place preservation of parliamentary rule above partisan interests that led the Reichstag to abdicate its control over the government in 1930. In the absence of the shift of authority from the parliament to the presidency that ensued, Hitler would have stood little or no chance of realizing his goal of untrammeled power. His party never came close to achieving a majority in a free election, and he was unwilling to settle for a share of power in parliamentary coalition with other parties.

The performance in January 1933 of the remaining two parties that clung to what was left of the republic, the Catholic Center and the Social Democrats, was marked by abysmal ineptitude. By that time, their leaders had lost touch with political realities. They were rendered politically impotent by their fixation on a sterile defense of the legalities of a constitution that had long since been hollowed out by the shift of power from the parliament to the presidency and by the defection of a majority of voters to extremists of Right and Left. The failure of republican leaders to recognize that an unconstitutional interlude under a general like Kurt von Schleicher would be by far a lesser evil than the constitutional installation of a dictatorial fanatic like Adolf Hitler ranks as one of the greatest political blunders of all time.

A much larger measure of responsibility must be assigned to the millions of Germans who freely gave their votes to Hitler and his party. Here too, however, there was an element of inadvertency. Many of those who supported the Nazis did so not out of commitment to the program of Hitler's party so much as out of protest against what were widely perceived as the failures of the republican regime. Others voted for the Nazis out of fear of communism. Particularly after the onset of the Great Depression, that is, there was a large negative component in the ballooning Nazi vote. Few of those who cast ballots for Hitler and his party were opting for Auschwitz and World War II. As they approached power, the Nazis dampened their anti-Semitism in their quest for votes, knowing that they already had the support of anti-Semites and realizing that many Germans were repelled by that aspect of their party's program.

Recognizing that a large part of the public still recoiled from the prospect of military conflict in the wake of the battlefield horrors of World War I, Hitler also concealed his plans for armed aggression. Nevertheless, for those who wished to see it, abundant evidence was available, in *Mein Kampf* and other Nazi utterances, to indicate that he and his party were committed to a foreign policy that would make a large-scale war very likely. By their violent actions, moreover, the Nazis abundantly demonstrated their scorn for law and their readiness to employ force to crush those who dared to oppose them. Nor did Hitler and his henchmen make any secret of their determination to deprive the German people of a voice in their government by destroying the democratic republic and replacing it with dictatorial, one-party rule. The readiness of millions to surrender their fate to such a movement revealed that a large part of the German public had failed to grasp how essential it is for citizens to retain the means to recall and replace those who govern.

The greatest responsibility for Germany's catastrophe lay, of course, with principal figures in the drama of January 1933. Behind their folly lay an appalling ignorance of Nazism. Normally, such highly placed individuals would be expected to draw upon an abundance of information before forming judgments about the leader of such a dynamic mass movement. Yet there is no evidence that Hindenburg, Schleicher or Papen, or indeed any of the others directly involved, ever read Hitler's book *Mein Kampf* or even consulted with anyone who had. Nor did they request analyses of Nazism by competent experts in the high civil service. The republican government of the state of Prussia had commissioned several such studies after Hitler's party became a major factor in national politics. The resulting inquiries revealed a violent movement bent not only on imposing dictatorial rule on Germany but also on abolishing the rule of law and subjecting Jewish citizens to persecution. But from all indications, the men who made the decisions that resulted in Hitler's installation in the chancellorship failed to draw upon those or any other searching inquiries into the nature of Nazism.

With regard to individual responsibility, the least culpable of the principal figures was the inept Schleicher. He bears the heavy historical burden of having lifted from well-deserved obscurity to political prominence the man who became his nemesis and Hitler's savior: Franz von Papen. But although Schleicher's role in the events of January was crucial, his contribution was the result not of intention but rather of a deficiency of political ability and judgment. After falling from the chancellorship, to be sure, he came to favor Hitler's candidacy over Papen's. But by that time he no longer wielded any direct influence on the course of events. By giving rise to the rumors of a putsch on his part, Schleicher's clumsy, last-minute attempt to curry favor with Hitler did, however, contribute indirectly to the outcome by enabling Papen to stampede Hindenburg into hurriedly bestowing the chancellorship on the Nazi leader. Schleicher won no gratitude from Hitler either for that inadvertent boost or for his indulgent attitude toward the Nazi Party while chancellor. In late June 1934, at the time of the wave of officially sanctioned murders that became known as the night of long knives, he and his wife were gunned down in their home by agents of the dictator's regime.

Heavier culpability weighs upon Oskar von Hindenburg, Otto Meissner, and Alfred Hugenberg. The president's son committed the cardinal political error of allowing his personal animus toward Schleicher to color his views on matters of the highest national importance. A similar, if lesser, degree of culpability rests with the president's chief aide, Otto Meissner. But whereas Oskar von Hindenburg was in large measure emotionally motivated, Meissner acted opportunistically out of self-interest. Having sensed that Schleicher's star was fading, he looked about for a new master and placed his bet on Hitler. Hugenberg, too, was motivated mainly by opportunistic considerations, in his case by a desperate desire to gain a measure of power as he approached the end of a frustrating political career.

After helping to hoist Hitler into power, Hugenberg soon developed misgivings, reportedly telling a friend only a day later: "I yesterday committed the greatest stupidity of my life: I allied myself with the greatest demagogue in world history." His alliance with Hitler would last less than five months. In June 1933, with his German-National Party collapsing as a consequence of defections to the Nazis and his aspirations to become economic dictator of Germany thwarted within the Hitler cabinet, Hugenberg resigned the offices he had so avidly sought and withdrew to private life. Oskar von Hindenburg, too, was soon consigned to obscurity, but not before proclaiming Hitler his father's chosen successor in a radio address to the nation following the president's death in August 1934. Otto Meissner continued throughout the Nazi dictatorship as what he had been during the republic, an obsequious servant to the head of state, now Adolf Hitler. He, along with Hugenberg and Oskar von Hindenburg, survived the Third Reich, and all three remained to the end of their lives unrepentant about their complicity in bringing it into being.

In the case of Franz von Papen, guilt—in the sense of responsibility for commission of a grave offense—applies. He was the key figure in steering the course of events toward the disastrous outcome, the person who more than anyone else caused what happened. None of what occurred in January 1933 would have been possible in the absence of his quest for revenge against Schleicher and his hunger for a return to power. Papen's actions abundantly confirm the verdict of Konrad Adenauer, who as a fellow Center Party politician found him "an extremely ambitious person whose primary concern was to achieve prominence." As Adenauer noted, "matters of principle never interested him." Motivated by nothing other than his own ambition, Papen ruthlessly exploited his sole asset: his hold over the elderly president. His repeated resort to the most brazen sort of mendacity bears out the verdict of another acquaintance, who characterized him as "probably one of the most consummate liars who ever lived." To attribute Papen's readiness to conspire with Hitler to cynicism is to credit him with more by way of intellectual depth than is merited. His behavior was characterized above all by a boundless overestimation of himself and a heedless disregard for the menace of Hitler and his movement.

Although Papen never joined the Nazi Party, he loyally served the Third Reich throughout its tumultuous duration. In the spring of 1934 he displayed a spark of conscience and offended Hitler by delivering a speech in which he expressed misgivings about the disregard shown for law and civil rights by the regime he had been so instrumental in creating. But even though he was placed under house arrest and two of his aides were murdered at the time of the night of long knives, he continued to cling to the empty title of deputy chancellor. In August 1934 he was shunted into the diplomatic corps and went on to represent Hitler's regime in ambassadorial posts to the end of the Third Reich. Acquitted of war crimes by the International Military Tribunal at Nuremberg in 1947, Papen was classified as heavily implicated in the regime by a German de-Nazification court and sentenced to eight years' imprisonment. He served only a fraction of that sentence, however, for the most part in hospitals. Appeals courts twice lowered the degree of his culpability and restored to him most of the property confiscated under the earlier ruling. Before his death in 1969 at age eighty-nine, Papen sought to retouch the record of his disastrous career in two volumes of self-serving memoirs, sniped at the policies of the postwar West German republic, and received an honorific title from the Vatican.

Greater even than Papen's guilt was that of the ultimate decision maker, President Paul von Hindenburg. Contrary to his public image of strength and wisdom, he proved, at the crucial point in his political career, weak and fatally susceptible to manipulation. Having installed Schleicher as head of government, the president abandoned him not because of any scruples about Schleicher's proposal to violate the constitution but because of a personal aversion abetted by the conspiracy against the chancellor led by Franz von Papen. By dismissing Schleicher, the president created a crisis for which he had no realistic solution in mind. Then, in a display of abysmal political judgment, he relied for guidance in the highest matters of state on the foolhardy Papen. Despite the latter's own earlier failure as chancellor, Hindenburg was quite ready to reappoint him until he withdrew in favor of Hitler. Had Hindenburg held to his initial, intuitive mistrust of Hitler, Germany and much of the rest of the world would have been spared much misery and destruction. Instead, he gave into the urgings of Papen, his son Oskar and his chief of staff Otto Meissner and took the fatal step of installing the Nazi leader as the head of government.

Even with allowance for the mitigating factors of advanced age and Papen's last-minute deception about the nature of Hitler's appointment, Hindenburg must bear ultimate historical responsibility for bestowing power on the Nazi leader. The authority to appoint chancellors was his alone. In assigning that high office to a man who had made no secret of his resolve to destroy the German republic, the president betrayed not only his oath to uphold its constitution but also the millions of republicans whose votes had helped to reelect him the previous year. Moreover, his actions during the remaining eighteen months of his life would serve to legitimate the Nazi dictator's tyrannous rule in the eyes of millions of Germans. It was a fitting irony that the ruinous policies of the man Hindenburg entrusted with power on January 30, 1933, would ultimately result in the obliteration of the proud German national state whose creation the old president had personally witnessed in 1871.

ONLY through the political blindness and blunders of others did Adolf Hitler gain the opportunity to put his criminal intentions into effect between 1933 and 1945. This is not to say that he alone was responsible for the heinous crimes committed during his rule. To the everlasting shame of the German nation, Hitler found large numbers of lackeys eager to persecute, subjugate and slaughter people deemed dangerous or inferior by the perverted standards of his regime. If his bid for power had been thwarted, men such as Heinrich Himmler, Reinhard Heydrich, and Adolf Eichmann would still have walked the earth. But without governmental endorsement, they could never have become mass murderers. Had Hitler failed to attain the chancellorship, they and others like them would have instead lived out their days as malicious but frustrated nobodies.

Although the Nazi dictator's career left only a negative legacy, it provides a powerful example for subsequent generations of the crucial need to exercise the utmost care in selecting those to whom control is granted over the most powerful—and potentially the most lethal—institution created by humanity: the modern state. As for how Hitler got the power to commit his crimes, that story serves as a reminder that nothing except change itself is inevitable in human affairs, that the acts of individuals make a difference, and that heavy moral responsibility weighs upon those who wield control over the state.

APPENDIX:

The Moscow Document

A MAJOR HANDICAP to the research for this book has been the paucity of surviving documentation on Kurt von Schleicher's chancellorship. Schleicher habitually committed little to paper, and whatever remained after his murder by way of personal documents was apparently confiscated by the Nazi regime and has disappeared. The surviving official documentation is unusually thin and sheds little light on Schleicher's thinking and intentions.

In an effort to establish Schleicher's aims, I have therefore had to rely heavily at many points on accounts written at the time by journalists shortly after they talked with him or members of his staff. One of the most extensive and informative of these accounts is located in folder number 5 of the Papen papers recently discovered in a hitherto secret Soviet archive in Moscow (Tsentralnyi Gosudarstvennyi Arkhiv, or TsGA). Since the account is anonymous, I have cited it in the notes to this book as the Moscow Document. It is a six-page, single-spaced typescript report, dated "14.1." (January 14), with the underlined heading *"Vertraulich!"* (confidential). It is an account of what Schleicher said in the course of a dinner he hosted for a group of invited journalists on the evening of January 13, 1933, in the reception rooms (*Gesellschaftsräume*) of the press section of the Chancellery.

Ordinarily, such a document of uncertain authorship would be a questionable source of information, but in this case there is conclusive corroboration of authenticity provided by two additional accounts of what Schleicher said at the same dinner, written by journalists who were also present. One of these was Josef Reiner of the Ullstein Verlag, which published the republican Berlin newspaper *Vossische Zeitung*. After attending the dinner with Schleicher, Reiner composed a four-page, double-spaced typescript report for the chief executive at Ullstein, Hans Schäffer. It bears the handwritten heading "13.I.33" and is located in volume 33 of Schäffer's papers (ED 93) in the archive of the Institut für Zeitgeschichte, Munich.

The third journalist who wrote a report about the dinner on January 13 was Georg Dertinger, who later worked in Goebbels' Propaganda Ministry and then, after the war, became the first foreign minister of the East German Communist regime. In January 1933 Dertinger worked for a conservative press service, Dienatag, which distributed news from the capital to subscribing papers elsewhere: see Hans Bohrmann, ed., *NS-Presseanweisungen der Vorkriegszeit* (4 vols., Munich, 1984), vol. 1, pp. 60–65. Dertinger's four-page, double-spaced typescript report on what Schleicher said at the dinner on January 13, entitled "Informationsbericht vom 14. Januar," is located, along with other similar reports of his, in the German Federal Archives (Bundesarchiv), Koblenz, in the "Sammlung Brammer" (ZSg 101/26).

A comparison of the Moscow Document with the reports by Reiner and Dertinger leaves no doubt that it was indeed written by someone who was present on the evening of January 13 and who had the ability of a good journalist to register and convey information accurately, if from a somewhat rightist point of view. All three documents display a close parallelism with regard to the subjects discussed by Schleicher and the views attributed to him. Since the Moscow Document is the most detailed of the three, I have relied heavily on that unusual but extremely informative source in my efforts to reconstruct the elusive Schleicher's thinking, despite the anonymity of the author. Its presence in the papers of Franz von Papen raises the intriguing question of how and when it came into the possession of Schleicher's archenemy, thereby alerting Papen to his views. Unfortunately, neither the Moscow Document itself nor the other documents in the small collection of Papen papers in the former Soviet archive provide clues on that count.

ABBREVIATIONS

AdR	Archiv der Republik (Vienna)
AdRk/KvP	*Akten der Reichskanzlei: Kabinett von Papen,* edited by Karl Dietrich Erdmann and Hans Booms (2 vols., Boppard, 1989)
AdRk/KvS	*Akten der Reichskanzlei: Kabinett von Schleicher,* edited by Karl Dietrich Erdmann and Hans Booms (Boppard, 1986)
AHR	*American Historical Review*
AzDAP	*Akten zur Deutschen Auswärtigen Politik*
BA/FA	Bundesarchiv/Filmarchiv (Berlin)
BAK	Bundesarchiv Koblenz
BA/MA	Bundesarchiv/Militärarchiv (Freiburg i. Breisgau)
BAP	Bundesarchiv Potsdam
BDC	Berlin Document Center
BPKb	Bildarchiv Preussischer Kulturbesitz
BSB	Bayerische Staatsbibliothek
BSV	Bilderdienst Süddeutscher Verlag
BT	*Berliner Tageblatt*
BVz	*Bayerische Volkszeitung* (Nuremberg)
CEH	*Central European History*

DA	*Der Angriff*
DAZ	*Deutsche Allgemeine Zeitung*
DB-Z	*Deutsche Bergwerks-Zeitung*
DBFP	*Documents on British Foreign Policy*
DDF	*Documents Diplomatiques Française*
DDS	*Documents Diplomatiques Suisse*
DHM	Deutsches Historisches Museum
DoN	*Documents on Nazism* 1919–1945, edited by Jeremy Noakes and Geoffrey Pridham (New York, 1974)
FAHV	F. A. Herbig Verlagsbuchhandlung
FAZ	*Frankfurter Allgemeine Zeitung*
FH	*Frankfurter Hefte*
FZ	*Frankfurter Zeitung*
G	*Germania*
GiW&U	*Geschichte in Wissenschaft und Unterricht*
IfZ	Institut für Zeitgeschichte
IMT	International Military Tribunal (Nuremberg)
Jd	*Der Jungdeutsche* (Berlin)
JCH	*Journal of Contemporary History*
JMH	*Journal of Modern History*
KV	*Kölnische Volkszeitung*
KZ	*Kölnische Zeitung*
LbsB	Landesbildstelle Berlin
MM	*Militärgeschichtliche Mitteilungen*
MNN	*Münchner Neueste Nachrichten*
MZ	*Münchener Zeitung*
NAUSA	National Archives, Washington, D.C.

NFP	*Neue Freie Presse* (Vienna)
NPA	Neues Politisches Archiv (in Archiv der Republik, Vienna)
NPZ	*Neue Preussische Zeitung* (Berlin)
NSHSAH	Niedersächsisches Hauptstaatsarchiv Hannover
PS	*Politische Studien*
RA	*Regensburger Anzeiger*
RF	*Rote Fahne* (Berlin)
R-MVz	*Rhein-Main Volkszeitung*
SBWB	Senatsverwaltung für Bau- und Wohnungswesen Berlin
SEG	*Schulthess' Europäischer Geschichtskalender*
TbJG	*Die Tagebücher von Joseph Goebbels: Sämtliche Fragmente,* edited by Else Fröhlich (Munich, 1987ff)
TR	*Tägliche Rundschau* (Berlin)
TsGA	Tsentralnyi Gosudarstvennyi Arkhiv, Moscow
UB	ULLSTEIN Bilderdienst
V	*Vorwärts* (Berlin)
VB	*Völkischer Beobachter*
VfS&Wg	*Vierteljahrschrift für Sozial- und Wirtschaftsgeschichte*
VfZ	*Vierteljahrshefte für Zeitgeschichte*
VZ	*Vossische Zeitung* (Berlin)
ZfM	*Zeitschrift für Militärgeschichte*
ZS	Zeugenschriftum (IfZ)
ZSg	Zeitgeschichtliche Sammlungen (BAK)

$$===$$

NOTES

1. Prologue: The Field Marshal, the Corporal, and the General

... **"The mighty Nazi assault"** ... *FZ*, January 1, 1933 (#1–2).

... **"The republic has been rescued"** ... *VZ*, January 1, 1933 (#1).

... **"Hitler's Rise and Fall"** ... *V*, January 1, 1933 (#1).

... **major Catholic paper** ... *KV*, January 1, 1933 (#1).

... **"Everywhere, throughout the whole world"** ... *BT*, January 1, 1933 (#1).

... **Throughout its turbulent fourteen years** ... The most recent histories of the republic are Heinrich August Winkler, *Weimar 1918–1933* (Munich, 1993), and Hans Mommsen, *The Rise and Fall of Weimar Democracy* (Chapel Hill, NC, 1996).

... **The president in whose hands** ... There is no up-to-date biography of Hindenburg. Although superseded in numerous respects by more recent research, a useful introduction is Andreas Dorpalen's *Hindenburg and the Weimar Republic* (Princeton, N.J., 1964).

... **When the political deadlock of 1930** ... On this and the following, see Winkler, *Weimar,* pp. 334ff.

... **Instrumental in bringing about Brüning's fall** ... Winkler, *Weimar,* 462ff.

... At Schleicher's urging ... Franz von Papen ... Thilo Vogelsang, *Reichswehr, Staat und NSDAP* (Stuttgart, 1962), pp. 203ff; Winkler, *Weimar,* pp. 477f.

... Papen's qualification ... was questionable ... See Jürgen A. Bach, *Franz von Papen in der Weimarer Republik* (Düsseldorf, 1977).

... Officially ... National Socialist German Workers' Party ... For the origins and development of the party, see Dietrich Orlow, *The History of the Nazi Party* (2 vols., Pittsburgh, 1969–73).

... By the summer of 1932 Hitler ... The best biographies are Alan Bullock, *Hitler: A Study in Tyranny* (London, 1952ff.) and Joachim Fest, *Hitler* (New York, 1974).

... In hopes of gaining Nazi support, ... See Winkler, *Weimar,* pp. 478ff.

... After the July election, Hitler reneged ... See Winkler, *Weimar,* pp. 510f.

... man he referred to in private as "the corporal" ... Although it is often asserted that the president described Hitler as "the Austrian corporal" or "the Bohemian corporal," Hindenburg's son Oskar insisted at his de-Nazification trial on March 14, 1949, that his father had spoken only of "the corporal": NSHSAH, Spruchkammerverfahren gegen Oskar von Hindenburg, Nds. 171 Lüneburg, Uzn/Nr. 11363, Bd. 3, p. 58.

... Neither Hindenburg's conscience ... *AdRk/KvP,* I, p. 392, n. 5.

... The trust republicans placed in Hindenburg ... See Winkler, *Weimar,* pp. 518f.

... Papen's plan to circumvent the constitution was derailed ... *ibid.,* pp. 522ff.

... When Hindenburg sounded out Hitler ... *AdRk/KvP,* vol. 2, pp. 984–86, 988–1000.

... open letter ... president's office ... sent to the Nazi leader ... *ibid.,* pp. 988–1000.

... One member of his cabinet reportedly quipped ... Rudolf Fischer, *Schleicher: Mythos und Wirklichkeit* (Hamburg, 1932), p. 54. This journalistic account traces Schleicher's career up to his chancellorship.

... Hindenburg was "firmly resolved to take all measures" ... *AdRK/KvP,* vol. 2, p. 1017.

... "I'm not the soul of the cabinet" ... Fischer, *Schleicher,* p. 25.

... Schleicher set about undermining ... Winkler, *Weimar,* pp. 546ff.

... Fifty years old ... Kurt von Schleicher ... There is still no reliable, full biography of Schleicher; useful are the short sketch by Thilo Vogelsang, *Kurt von Schleicher: Ein General als Politiker* (Göttingen, 1965). Highly informative and insightful is the article by Peter Hayes, " 'A Question Mark with Epaulettes'? Kurt von Schleicher and Weimar Politics," *JMH* 52 (1980), pp. 35–65. A Ph.D. dissertation by Theodore Albert Cline, "The Chancellorship of General Kurt von Schleicher" (University of Texas, 1976), is informative but now outdated on many points. Less reliable are the hagiographic biography by Friedrich-Karl von Plehwe, *Reichskanzler Kurt von Schleicher* (Esslingen, 1983) and the journalistic accounts of Hans Rudolf Berndorff, *General Zwischen Ost und West* (Hamburg, 1951), and Kurt Caro and Walter Oehme, *Schleichers Aufstieg* (Berlin, 1933).

... "He has the gift" ... Fischer, *Schleicher,* p. 11 (quoting the conservative journalist Adolf Stein, who published under the pseudonym Rumpelstilzchen).

... "What Germany needs today" ... John W. Wheeler-Bennett, *The Nemesis of Power* (London, 1956), p. 237f., n. 3.

... "sphinx in uniform" ... Quoted from *Acht-Uhr Abendblatt* of Berlin, in *DA,* December 6, 1932 (#254).

... Trotsky ... "a question mark with ... epaulettes" ... Hayes, "A Question Mark," p. 35.

... "Republic or monarchy is not the question now," ... Vogelsang, *Reichswehr,* p. 410.

... Schleicher enjoyed ... political honeymoon ... Winkler, *Weimar,* pp. 559f, 562.

... he had no intention ... to alter the constitution ... *AdRk/KvS,* p. 26, n. 4.

... So did the leaders of the Christian trade unions ... See William L. Patch, Jr., *Christian Trade Unions in the Weimar Republic, 1919–1933* (New Haven, Conn., 1985), p. 215.

... Heartened by ... responses from organized labor ... Schleicher's
Chancellery press secretary, Erich Marcks, boasted to a journalist on January
10 that the chancellor had successfully achieved his goal of breaking up the
constellation of extraparliamentary forces that had coalesced against the
Papen cabinet: "Informationsbericht vom 11. Januar 1933," by Georg Dertinger, in BAK, Sammlung Brammer, ZSg 101/26.

... "troublesome types" ... Schleicher to Wilhelm Groener, March 25,
1932, in Gordon A. Craig, "Briefe Schleichers an Groener," *Die Welt als
Geschichte* 11 (1951), p. 130.

... respected Jewish figures ... Among those who favored admitting the
Nazis to government were the Social Democratic leader and former finance
minister Rudolf Hilferding, who told the German-National politician Reinhold Quaatz on November 18, 1932, that this approach would be the best
way to dampen Nazi radicalism. See *Die Deutschnationalen und die Zerstörung
der Weimarer Republik,* edited by Hermann Weiss and Paul Hoser (Munich,
1989), p. 211; see also the remarks of the Berlin banker Oskar Wassermann to
the British ambassador in April 1932: *DBFP 1919–1939,* series 2, vol. 3
(London, 1948), p. 128. Similar views were expressed in September 1932 by
the Hamburg banker Carl Melchior and Hans Schäffer, head of the Ullstein
publishing firm and formerly a high official in the Finance Ministry. See
Henry Ashby Turner, Jr., *German Big Business and the Rise of Hitler* (New
York, 1985), p. 277.

... Fearing that if the Nazi party broke up ... Hayes, "A Question
Mark," p. 43; also reports of the British ambassador, December 21, 1932,
and January 11, 1933: *DBFP, 1919–1939,* series 2, vol. 4 (London, 1950),
pp. 383f., 386.

... "If they did not exist" ... Schleicher to Wilhelm Groener, March 25,
1932, in Craig, "Briefe Schleichers," p. 130.

... Schleicher based his optimism ... Hayes, "A Question Mark," pp. 48f.

... The Nazis also fit into Schleicher's plans ... *ibid.,* pp. 45f.; Michael
Geyer, "Das zweite Rüstungsprogramm (1930–1934)," *MM* 17 (1975),
pp. 125–72; Edward W. Bennett, *German Rearmament and the West* (Princeton, N.J., 1979), pp. 284–88.

... Schleicher had ... maintained covert contact with ... the SA ... See
the papers of Schleicher's aide at the Defense Ministry, Ferdinand von
Bredow, in BA/MA, esp. the "Kurzorientierungen" of July 26, 1932

(N97/1), December 19, 1932 (N97/2), and January 5, 6, 16, 20, and 23, 1933 (N97/3). Also Schleicher's letter to Röhm of November 4, 1931, in Carl Severing, *Mein Lebensweg* (Cologne, 1950), vol. 2, p. 322.

... **"an interesting man"** ... Quoted in 1946 by one of Schleicher's Defense Ministry aides, Hanshenning von Holtzendorff, in his "Die Politik des Generals von Schleicher gegenüber der NSDAP 1930–33," manuscript, IfZ, ZS/A 36/1, p. 5.

... **ready to see Hitler installed as chancellor** ... Hayes, "A Question Mark," pp. 49f.

... **sounded out Hitler about becoming vice chancellor** ... Schleicher reported on his meeting with Hitler, which took place on November 23, at the session of the Papen cabinet on November 25: *AdRk/KvP*, vol. 2, p. 1013. On the eve of his appointment as chancellor, he dispatched a Defense Ministry aide to renew his offer to Hitler, with the same negative result: Vogelsang, *Reichswehr*, p. 330.

... **Schleicher turned his attention to ... Gregor Strasser** ... On Strasser, see Udo Kissenkoetter, *Gregor Strasser und die NSDAP* (Stuttgart, 1978) and Peter Stachura, *Gregor Strasser and the Rise of Nazism* (London, 1983).

... **observers erroneously concluded ... 'labor axis'** ... The notion of a labor axis as the goal of Schleicher's strategy seems to have originated with Hans Zehrer, editor in chief of the Berlin daily, *Tägliche Rundschau*. Although Schleicher may possibly have diverted some funds toward purchase of the paper by Zehrer and his group in the summer of 1932, there is no evidence that Zehrer spoke for Schleicher or was even in close contact with him during his chancellorship; for the contrary view, see Ebbo Demant, *Von Schleicher zu Springer* (Mainz, 1971), pp. 101–11. Papen's notoriously unreliable memoirs have frequently been invoked as a source on this subject, but there are no grounds for according him either credibility on the matter or knowledge of it.

... **Schleicher had in mind an elaborate scheme** ... See Otto Braun, *Von Weimar bis Hitler* (New York, 1940), pp. 431ff. Braun's recollection of what Schleicher told him on December 8, 1932, is corroborated by contemporaneous sources. See Vogelsang, *Reichswehr*, pp. 341f. See also the reports of two journalists with access to the chancellor's staff: Heinz Brauweiler, "A.-Brief Nr. 311," December 7, 1932, in Nachlass Brauweiler, IfZ, 102/2; and R.K. (Robert Kircher), "Ein vergeblicher Fühler Goerings," *FZ,* December

13, 1932. (#930). See also Goebbels's diary entry of December 13, 1932, *TbJG*, part I, vol. 2, p. 304.

... Hitler swiftly scotched this scheme ... Kissenkoetter, *Gregor Strasser,* pp. 170f.

... crushing setback at the polls ... in ... Thuringia ... "38.1 Prozent Verlust," *VZ*, December 31, 1932 (#628), an analysis of the official results.

... Coming on top of losses in local balloting ... Elections were held in Lübeck and Saxony on November 13. See Cuno Horkenbach, *Das Deutsche Reich von 1918 bis heute* (Berlin, 1932), p. 378. Local elections in Bremen took place on November 27. See "Flucht aus der Nazipartei," *V*, November 29, 1932 (#561).

... Strasser argued ... on December 5 ... Goebbels, *TbJG*, part I, vol. 2, pp. 292f.

... When the new Reichstag convened ... Winkler, *Weimar*, pp. 559f.

... On December 7, Schleicher confidently predicted ... *AdRk/KvS*, pp. 22–24 (minutes of the cabinet).

... December 8 ... Hitler was staggered ... Goebbels, *TbJB*, part I, vol. 2, p. 295.

... letter from Gregor Strasser ... The original letter has never been located, but a draft has been preserved. See Kissenkoetter, *Gregor Strasser,* pp. 202f.

... Strasser had denounced Hitler's all-or-nothing strategy ... The group to whom Strasser spoke was made up of the *Landesinspekteure* he had recently appointed. See the later account by one of those present, Hinrich Lohse, in *DoN* (1974), pp. 141f.

... similar letter from ... Gottfried Feder ... Kissenkoetter, *Gregor Strasser*, p. 173.

... "If the party falls apart" ... Goebbels, *TbJG*, part I, vol. 2, p. 295. The specification of the weapon was added by Goebbels in the published version of his diary, *ibid*, p. 297.

... he delivered an impassioned appeal ... See the later account by Hinrich Lohse in *DoN* (1974), pp. 143–46.

... Hitler brought the Nazi Reichstag deputies to heel ... Goebbels, *TbJG,* part I, vol. 2, pp. 298–300.

... he released to the press a statement ... "Gregor Strassers Beurlaubung," *DA,* December 9, 1932 (#257). Later in the month, the Nazis publicized a denial of rumors about his departure, purportedly at Strasser's request, which contradicted the original statement by referring to his resignation (*Rücktritt*). See "Alles Kombinationen!" *VB,* December 21, 1932 (#356).

... Strasser departed for a vacation ... Kissenkoetter, *Gregor Strasser,* p. 177.

... Feder quickly recanted ... "Eine Erklärung Feders," *FZ,* December 10, 1932 (#923); Goebbels, *TbJG,* part I, vol. 2, pp. 298–99.

... To bolster morale, [Hitler] hurried about the country ... Ulrich Wörtz, "Programmatik und Führerprinzip: Das Problem des Strasser-Kreises in der NSDAP" (Ph.D. diss., Erlangen-Nurnberg, 1966), pp. 236f.

... the value of shares and bonds ... "Die Börse im Jahre 1932," *Wirtschaft und Statistik,* January 25, 1933 (vol. 13, no. 2), p. 61.

... "The slump has ended" ... Quarterly report of the Institut für Konjunkturforschung, quoted in the "Frankfurter Handelsblatt" of the *FZ,* January 1, 1933 (#1–2).

... "Land in Sight!" ... *ibid.*

... "1932 ... one long streak of bad luck" ... Goebbels, *TbJG,* part I, vol. 2, p. 314.

2. A Conspiracy against the Chancellor Is Hatched

... Hitler attended ... *Die Meistersinger* ... This paragraph and the next are based on the memoirs of Ernst Hanfstaengl, *Hitler: The Missing Years* (London, 1957), pp. 194f.; Münchner Stadtmuseum, *München—"Hauptstadt der Bewegung"* (Munich, 1993), p. 124 (catalog published for an exposition with the same title).

... "This year belongs to us" ... Hanfstaengl, *Hitler,* p. 195.

... Hitler was ... a quite prosperous man ... See Oren J. Hale, "Adolf Hitler: Taxpayer," *AHR* 60 (1955), pp. 830–42.

... **"with the certainty of a sleepwalker"** ... Speech of March 14, 1936, in Max Domarus, *Hitler: Reden und Proklamationen 1932–1945* (Munich, 1965), vol. 2, p. 606.

... **Hitler's vision of Germany's future** ... The best introduction is Eberhard Jäckel, *Hitler's Weltanschauung* (Middletown, Conn., 1972).

... **"I have no time to wait!"** ... Albert Krebs, *Tendenzen und Gestalten der NSDAP* (Stuttgart, 1959), p. 137.

... **"They want to give us a share of government,"** ... "Adolf Hitlers Kampfbotschaft für 1933," *VB*, January 1–2, 1933 (#1–2).

... **"Scathing toward the defeatists"** ... Goebbels, *TbJG,* part I, vol. 2, p. 319f.

... **January 4 ... Reichstag's agenda committee** ... "Reichstag am 24. Januar," *FZ*, January 5, 1933 (#13); "24. Januar Reichstag," and "In Verlegenheit," *BT,* January 5, 1933 (#7); "Reichstag erst am 24. Januar," *V,* January 5, 1933 (#7).

... **January 4, Hitler arrived in ... Bonn** ... See Otto Dietrich, *Mit Hitler in die Macht* (Munich, 1934), pp. 169f.

... **Papen's background** ... There are two recent biographies: Joachim Petzold, *Franz von Papen* (Munich and Berlin, 1995) and Richard W. Rolfs, *The Sorcerer's Apprentice* (Lanham, Md., 1996). Less reliable is the hagiographic biography by Henry M. and Robin K. Adams, *Rebel Patriot* (Santa Barbara, Calif., 1987). See also Papen's two volumes of memoirs, the second of which repeats much of the first: *Der Wahrheit eine Gasse* (Munich, 1952) and *Vom Scheitern einer Demokratie* (Mainz, 1968).

... **"No one wanted to believe it,"** ... André François-Poncet, *Souvenirs d'une ambassade à Berlin* (Paris, 1946), pp. 42f.

... **Swiss envoy in Berlin ... "I left Herr von Papen"** ... *DDS, 1848–1945,* vol. 10, (Bern, 1982), p. 505.

... **Sir Horace Rumbold ... "the wonder of an observer"** ... *DBFP,* 2d series, vol. 4, pp. 389f.

... **Konrad Adenauer ... "I always gave him the benefit"** ... Adenauer to Countess Fürstenberg-Herdringen, October 22, 1946, in Adenauer, *Briefe 1945–1947* (Bonn, 1983), p. 350.

... **"Papen sometimes served as the butt of their jokes"** ... François-Poncet, *Souvenirs,* p. 44.

... **"It's he who is the preferred one"** ... François-Poncet, *Souvenirs,* p. 44.

... **Hindenburg expressed his sense of loss** ... Papen, *Gasse,* pp. 250f.

... **presented him with an autographed photograph** ... It is reproduced opposite p. 225 of Papen, *Gasse.*

... **"He doesn't need a head"** ... Lutz Count Schwerin von Krosigk, finance minister under Papen, Schleicher and Hitler, related this anecdote at third hand in an interview on April 24, 1952: IfZ, ZS 145. It was also recounted in 1951 by another contemporary who claimed to have heard it from Schleicher: Karl Dietrich Bracher, *Die Auflösung der Weimarer Republik* (Stuttgart and Düsseldorf, 1957), p. 519, n. 179.

... **"What do you say about that"** ... This was recalled in an interview on January 28 and 31, 1953, by Hermann Foertsch, who was one of Schleicher's aides at the Defense Ministry in 1932 and 1933: IfZ, ZS 37, p. 10.

... **"knight without fear or blemish"** ... *AdRk/KvS,* p. 102.

... **"my dear Fränzchen ... the banner-bearer in decisive battles"** ... Papen, *Scheitern,* pp. 336f.

... **Following a speech to the ... Gentlemen's Club** ... On this and the following, see Turner, *German Big Business,* pp. 315ff.; Heinrich Muth, "Das 'Kölner Gespräch' am 4. Januar 1933," *GiW&U* 37 (1986), pp. 463–80, 529–41.

... **Upon arriving at ... Schröder's ... townhouse** ... See Schröder's affidavit of July 21, 1947, for the American war crimes prosecution at Nuremberg: NAUSA, RG 238, NI-7990.

... **As Hitler disclosed to Goebbels** ... Goebbels, *TbJG,* part I, vol. 2, p. 332, entry of January 10.

... **When Papen and Hitler turned to the future** ... This is based upon Schröder's affidavit of July 21, 1947, for the American war crimes prosecution at Nuremberg: NAUSA, RG 238, NI-7990. Papen's versions in his two volumes of memoirs, *Gasse,* p. 256, and *Scheitern,* pp. 334–39, are untrustworthy. Günther Gereke, commissioner for job creation in the Schleicher cabinet, told a journalist on January 5 that President von Hindenburg had informed him between Christmas and New Year's that he had approved of Papen's plans to meet with Hitler. See BAK, Sammlung Brammer, ZSg 101/26, "Informationsbericht vom 5. Januar," by Georg Dertinger. It seems unlikely that this was true, however; for if Hindenburg had in fact approved of the meeting in advance, Papen would presumably have invoked that approval, at the latest after the war, to defend himself against charges of plotting on his own against Schleicher.

... president had urged him ... to turn down ... ambassadorship ... Papen, Gasse, p. 251.

... day before, a Berlin newspaper predicted ... "Hitler schwenkt zu Papen," *Jd,* January 3, 1933 (#2).

... Papen at once issued a flat denial, ... "Aufmarsch zum Wahlkampf," *Jd,* January 5, 1933 (#4), citing Papen's statement to the Telegraphen-Union, a wire service.

... as did Goebbels' tabloid newspaper ... "Keine Unterredung Hitler-Papen," *DA,* January 3, 1933 (#2).

... unpleasantly surprised to find a photographer ... Papen complained about this in a letter of May 21, 1933, to Major Müldner von Mülnheim, an intermediary who sought unsuccessfully to mediate between him and Schleicher: Papen Papers, TsGA, vol. 5. See also Papen, *Gasse,* p. 255, where Papen describes the photographer as a detective.

... politically well-connected Berlin dentist ... The dentist was Hellmuth Elbrechter; see his statement of 1945 and Brüning's letter of January 10, 1953, in Kissenkoetter, *Gregor Strasser,* pp. 205–7. See also Gottfried Treviranus, *Das Ende von Weimar* (Düsseldorf, 1968), pp. 346f., 355f.

... Brüning ... learning of it ... from Gregor Strasser ... Brüning, *Memoiren, 1918–1934* (Stuttgart, 1970), p. 639.

... "Hitler and Papen against Schleicher" ... *TR,* January 5, 1933. (#4) Copies of the paper printed earlier that day bore the same date and number but carried in the space atop the front page a story with the headline "Reichstag erst am 24, Januar."

... On January 5 Papen issued a statement ... "Eine Erklärung von Papens," *KV,* January 6, 1933 (#6).

... On January 6 Baron von Schröder announced ... "Eine Auslassung des Freiherrn von Schröder," *FZ,* January 7, 1933 (#19).

... **"possibility of a broad nationalist political unity front"** ... "Eine gemeinsame Erklärung Papens und Hitlers," *FZ*, January 7, 1933 (#19).

... **same day, Goebbels'** ... *Der Angriff* **stated** ... "Die Unterredung Hitler-Papen," *DA*, January 6, 1933 (#5).

... **"casual conversation"** ... "Das Zusammentreffen Adolf Hitlers mit Papen," *VB*, January 6, 1933 (#6).

... **"interesting details"** ... "Das Zusammentreffen Adolf Hitlers mit Papen," *VB*, January 7, 1933 (#7).

... **press fell victim to the anticapitalist sentiment** ... See Turner, *German Big Business*, pp. 316f.

... **"Caught In Flagrante!"** ... "Hitler beim Herrenklub. In flagranti (sic) ertappt," *V*, January 6, 1933 (#10).

... **"Since Hitler has been heavily financed"** ... "Bei den 'feinen Leuten'," *RF*, January 6, 1933 (#5).

... **imaginative ... allegations of ... machinations** ... See, for examples, "Geheime Verhandlungen Hitler-Papen bei rheinischen Bankfürsten," *RF*, January 6, 1933 (#5); "Der Agent der Grossindustrie," *V*, January 7, 1933 (#11); "Die Unterredung v. Papen Hitler," *Jd*, January 7, 1933 (#6). Even Schleicher came to suspect capitalist involvement. On January 10 he told a journalist that "it had become known" that former Reichsbank president Hjalmar Schacht had been behind the meeting: IfZ, ED 93, Bd. 33, "Dienstag, den 10. Januar 1933 Unterhaltung mit Reichskanzler von Schleicher," by Josef Reiner of the Ullstein Verlag.

... **Some journalists accepted the denials** ... "Die Unterredung Hitler-Papen," *FZ*, January 6, 1933 (#16); "Hitler klopft an die Hintertüren," *VZ*, January 6, 1933 (#9); "Anderthalbstündige Aussprache Schleicher-Papen," *DAZ*, January 9, 1933 (#14); "Die Lage des Kabinetts Schleicher," *FZ*, January 10, 1933 (#26).

... **others speculated that Papen** ... "Reichsregierung und Nationalsozialisten," *KV*, January 6, 1933 (#6).

... **Only a minority recognized** ... "Was war in Köln?" *BT*, January 6, 1933 (#10); "Das Komplot," *BT*, January 6, 1933 (#9).

... **[Schleicher] complained to President von Hindenburg** ... Otto Meissner, *Staatssekretär unter Ebert—Hindenburg—Hitler* (Hamburg, 1950), p. 261.

... **"Let him talk"** ... Theodor Eschenburg, *Die improvisierte Demokratie* (Munich, 1963), p. 280.

... **Schleicher ... France should be conciliated** ... See Gaines Post, Jr., *The Civil-Military Fabric of Weimar Foreign Policy* (Princeton, N.J., 1973), pp. 302–3; also Michael Geyer, *Aufrüstung oder Sicherheit* (Wiesbaden, 1980), pp. 47, 181.

... **"He is frivolous"** ... François-Poncet's dispatch to Paris of January 7, 1933: *DDF, 1932–1939,* series 1, vol. 2, p. 375.

... **On ... January 9, Papen ... called on Schleicher** ... Papen, *Gasse,* p. 260.

... **Schleicher ... speaking off the record** ... See the report by one of those present, "Informationsbericht vom 14. Januar 1933," by Georg Dertinger: BAK, Sammlung Brammer, Zsg 101/26. Also, Moscow Document (see Appendix).

... **Goebbels ... recorded in his diary** ... Goebbels, *TbJG,* part I, vol. 2, p. 332 (entry of January 10).

... **"I was fool enough to believe him."** ... "Schleicher's Political Dream," *The New Statesman and Nation,* July 7, 1934. The authenticity of this anonymous account of a conversation with Schleicher in March 1933 is corroborated by a variety of other evidence.

... **Meissner ... recalled in his memoirs** ... Meissner, *Staatssekretär,* p. 261.

... **According to Papen's memoirs** ... Papen, *Gasse,* p. 261.

... **"acutely offended"** ... François-Poncet's dispatch to Paris of January 7. *DDF, 1932–1939,* series 1, vol. 2, p. 375.

... **According to Meissner ... the president instructed him** ... See Meissner's Nuremberg testimony of May 4, 1948: NAUSA, RG 238, Case 11, p. 4612; also Meissner, *Staatssekretär,* pp. 261f.

3. Hitler Scores a Dubious Triumph amid a Nazi Crisis

... **Hitler plunged ... into the campaign** ... Arno Schröder, *"Hitler geht auf die Dörfer"* (Detmold, 1938), p. 131.

... **During the next eleven days** ... Jutta Ciolek-Kümper, *Wahlkampf in Lippe* (München, 1976), pp. 313–15.

... **As observant journalists noticed** ... "Adolf Hitler diniert und konferiert," *V*, January 7, 1933 (#12); "Sturm über Lippe," *V*, January 9, 1933 (#14).

... **no fewer than six special trains** ... Ciolek-Kümper, *Wahlkampf*, pp. 164f.

... **between six and seven hundred Nazi stormtroopers** ... *ibid.*, pp. 137f.

... **Hitler ... lived ... in a castle** ... Hans Hüls, *Wähler und Wahlverhalten im Land Lippe während der Weimarer Republik* (Detmold, 1974), pp. 79f.

... **Alfred Hugenberg, ... refrained from attacks** ... John A. Leopold, *Alfred Hugenberg* (New Haven, Conn., 1977), p. 133.

... **Nazis turned ... rallies into theatrical performances** ... Ciolek-Kümper, *Wahlkampf*, 165f. For other examples, see William Sheridan Allen, *The Nazi Seizure of Power* (rev. ed., New York, 1984), p. 80f., 124.

... **British ambassador ... "... jazz band"** ... Sir Horace Rumbold to Arthur Henderson, December 17, 1929. See *DBFP, 1919–1939*, series IA, vol. 7, p. 261.

... **Nazi campaign speeches in Lippe** ... See Ciolek-Kümper, *Wahlkampf*, 233ff.

... **republican *Vossische Zeitung* of Berlin pointed out,** ... Quoted in Arno Schröder, *Mit der Partei vorwärts* (Detmold, 1940), p. 40.

... **as a paper in nearby Bielefeld observed,** ... *Bielefelder Volkswacht*, quoted in Schröder, *Mit der Partei*, pp. 42f.

... **His first speech ... January 4** ... Ciolek-Kümper, *Wahlkampf*, pp. 324ff.; Schröder, *Mit der Partei*, pp. 30f.

... **republican political police ... Nazi Party in Munich,** ... Quoted in Geoffrey Pridham, *Hitler's Rise to Power* (New York, 1974), p. 291.

... **Previously, Nazism ... largely self-supporting operation,** ... Turner, *German Big Business*, pp. 111ff.

... **Now ... influx of new members dwindled** ... *ibid.*, pp. 292f; Walter

Struve, *Aufstieg und Herrschaft des Nationalsozialismus in einer industriellen Kleinstadt* (Essen, 1992), pp. 155f.

… defections multiplied … *ibid.;* Jeremy Noakes, *The Nazi Party in Lower Saxony, 1921–1933* (London, 1971), pp. 233f.; Allen, *Nazi Seizure*, p. 133.

… party rallies … attendance fell off … Noakes, *Lower Saxony*, p. 235; Allen, *Nazi Seizure*, p. 138f.; Struve, *Kleinstadt*, p. 162.

… local party officials … dunned by merchants … See Lawrence D. Stokes, *Kleinstadt und Nationalsozialismus* (Neumünster, 1984), p. 365.

… staff of the national headquarters alone grew … Speech by party treasurer Franz Xaver Schwarz to the Nuremberg party congress of 1935, September 13, 1935: BDC, Non-Biographic Collection, Ordner 266.

… accusations of misappropriation of funds … Allen, *Nazi Seizure*, p. 139; Rainer Hambrecht, *Der Aufstieg der NSDAP in Mittel- und Oberfranken (1925–1933)* (Nuremberg, 1976), p. 385; Stokes, *Kleinstadt*, p. 366; Goebbels, *TbJG*, part I, vol. 2, p. 329.

… Friction … between components of the movement … Stokes, *Kleinstadt*, pp. 364–66.

… stormtroopers … rattling cans … Ciolek-Kümper, *Wahlkampf*, p. 90f.; Schröder, *Dörfer*, p. 104; " 'Kampfschatz' gepfandet," *V*, January 9, 1933 (#14); "Die demoralisierte SA," *BT*, January 11, 1933 (#17).

… party units conducted lotteries … Noakes, *Lower Saxony*, p. 243; Allen, *Nazi Seizure*, p. 134.

… elaborate, intense campaign … On the following, see Ciolek-Kümper, *Wahlkampf*, pp. 88–91.

… three rented tents … *ibid.*, p. 141.

… Hitler had to dip into the royalties … *ibid.*, p. 140.

… one of his aides desperately approached … Otto Dietrich, *12 Jahre mit Hitler* (Cologne, [1955]), p. 187.

… a bailiff sequestered the box-office receipts … Schröder, *Dörfer*, p. 192.

… Some of Strasser's admirers … refused to give up … Kissenkoetter, *Gregor Strasser*, pp. 185–90; Volker Hentschel, *Weimars letzte Monate* (Düsseldorf, 1978), pp. 150–54.

... **gauleiter of Hesse-Darmstadt** ... "Strasser-Krise greift um sich," *VZ*, December 17, 1932 (#603); "1600 Austritte in Hessen," *FZ*, December 18, 1932 (#945); See also the letter, purportedly by the gauleiter, Karl Lenz, which stated that he had resigned for reasons of health: "Aus allem wird eine 'Sensation'," *VB*, December 21, 1932 (#356). Lenz nevertheless soon began contributing articles to pro-Strasser, oppositional publications. See Kissenkoetter, *Gregor Strasser,* pp. 185f.

... **reports ... pro-Strasser sentiment ... Hamburg** ... Goebbels, *TbJG*, part I, vol. 2, p. 333.

... **"Strasser wants to fight under the slogan"** ... *ibid.*

... **"Strasser is plotting."** ... *ibid.,* pp. 334, 336–38.

... **On ... January 12, embarrassing evidence** ... Ciolek-Kümper, *Wahlkampf,* pp. 217–26; Hüls, *Wähler,* p. 161; "Die Abtrünnigen," *BT,* January 13, 1933 (#22).

... **Hitler faced ... dissension in ... stormtrooper auxiliary,** ... Peter Longerich, *Die braunen Bataillone* (Munich, 1989), pp. 161f.; Robert Lewis Koehl, *The Black Corps* (Madison, 1988), pp. 56–58; "Die demoralisierte SA," *BT,* January 11, 1933 (#17). See also the memoirs of a Berlin SA man: Fritz Stelzner, *Schicksal SA* (Berlin, 1936), pp. 137–39.

... **Where acts of terrorism ... had been particularly numerous** ... Richard Bessel, *Political Violence and the Rise of Nazism* (New Haven, Conn., 1984), pp. 92–96.

... **Party officials ... complained of inadequate participation** ... Thomas Childers, "The Limits of National Socialist Mobilisation," in *The Formation of the Nazi Constituency, 1919–1933,* edited by Thomas Childers (Totowa, N.J., 1986), p. 249f.

... **a high SA commander took ... extraordinary step** ... "Partei oder Kampfbund?" *TR,* January 3, 1933 (#2), signed by "v.F.", who was presumably Werner von Fichte, leader of Gruppe Nord, with his base in Düsseldorf.

... **major outbreak of stormtrooper insubordination....** On the "Stegmann Revolt," see Hambrecht, *Der Aufstieg,* pp. 323f., 371–89; Eric G. Reiche, *The Development of the SA in Nürnberg, 1922–1934* (New York, 1986), pp. 146–63; Pridham, *Hitler's Rise,* pp. 291ff.; Wolfgang Horn, *Führerideologie und Parteiorganisation in der NSDAP* (Düsseldorf, 1972), pp. 411f.

... The dispute in Franconia burst into the headlines ... "Revolte in der fränkischen SA," *V*, January 12, 1933 (#19); "S.A. Franken," *BT*, January 12, 1933 (#20); "Schwerer Konflikt in der SA," *VZ*, January 12, 1933 (#19); "Die Abtrünnigen," *BT*, January 13, 1933 (#22); "Stegmann wird degradiert," *VZ*, January 13, 1933 (#21); "NSDAP in der Krise," *NPZ*, January 15, 1933 (#15).

... A Catholic newspaper in nearby Paderborn ... Schröder, *Mit der Partei*, p. 49.

... "the result has something artificial about it" ... *DDF, 1932–1939*, series 1, vol. 2, p. 479, dispatch of January 19, 1933.

... "In truth ... a fly impaled on the tip of his sword" ... "Der gefährliche Bülowplatz," *BT*, January 22, 1933 (#37).

... outcome "cannot be assessed too highly" ... "Für faule Kompromisse weniger die Zeit denn je!" *VB*, January 17, 1933 (#17).

... "From this little sector of the trenches" ... "Signal Lippe!", *DA*, January 16, 1933 (#13).

... On the afternoon of January 15 ... Hitler greeted ... Ciolek-Kümper, *Wahlkampf*, pp. 365f.

... Hitler addressed a closed-door gathering ... "Hitler wiederholt seine Kampfansage," *FZ*, January 17, 1933 (#45).

... "brusque intransigence" ... Goebbels, *TbJG*, part I, vol. 2, p. 340.

... "At the end, everyone went wild" ... *ibid.*

... Within days ... word ... had reached ... Schleicher ... *AdRk/KvS*, p. 233, n. 13. Letter from a Nazi informant to Prince Wilhelm, January 17, 1933, forwarded by the latter to Schleicher on January 19.

... [Strasser] ... suffered under the paralyzing handicap ... Kurt Ludecke, *I Knew Hitler* (New York, 1937), pp. 499, 502; Heinrich Muth, "Schleicher und die Gewerkschaften 1932," *VfZ* 29 (1981), p. 206.

... [Strasser] ... meekly approached Göring ... Goebbels, *TbJG*, part I, vol. 2, pp. 343, 346.

... Strasser withdrew from politics altogether ... Kissenkoetter, *Gregor Strasser*, pp. 192f.

... **[Strasser] ... was murdered** ... *ibid.,* p. 194.

... **The two men had a troubled relationship** ... On the following, see Leopold, *Hugenberg*.

... **In December the two met secretly** ... Hugenberg to Hitler, December 28, 1932, and January 4, 1933. In BAK, Nachlass Schmidt-Hannover, file 72.

... **Hugenberg had conferred with ... Schleicher** ... *AdRk/KvS,* p. 234, n. 15; p. 282, n. 1.

... **Hugenberg ... proved unresponsive** ... Goebbels, *TbJG,* part I, vol. 2, p. 341.

... **"a phonograph record"** ... This is based on Hugenberg's version of the meeting, as recorded in the diary of Reinhold Quaatz, in Weiss and Hoser, eds., *Deutschnationalen,* p. 223.

... **"Rubbish!"** ... Goebbels, *TbJG,* part I, vol. 2, p. 341.

... **Joachim von Ribbentrop** ... See Michael Bloch, *Ribbentrop* (London, 1992).

... **bought his name and married his money** ... Rudolf Semmler, *Goebbels—the man next to Hitler* (London, 1947), p. 18f.; Hans-Adolf Jacobsen, *Nationalsozialistische Aussenpolitik, 1933–1938* (Frankfurt, 1968), pp. 255f.

... **summer of 1932 Ribbentrop had approached Hitler** ... Joachim von Ribbentrop, *Zwischen London und Moskau* (Leoni am Starnberger See, 1961), p. 36f.

... **When Hitler's staff asked Ribbentrop** ... *ibid.,* p. 37.

... **But Hitler instructed Ribbentrop** ... *ibid.,* p. 38: Goebbels, *TbJG,* part I, vol. 2, pp. 333f.

... **Over lunch at Ribbentrop's on January 18** ... Ribbentrop, *Zwischen,* p. 39.

... **Nazis again sought to keep the meeting secret** ... See "Hitler und Thyssen bei Kerrl," *VZ,* January 19, 1933 (#31); NAUSA, RG 238, NI-220, Wilhelm Keppler to Baron Kurt von Schröder, January 21, 1933.

... **Some journalists ... got wind of the meeting** ... "Aussprache Papens mit Hitler," *MNN,* January 19, 1933 (#18); "Papen—Hitler—Schleicher," *VZ,* January 18, 1933 (#30); "Noch kein Fortschritt," *G,* January 19, 1933

(#19); "Wieder Hitler und Papen," *KZ*, January 19, 1933 (#36); "Trommelfeuer auf Schleicher," *TR*, January 20, 1933 (#17).

... the chargé d'affaires at the American embassy ... Alfred Kliefoth to secretary of state, January 23, 1933. NAUSA, State Department Central Files, 862.00/2892.

... Party newspapers lost subscribers ... Oren J. Hale, *The Captive Press in the Third Reich* (Princeton, N.J., 1964), pp. 59f.; BAP, Nachlass Bracht, Bd. 2, Bl. 177, memorandum, "vertraulich," to Franz Bracht by Scholtz, November 9, 1932.

... Accusations of cronyism and financial irregularities ... Allen, *Nazi Seizure*, p. 139; Stokes, *Kleinstadt*, p. 366; "Neue Umgruppierungen der Hitlerfront," *VZ*, January 21, 1933 (#36).

... Stegmann ... bolted again ... Hambrecht, *Der Aufstieg*, pp. 384–89; Reiche, *SA in Nürnberg*, pp. 160–63; Kissenkoetter, *Gregor Strasser*, pp. 183f.; "Stegmanns Freikorps Franken," *VZ*, January 20, 1933 (#34); "Stegmann hält Generalprobe in Nürnberg," *BVz*, January 23, 1933 (#18).

... The "movement's historic moment ... missed" ... Hambrecht, *Der Aufstieg*, p. 388; Reiche, *SA in Nürnberg*, p. 162; " 'Freikorps Franken'," *FZ*, January 26, 1933 (#68–69).

... Appeals for support ... by Stegmann ... Kissenkoetter, *Gregor Strasser*, pp. 184, 187.

... In the state of Hesse, repeated mutinies ... *ibid.*, pp. 137–42; "Die Meuterei in der Kasseler S.A.," *BT*, January 3, 1933 (#3); "Die SA-Meuterei in Kassel," *FZ*, January 3, 1933 (#5–6); "SA-Meutereien in Kassel," *R-MVz*, January 3, 1933 (#2).

... the Hessian dissidents established a paramilitary organization ... Eberhard Schön, *Die Entstehung des Nationalsozialismus in Hessen* (Meisenheim am Glan, 1972), p. 139.

... hostel and soup kitchen ... in Stuttgart ... "Bewegung im Abstieg," *RA*, January 24, 1933 (#24).

... On January 21, the Munich police reported ... Conan Fischer, *Stormtroopers* (London, 1983), p. 210.

... In Berlin, partisans of Gregor Strasser ... waited ... Kissenkoetter, *Gregor Strasser*, p. 184.

... **SA units ... clashed with ... SS ...** "Hitlers SA schlägt SA.-Köpfe ein," *V*, January 3, 1933 (#3); "SS gegen SA.!" *V*, January 7, 1933 (#11). On the rivalry, see Schön, *Die Entstehung*, pp. 142–44; Andreas Werner, "SA und NSDAP" (Diss., Erlangen-Nürnberg, 1964), p. 586.

... **SS ... resignation en bloc ... in ... Meissen ...** "Die Hintermänner des Fememordes," *BT*, January 2, 1933 (#2); "Der grosse Katzenjammer," *V*, January 5, 1933 (#8).

... **Nazi stormtroopers defected to the Communists ...** Fischer, *Stormtroopers*, pp. 208–17; Wilfried Böhnke, *Die NSDAP im Ruhrgebiet* (Bonn, 1974), p. 157.

... **secret, internal Nazi analysis ...** Childers, "Limits," pp. 234–55.

... **permanent undersecretary in the Foreign Ministry ...** Bernhard von Bülow to Friedrich von Prittwitz und Gaffron, German ambassador in Washington, January 19, 1933. In *AzDAP*, series C, vol. 1, p. 22, n. 2.

... **the Austrian consul general in Munich ...** Engerth to Dollfuss, December 19, 1932: AdR, NPA 57.

... **leading dissident Nazis were not impressed ...** Kissenkoetter, *Gregor Strasser*, p. 188.

... **An expert on the history of the SA ...** Fischer, *Stormtroopers*, p. 210.

... **a rally ... on January 20 at the Sportpalast ...** "Der Weg zur Freiheit muss erkämpft werden," *VB*, January 22–23, 1933 (#22–23).

... **Ambassador François-Poncet ... note of skepticism ...** *DDF, 1932–1939*, series 1, vol. 2, p. 528.

... **[Hitler's] evenings ...** Goebbels, *TbJG*, part I, vol. 2, pp. 343f., 354.

... **Hitler went to see a new motion picture, ...** *ibid.*, pp. 342f.

... **"excludes surrender, ... does not preclude defeat" ...** Siegfried Kracauer, *From Caligari to Hitler* (New York, 1960), pp. 261–63.

... **"I have chosen this task" ...** "Der Weg zur Freiheit muss erkämpft werden," *VB*, January 22–23, 1933 (#22–23).

4. *Schleicher Falls Victim to Illusions*

... Schleicher attended ... *La Princesse de Trébizonde* **...** "Politische Hellseherei," *V*, January 3, 1933 (#3).

... a seamstress ... died after being shot by a Nazi ... "Eine blutige Silvesternacht," *V*, January 2, 1933 (#2); "Mörder aus der Ackerstrasse verhaftet," *V*, January 8, 1933 (#19).

... the murderer ... later testified ... "Die Bluttat in der Sylvesternacht," *FZ*, January 10, 1933 (#24–25).

... another Nazi stabbed a ... Communist ... "Drei politische Morde," *BT*, January 2, 1933 (#2); "Drei Todesopfer der Neujahrsnacht," *VZ*, January 2, 1933 (#2).

... a sixteen-year-old member of the Hitler Youth ... succumbed ... *ibid.*

... more than half of the jobless in Berlin ... Eve Rosenhaft, "The Unemployed in the Neighborhood," in *The German Unemployed*, edited by Richard J. Evans and Dick Geary (London, 1987), p. 207.

... An American journalist calculated ... Hubert R. Knickerbocker, *The German Crisis* (New York, 1932), pp. 23–25.

... Malnutrition, especially among children ... Rosenhaft, "The Unemployed," pp. 207f.; Ruth Weiland, *Die Kinder der Arbeitslosen* (Berlin, 1933), pp. 8–15.

... many had lost their homes ... Bruno Nelissen Haken, *Stempelchronik* (Hamburg, 1932); Knickerbocker, *Crisis*, pp. 26–28.

... radio address to the nation ... *AdRk/KvS*, pp. 101–17.

... [Schleicher] would need at least two years free ... IfZ, ED 93, Bd. 33, "Dienstag, den 10. Januar 1933 Unterhaltung mit Reichskanzler von Schleicher," by Josef Reiner of the Ullstein Verlag; BAK, Sammlung Brammer, ZSg 101/26, "Informationsbericht vom 14. Januar 1933," by Georg Dertinger; Moscow Document (see Appendix).

... By focusing public attention on national security ... Schleicher's press aide explained this strategy to a journalist on January 10. See BAK,

Sammlung Brammer, ZSg 101/26, "Informationsbericht vom 11. Januar 1933," by Georg Dertinger.

... Schleicher's view ... formation of a compulsory militia ... In a "Kurzorientierung" prepared for Schleicher on January 21, 1933, his aide at the Defense Ministry, Colonel Ferdinand von Bredow, reported having promoted "our concept" of "compulsory militia and retention of the professional army," to which Schleicher responded with the marginal notation, "good": Bredow Papers, BA/MA, N 97/3. At dinner with journalists on January 13, Schleicher specified that he saw a militia as a means of achieving universal military conscription: IfZ, ED 93, Bd. 33, "13.I.33," by Josef Reiner of the Ullstein Verlag.

... Otto Braun ... paid the chancellor a visit ... Braun, *Von Weimar,* pp. 436–38; Heinrich August Winkler, *Der Weg in die Katastrophe* (Berlin, 1987), p. 831, n. 143.; Hagen Schulze, *Otto Braun oder Preussens demokratische Sendung,* (Frankfurt/Main, 1977), pp. 773–76.

... "modus vivendi" ... Schleicher's draft of a letter to the *Vossische Zeitung,* January 30, 1934, Thilo Vogelsang, "Zur Politik Schleichers gegenüber der NSDAP 1932," *VfZ* 6 (1958), p. 90.

... As Schleicher ... explained to a gathering of generals ... Thilo Vogelsang, "Neue Dokumente zur Geschichte der Reichswehr," *VfZ* 2 (1954), pp. 426–29.

... feared its breakup would release energy and talent ... IfZ, ED 93, Bd. 33, "Dienstag, den 10. Januar 1933 Unterhaltung mit Reichskanzler von Schleicher," by Josef Reiner of the Ullstein Verlag; *DBFP, 1919–1939,* 2d series, vol. 4, p. 386, Rumbold to Simon, January 11, 1933.

... view shared by many observers and accepted by ... historians ... Among those who thought Schleicher was seeking to split the Nazi Party were Papen (*Gasse,* p. 244) and Meissner (Quaatz diary entry of December 16, 1932), in Weiss and Hoser, eds., *Deutschnationalen,* p. 218. Schleicher's finance minister, Lutz Graf Schwerin von Krosigk, still believed that had been Schleicher's aim when he wrote his memoirs many years later. See Schwerin von Krosigk, *Staatsbankrott* (Göttingen, 1974), p. 156.

... visit with Hindenburg ... for Strasser ... This meeting has been variously dated, but Schleicher's Chancellery press aide specified to a journalist on January 10 that it had occurred on January 6. BAK, Sammlung Brammer, ZSg 101/26, "Informationsbericht vom 11. Januar 1933," by

Georg Dertinger. On the secrecy, see Gustav Stolper, "Umsturz," *Der Deutsche Volkswirt* 7 (1933), p. 564.

... **president ... expressed relief at finding nothing radical about Strasser** ... Meissner, *Staatssekretär,* pp. 251f.; also Meissner's testimony at Papen's de-Nazification trial, January 31, 1947: Amtsgericht München, Spruchkammerakten F. von Papen, S. 218.

... **Schleicher himself estimated ... about 60 of the 196** ... Moscow Document (see Appendix).

... **As Schleicher admitted to his cabinet** ... *AdRk/KvS,* pp. 233, 235.

... **Meanwhile, Schleicher encouraged talk of a split** ... See Braun, *Von Weimar,* p. 432; see also *DDF, 1932–1939,* series 1, vol. 2, p. 375, dispatch of January 7 by Ambassador François-Poncet, who recognized that Schleicher was seeking to exert pressure on Hitler.

... **he had his staff indicate to the press** ... BAK, Sammlung Brammer, ZSg 101/26, "Informationsbericht vom 11. Januar 1933" by Georg Dertinger (reporting on long conversation with Erich Marcks, Schleicher's Chancellery press spokesman, on January 10); Moscow Document (see Appendix); "Die Lage des Kabinetts," *FZ,* January 15, 1933 (#39–40).

... **To discourage Hitler from stalling** ... BAK, Sammlung Brammer, ZSg 101/26, "Informationsbericht vom 14. Januar 1933," by Georg Dertinger; "Gregor Strasser war bei Hindenburg," *DAZ,* January 12, 1933 (#19); "Schleicher warnt," *DAZ,* January 14, 1933 (#24); "Die Lage des Kabinetts," *FZ,* January 15, 1933 (#39–40); "Kaas bei Schleicher," *BT,* January 17, 1933 (#27); "Dem neuen Kampf entgegen," *FZ,* January 18, 1933 (#17); *DBFP, 1919–1939,* 2d series, vol. 4, p. 387, Rumbold to Simon, January 16, 1933.

... **"Hitler's on the verge of desperation"** ... IfZ, ED 93, Bd. 33, "Dienstag, den 10. Januar 1933 Unterhaltung mit Reichskanzler von Schleicher," by Josef Reiner of the Ullstein Verlag.

... **"I'll take care of them"** ... Moscow Document (see Appendix).

... **His goal, ... force ... Nazis to abandon their "messianic beliefs"** ... BAK, Sammlung Brammer, ZSg 101/26, "Informationsbericht vom 14. Januar 1933," by George Dertinger; Moscow Document (see Appendix).

... **"He perhaps inclines to underestimate"** ... Diary of Colonel von Thaer for July 1918, quoted in Vogelsang, *Schleicher,* p. 18.

... "Hitler has almost as bad an effect on Hindenburg ..." IfZ, ED 93, Bd. 33: "Dienstag, den 10. Januar 1933 Unterhaltung mit Reichskanzler von Schleicher," by Josef Reiner of the Ullstein Verlag.

... [Hitler] did not "at the bottom of his heart" want the office ... Vogelsang, "Neue Dokumente," p. 426.

... Nazi leader's demands ... meant for Hindenburg's ears ... BAK, Sammlung Brammer, ZSg 101/26, "Informationsbericht vom 14. Januar 1933," by Georg Dertinger; Moscow Document (see Appendix).

... suspected that their telephones were tapped ... Brüning, *Memoiren*, pp. 395–98; Papen, *Gasse*, p. 280; Magnus von Braun, *Weg durch vier Zeitepochen* (Limburg/Lahn, 1965), p. 258; Erasmus Jonas, *Die Volkskonservativen, 1928–1933* (Düsseldorf, 1965), p. 148, n. 8.

... letters forwarded ... by former ... crown prince ... The prince's informant was ex-major general Franz Ritter von Hörauf, who headed the "Wehramt" of the Nazi Party. See, for examples of his letters, Hentschel, *Weimars letzte Monate*, pp. 150–54; *AdRk/KvS*, pp. 154–56, 221–24, 233, n. 13.

... On January 10 ... [Schleicher] and his press secretary planted reports ... BAK, Sammlung Brammer, ZSg 101/26: "Informationsbericht vom 11. Januar 1933," by Georg Dertinger; IfZ, ED 93, Bd. 33: "Dienstag, den 10. Januar 1933 Unterhaltung mit Reichskanzler von Schleicher," by Josef Reiner of the Ullstein Verlag.

... Schleicher specified in briefing one journalist ... *ibid.* (Reiner).

... To ratchet up the pressure on Hitler ... BAK, Sammlung Brammer, ZSg 101/26: "Informationsbericht vom 11. Januar 1933," by Georg Dertinger. See also "Gregor Strasser war bei Hindenburg," *DAZ*, January 12, 1933 (#19).

... [Schleicher] did not intend to initiate a meeting with Hitler ... IfZ, ED 93, Bd. 33: "Dienstag, den 10. Januar 1933 Unterhaltung mit Reichskanzler von Schleicher," by Josef Reiner of the Ullstein Verlag; *AdRk/KvS*, p. 230, n. 3 (quotation from *MZ* of January 13–14).

... Informed political observers immediately responded ... *ibid.;* BAK, Sammlung Brammer, ZSg 101/26: "Informationsbericht vom 11. Januar 1933," by Georg Dertinger; "Dreigespann Strasser-Hugenberg-Stegerwald?", *VZ*, January 14, 1933 (#23); Peter Reinhold, "Das System,"

VZ, January 15, 1933 (#25); *DBFP, 1919–1939*, 2d series, vol. 4, p. 387, Rumbold to Simon, January 16, 1933.

... Schleicher offered [Hugenberg] the ministries of agriculture and economics ... See Quaatz's diary entry of January 21, 1933: Weiss and Hoser, eds., *Deutschnationalen*, p. 224.

... Hugenberg ... willing to enter the cabinet only if ... *AdRk/KvS*, p. 234, n. 15; "Wird Hugenberg Krisenminister?" *NPZ*, January 14, 1933 (#14); "Unsere Meinung," *DAZ*, January 17, 1933 (#28).

... newspaper of the Christian Unions announced ... *Der Deutsche*, January 16, quoted in "Was wird Schleicher tun?" *FZ*, January 17, 1933 (#45).

... Monsignor Ludwig Kaas, visited the chancellor ... "Kaas bei Schleicher," *VZ*, January 17, 1933 (#27); "Kaas drängt auf Entscheidung," *VZ*, January 17, 1933 (#28); *AdRk/KvS*, p. 234; Rudolf Morsey, "Die deutsche Zentrumspartei," in *Das Ende der Parteien 1933*, edited by Erich Matthias and Rudolf Morsey (Düsseldorf, 1960), p. 335.

... [Schleicher's] sole concession to reality ... *AdRk/KvS*, p. 234.

... Hugenberg came under increasing pressure ... Weiss and Hoser, eds., *Deutschnationalen*, pp. 224f.

... [Hugenberg] agreed to a strongly worded party resolution ... The published text is in *SEG* (1933), p. 26. A slightly different version, found in Hugenberg's papers, is in *AdRk/KvS*, pp. 282f.

... a copy was personally delivered ... on January 21 ... Otto Schmidt-Hannover, *Umdenken oder Anarchie* (Göttingen, 1959), pp. 323f.

... By the 21st the chancellor was himself disclaiming ... See Quaatz's diary entry for that date: Weiss and Hoser, eds., *Deutschnationalen*, p. 224.

... [Schleicher] ... reacted angrily to rightist charges ... BAK, Sammlung Brammer, ZSg 101/26, "Informationsbericht vom 11. Januar 1933," by Georg Dertinger, to whom Schleicher's press aide, Erich Marcks, relayed on January 10 the chancellor's resentment at attacks on him two days earlier in the *Hamburger Nachrichten* and the *Allgemeine Zeitung* of Chemnitz. See also the report on Schleicher's outburst against one of the same rightist journalists on January 13: Moscow Document (see Appendix).

... Schleicher also undercut his threat ... IfZ, ED 93, Bd. 33, "13.I.33," by one of those present, Josef Reiner of the Ullstein Verlag. Also, Moscow Document (see Appendix).

... January 16, Schleicher said ... same thing to his cabinet ... *AdRk/ KvS,* p. 231.

... possibility ... violation of the constitution by the chancellor ... See, for examples, "Hitler in Berlin," *DAZ,* January 17, 1933 (#28); "Schleicher und Hitler kampfbereit," *FZ,* January 20, 1933 (#54); *AdRk/KvS,* p. 267, n. 2.

... idea of ... "presidential party" ... *AdRk/FvP,* vol. 1, p. 477 (Schleicher to cabinet meeting of August 30, 1932); IfZ, ED 93, Bd. 33, "Dienstag, den 10. Januar 1933 Unterhaltung mit Reichskanzler von Schleicher," by Josef Reiner of Ullstein Verlag.

... Apprehension about such a breach ... Catholic Center ... See the letter of Centrist leader Ludwig Kaas to Schleicher, January 26, 1933: *AdRk/ KvS,* pp. 304f.

... For the Social Democrats ... confirmed ... misgivings ... "Eine Warnung Breitscheids an Hitler," *FZ,* January 21, 1933 (#55–56).

... anti-republican conservatives greeted the reports ... "Unsere Meinung," *DAZ,* January 18, 1933 (#29); "Staatsnotstand," *NPZ,* January 22, 1933 (#22).

... Chancellery issued a denial ... Official statement of January 24. *SEG* (1933), p. 27.

... "Yes, sonny boy" ... IfZ, ZS 37, interview of Hermann Foertsch, press aide to Schleicher at the Defense Ministry, by Wolfgang Sauer, January 28 and 31, 1953, pp. 11f.

... increasingly infrequent cabinet meetings ... Whereas Papen's cabinet had met on the average more than twice a week, Schleicher's met less than once a week. See *AdRk/FvP* and *AdRk/KvS.*

... the experience ... of Günther Gereke ... Gereke complained about his treatment at the hands of Schleicher in a conversation with a journalist on January 5. BAK, ZSg 101/26, Sammlung Brammer, "Informationsbericht vom 5. Januar 1933," by Georg Dertinger.

... chancellor instructed the two ministers to ... compromise ... *AdRk/KvS,* p. 1, n. 5; p. 106.

… threats of resignation … See the letter of Agriculture Minister Magnus von Braun to Schleicher, January 5, 1933, in *AdRk/KvS,* pp. 186–89.

… minister of agriculture … "true torture" … von Braun, *Weg,* p. 261. For foreign consumption, von Braun portrayed Schleicher's cabinet in a much more positive light; see the report of British Ambassador Sir Horace Rumbold on a conversation with him on January 29: *DBFP, 1919–1939,* 2d series, vol. 4, p. 397.

… reports of coolness on the president's side … See, for examples, Weiss and Hoser, eds., *Deutschnationalen,* p. 218 (Quaatz diary, December 16, 1932); Jonas, *Volkskonservativen,* p. 129, n. 3.

… openly conceding … less cordial relations … See BAK, Sammlung Brammer, ZSg 101/26, "Informationsbericht vom 11. Januar 1933," by Georg Dertinger (report on conversation with Schleicher's Chancellery press spokesman Erich Marcks on January 10). That same day, Schleicher tried to put a good face on the matter by assuring another journalist that his relations with both the president and his son, Oskar, had improved: IfZ, ED 39, Bd. 33, "Dienstag, den 10. Januar 1933 Unterhaltung mit Reichskanzler von Schleicher," by Josef Reiner of the Ullstein Verlag.

… That view was widely held in the capital's political circles … When the subject came up in a journalist's conversation with Schleicher's Chancellery press spokesman, Erich Marcks, on January 10, the journalist remarked afterward that Marcks became "uncharacteristically excited" in denying the rumors that Schleicher had deserted Papen: BAK, Sammlung Brammer, ZSg 101/26, "Informationsbericht vom 11. Januar 1933," by Georg Dertinger.

… [Schleicher] would be … expected to defend his predecessor's record … BAK, R43 I/1504, Bl. 93: Meissner to Planck, December 14, 1932.

… By January he was making caustic comments … At dinner with journalists on January 13, Schleicher referred disparagingly to Papen's "romantic clichés." As a result of Papen's reckless statements, he told the journalists, there would have been a general strike if Papen had remained in office three days longer, in which case he (Schleicher) would have been forced to send the army into the streets with machine guns. See IfZ, ED 93, Bd. 33, "13.I.33," by Josef Reiner of the Ullstein Verlag. The similar report of one of the other journalists present soon reached Papen: Moscow Document (see Appendix).

... Gereke ... intimate of the Hindenburg family ... See Gereke's memoirs, *Ich war Königlich-preussischer Landrat* (Berlin, 1970), pp. 176ff.

... [Papen] stayed on in the apartment ... Hans-Otto Meissner, *30. Januar '33* (Esslingen, 1976), pp. 186–88.

... Hindenburg had ... taken over the apartment ... *ibid.*

... Schleicher did not reside in the Wilhelmstrasse complex ... *ibid.*, p. 187; Vogelsang, *Schleicher,* p. 72.

... Schleicher ... continued to rely ... on his military staff ... On constitutional questions, he called upon Lieutenant Colonel Eugen Ott. See *AdRk/KvP,* vol. 1, pp. 579–80, esp. n. 11. Schleicher assigned another officer, Hanshenning von Holtzendorff, to work on rural resettlement: IfZ, ZS/A, 36/2, Holtzendorff to Graf Borke, May 3, 1949. Schleicher's chief aide at the Defense Ministry, Colonel Ferdinand von Bredow, handled many matters of a more general political nature; See Bredow's papers: BA/MA, N 97/1–3.

... conversation with an Austrian diplomat ... AdR, NPA 11 (Gesandtschaftsberichte Berlin), Josef Meindl, Geschäftsträger, to Engelbert Dollfuss, February 9, 1933.

... Agrarian League, complained to [Hindenburg] on January 11 ... *AdRk/KvS,* pp. 206–08.

... Hindenburg responded ... by peremptorily summoning ... *ibid.*, pp. 208–14. See also a later version of the meeting by one of the Nazis among the League spokesmen present: Bracher, *Die Auflösung,* pp. 697f.

... the Nazis had infiltrated the League ... Horst Gies, "NSDAP und landwirtschaftliche Organisationen in der Endphase der Weimarer Republik," *VfZ* 15 (1967), pp. 341–76. Schleicher was aware of the Nazis' domination of the League. See his remarks to journalists on January 13: IfZ, ED 93, Bd. 33, "13.I.33," by Josef Reiner of the Ullstein Verlag.

... the League's ... harshly worded resolution ... *AdRk/KvS,* p. 214, n. 16.

... statement denouncing the League for a breach ... *ibid.*

... [Hindenburg] became a landowner ... See Wolfgang Wessling, "Hindenburg, Neudeck und die deutsche Wirtschaft," *VfS&Wg* 64 (1977), pp. 41–73.

... president received letters and telegrams ... Gies, "NSDAP und landwirtschaftliche Organisationen," p. 374, n. 164.

... the president addressed a cordial letter ... BAK, R43 II/192, Bl. 109. For the cabinet's action of January 17 on foreclosure protection, see *AdRk/ KvS,* pp. 247f.

... charges of fraud at Junker beneficiaries ... *SEG* (1933), pp. 23–24. See also *AdRk/KvS,* p. 237, n. 22; p. 319, n. 15.

... dismissed ... committee meetings ... as a "fool's game" ... Vogelsang, "Neue Dokumente," p. 427 (Schleicher to a meeting of generals, December 13–15, 1932).

... rumors ... damaging information leaked to the committee ... *DDF, 1932–1939,* series 1, vol. 2, p. 547 (François-Poncet to Paul-Boncour, February 1, 1933).

... "absolutely certain" ... BAK, Sammlung Brammer, ZSg 101/26, "Informationsbericht vom 11. Januar 1933," by Georg Dertinger.

... Schleicher spoke with such confidence about his plans ... Moscow Document (see Appendix); BAK, Sammlung Brammer, ZSg 101/26, "Informationsbericht vom 14. Januar 1933," by Georg Dertinger.

... Gereke ... revealed ... that Oskar von Hindenburg had ... confided ... *ibid.*

... flat assurance: Hindenburg had already granted ... Moscow Document (see Appendix).

... matter was simple ... Hindenburg had promised ... IfZ, interview of March 30, 1951, with Erich Freiherr von dem Bussche-Ippenburg, who headed the personnel office of the Defense Ministry from 1930 to 1933: IfZ, ZS 217. In the draft of a letter dated January 30, 1934, which he addressed to the *Vossische Zeitung* but which was apparently not sent, Schleicher referred to the sudden withdrawal of the "solemnly promised support of the president": Vogelsang, "Zur Politik Schleichers," p. 90. See also the account of Schleicher's sister: Vogelsang, *Reichswehr,* p. 336, n. 1590. According to another member of the Defense Ministry staff, Eugen Ott, Schleicher had expressed doubts during January about the extent of Hindenburg's confidence in him: IfZ, ZS 279, Ott's "Bemerkungen zu den Akten des Instituts für Zeitgeschichte," February 18, 1952, p. 7.

... Meissner cautioned that such a step would compromise ... *AdRk/ KvS,* p. 235.

... Schleicher mentioned in passing ... IfZ, ZS/A-20, Bd. 4, "The Beginning and the End" (excerpts from diary of Lutz Graf Schwerin von Krosigk), entry dated January 22, p. 11 (the conversation with Schleicher is not dated). In the draft of a letter to the editors of the *Vossische Zeitung* written by Schleicher in January 1934 but never published, he mentioned that fourteen days before his fall, the president had pressed him to dissolve the parliament: Vogelsang, "Zur Politik Schleichers," p. 90.

... press office ... conceded to journalists ... BAK, Sammlung Brammer, ZSg 101/26, "Informationsbericht vom 19. January 1933," by Georg Dertinger.

... To the frustration of Gereke, ... Gereke, *Landrat,* pp. 213ff.; Moscow Document (see Appendix); Helmut Marcon, *Arbeitsbeschaffungspolitik der Regierungen Papen und Schleicher* (Frankfurt/Main, 1974), pp. 303–10; Michael Schneider, *Das Arbeitsbeschaffungsprogramm des ADGB* (Bohn-Bad Godesberg, 1975), pp. 200–202.

... Schleicher temporized ... See the notes of Gustav Krupp von Bohlen und Halbach on his conversation with Schleicher on January 12, 1933: Krupp-Archiv, FAH 23/793, Bl. 226–29. Cf. Schleicher's remarks to the spokesmen of the Agrarian League a day earlier: *AdRk/KvS,* pp. 210–12.

... [Schleicher] spent most of the evening setting forth his strategy ... Moscow Document (see Appendix); IfZ, ED 93, Bd. 33, "13.I.33," by Josef Reiner of the Ullstein Verlag.

... On January 15 ... speech to ... retired army officers ... *SEG* (1933), pp. 19f., speech to Kyffhäuserbund in Berlin. See also Geyer, *Aufrüstung oder Sicherheit,* pp. 302f.

... Chancellery press office led journalists to believe ... "Aussprache Papens mit Hitler," *MNN,* January 19, 1933 (#18); "Papen-Hitler-Schleicher," *VZ,* January 18, 1933 (#30); "Wahlen am 19, Februar?" *NPZ,* January 19, 1933 (#19).

... January 20 ... agenda committee of the Reichstag met ... Goebbels, *TbJG,* part I, vol. 2, p. 344; "Vertagung bis 31. Januar," *VZ,* January 21, 1933 (#35); "Die NSDAP weicht aus," *FZ,* January 21, 1933 (#57); "Reichstag vertagt," *V,* January 21, 1933 (#35); "Unbequeme Wahrheit," *V,* January

21, 1933 (#36); "Reichstag vertagt sich wieder!" *TR,* January 21, 1933 (#18); "Reichstag am 31. Januar," *KZ,* January 21, 1933 (#40); "Acht Tage Aufschub," *BT,* January 21, 1933 (#35); "Ein kurzer Zeitgewinn," *G,* January 21, 1933 (#21); "Das schlechte Gewissen," *BT,* January 22, 1933 (#37).

... Frick was ... a cautious man ... Günter Neliba, *Wilhelm Frick* (Paderborn, 1992), pp. 66–68. Earlier in January, Frick said in a speech that he favored postponing the reconvening of the Reichstag: "Hitlers Abstecher nach Berlin," *FZ,* January 12, 1933 (#32).

... "We must gain time" ... *TbJG,* part I, vol. 2, p. 343.

... budget could not ... be ready before the spring ... "Hitlers Schwenkung," *BT,* January 11, 1933 (#18); "Das schlechte Gewissen," *BT,* January 22, 1933 (#37); "Kein Staatsnotstand!" *VZ,* January 24, 1933 (#40).

... Although ... enough support ... to approve Frick's motion ... On the Center Party's readiness, see Brüning, *Memoiren,* p. 645. On that of the German-Nationals, see remarks of Oskar Hergt in "Geldnot der N.S.D.A.P.," *BT,* January 12, 1933 (#19); also "Reichstag am 31. Januar," *KZ,* January 21, 1933 (#40).

... Planck telephoned former chancellor Brüning ... Brüning, *Memoiren,* p. 645.

5. The Conspiracy Widens and Schleicher Relinquishes Power

... policemen invaded Karl Liebknecht House ... The following descriptions are based on press reports: "Abgekapselt," *VZ,* January 23, 1933 (#38); "Bannmeile um den Bülowplatz," *V,* January 23, 1933 (#38); "Das Spiel mit dem Bürgerkrieg," *V,* January 23, 1933 (#38); "Berlin bleibt rot!" *V,* January 23, 1933; (#38); "Militärische Lage," *V,* January 24, 1933 (#39); "Wunder der Strategie," *BT,* January 24, 1933 (#39); "Bülowplatz 22. Januar," *BT,* January 24, 1933 (#39); "Ein kleineres Übel—riesengross," *VZ,* January 24, 1933 (#39).

... Berlin stormtrooper recalled it ... Stelzner, *Schicksal SA,* pp. 142f.

... "The Commies raging in the side streets" ... *TbJG,* part I, vol. 2, p. 347.

... Goebbels had feared ... government would put a stop ... *ibid.*, p. 345.

... republican observers suspected ... a conciliatory gesture ... "Anklage und Aufruf," *V*, January 22, 1933 (#37); Theodor Wolff, "Der gefährliche Bülowplatz," *BT*, January 22, 1933 (#37).

... "eerie fatalism" ... "Schöpferische Vorsicht?" *G*, January 22, 1933 (#22).

... "Olympian detachment" ... "Entweder—oder," *FZ*, January 24, 1933 (#64).

... January 22, two men and their wives took seats ... The following is based on the account attributed to Meissner after his death by his son: Hans-Otto Meissner, *30. Januar*, pp. 230f. Oskar von Hindenburg questioned this account of the visit to the opera in a letter to the magazine where the younger Meissner first published it: "Von Neudeck ist nicht gesprochen worden ... ," *Weltbild*, December 1957 (vol. 12, no. 26), p. 14. In the original draft of an affidavit of September 28, 1945, for the Nuremberg war crimes tribunal, however, the elder Meissner mentioned being at the opera before going to Ribbentrop's: NAUSA, RG 238, 3309-PS.

... Papen had set out to widen the conspiracy ... See Meissner's testimony at the trial of German Foreign Ministry officials before the American tribunal at Nuremberg, May 4, 1948: NAUSA, RG 238, Case 11, pp. 4612f.

... evening of January 20, Papen could inform Ribbentrop ... Ribbentrop, *Zwischen*, p. 39.

... "thick-featured, churlish and ill-educated" ... François-Poncet, *Souvenirs*, p. 43.

... "I foresee a great future" ... Vogelsang, *Schleicher*, p. 18.

... Something Schleicher said to the younger Hindenburg ... Asked about his relations with Schleicher while testifying at Papen's de-Nazification trial on January 28, 1947, Oskar said they had become estranged over a personal matter: Amtsgericht München, Spruchkammerakten F. von Papen, Bl. 104. On January 29, 1933, Gottfried Treviranus, a conservative politician who knew both men, told British Ambassador Sir Horace Rumbold that the trouble had started when the younger Hindenburg had "in an improper manner, transgressed his function as adjutant to his father": *DBFP, 1919–1939*, 2d series, vol. 4, p. 396. But a member of Schleicher's staff at the

Defense Ministry in 1932–33 who was questioned about the matter after the war attributed the estrangement to a mocking remark Schleicher had made to Oskar: IfZ, ZS 37, interview of Hermann Foertsch by Wolfgang Sauer, January 28 and 31, 1953, p. 9. Another officer who served at the Defense Ministry at the time, Erich Freiherr von Bussche-Ippenburg, similarly referred, in a letter written in 1953, to Schleicher's having mocked Oskar von Hindenburg: Kunrat von Hammerstein, "Schleicher, Hammerstein und die Machtübernahme 1933," *FH* 11 (1956), p. 119.

... baroness ... referred to Schleicher ... as "our Fouché" ... Magnus von Braun, *Weg,* p. 259.

... "an eerie personage ... florid-faced, puffed-up" ... François-Poncet, *Souvenirs,* p. 43f.

... late-evening gathering at Ribbentrop's on January 22 ... The following is based mainly on Meissner's accounts after the war: Meissner, *Staatssekretär,* pp. 263f.; NAUSA, RG 59, Microcopy M 679, roll 2, report on the interrogation of Meissner, October 26, 1945; NAUSA, RG 238, 3309-PS, affidavit of November 28, 1945; testimony of January 31, 1947, at Papen's de-Nazification trial, Amtsgericht München, Spruchkammer Akten F. von Papen, Bl. 222; testimony of May 4, 1948, at the trial of Foreign Ministry officials before the American tribunal at Nuremberg, NAUSA, RG 238, Case 11, pp. 4615f.; affidavit of February 3, 1949, for Oskar von Hindenburg's de-Nazification trial of March 14–17, 1949: NSHSAH, Nds. 171 Lüneburg Uzn/11363, Spruchkammer Verfahren gegen Oskar von Hindenburg, Bd. I, Bl. 2f. See also Oskar's testimony of March 14, 1949, at his own de-Nazification trial, Bl. 26f., and at Papen's de-Nazification trial on January 28, 1947 (see above), p. 110. Unreliable is Papen's testimony of March 15, 1949, at Oskar's de-Nazification trial: Bl. 133f.; also Papen, *Gasse,* pp. 265f.; *Scheitern,* pp. 369f.

... Two months earlier ... remarkably perceptive memorandum ... This document, identified as coming from the elder Hindenburg's papers and dated November 21, 1932, was read into the record of Oskar's de-Nazification trial on March 14, 1949 (see preceding note), Bl. 25–27. Günther Gereke testified that same day at the trial that during a long walk in the Tiergarten park in Berlin during January 1933 Oskar had strongly opposed Hitler's appointment as chancellor, Bl. 51. In his affidavit of February 3, 1949, for Oskar's trial, Meissner wrote that until the end of January, Oskar remained opposed to Hitler's appointment and favored a return by Papen, trial records, Bd. I, Bl. 2. In his testimony of May 4, 1948, at the trial of Foreign Ministry officials, Meissner had said the same thing: NAUSA, RG 238, Case 11, p. 4615.

... no plausible grounds for such blackmail ... It has repeatedly been contended that Hitler might have threatened to reveal that when the elder Hindenburg had been presented with his country estate in East Prussia in 1927, the title had been assigned to Oskar in order to avoid payment of an inheritance tax when the president died. That information had, however, already been made public in November 1932: Wessling, "Hindenburg, Neudeck," pp. 41–54.

... Oskar ... at his de-Nazification trial ... NSHSAH, Nds. 171 Lüneburg Uzn/11363, Spruchkammerverfahren gegen Oskar von Hindenburg, 14.-17. März 1949, Bl. 26–28.

... "the personification of stupidity" ... *TbJG,* part I, vol. 2, p. 349f.

... Meissner later recalled that during their taxi ride ... NAUSA, RG 59, Microcopy M679, report on interrogation of Meissner, October 26, 1945; *ibid.,* RG 238, 3309-PS, affidavit by Meissner, November 28, 1945; *ibid.,* Case 11, p. 4616, Meissner's testimony of May 4, 1948, at the trial of Foreign Ministry officials before the American tribunal at Nuremberg.

... January 23, Papen called on Hindenburg ... Ribbentrop, *Zwischen,* p. 39.

... As Hindenburg privately confided to a conservative ... Ewald von Kleist-Schmenzin, "Die letzte Möglichkeit," *PS* 10 (1959), p. 89.

... When the president called in Meissner and Oskar ... NAUSA, RG 238, Case 11, pp. 4614, Meissner's testimony at the trial of Foreign Office officials before the American tribunal at Nuremberg, May 4, 1948.

... January 23, Meissner received a telephone call from Schleicher ... NAUSA, RG 59, Microcopy M679, report on interrogation of Meissner, October 26, 1945; NAUSA, RG 238, 3309-PS, affidavit by Meissner, November 28, 1945.

... memorandum prepared by his staff at the Defense Ministry ... *AdRk/KvS,* pp. 241–43.

... a gap in the republic's constitution ... *ibid.,* p. 242, n. 39; Ernst Fraenkel, "Verfassungsreform und Sozialdemokratie," *Die Gesellschaft* 9 (1932), 486, 493–95; Walter Simons, "Die Stellung des Reichspräsidenten,"

Deutsche Juristen-Zeitung 38 (1933), pp. 22–27; Joseph Bendersky, *Carl Schmitt* (Princeton, N.J., 1983), pp. 180f.; Eberhard Kolb and Wolfram Pyta, "Die Staatsnotstandsplanung unter den Regierungen Papen und Schleicher," in *Die Deutsche Staatskrise 1930–33*, edited by Heinrich August Winkler (Munich, 1992), p. 157, n. 6.

... **Wilhelm Simpfendörfer** ... A deputy of the Christlich-Sozialer Volksdienst, Simpfendörfer first presented his proposal to Schleicher in person on January 19, then submitted it in a letter of January 24: *AdRk/KvS*, pp. 297–300.

... **Bavarian envoy ... made the same proposal** ... See the memorandum of Franz Sperr, December 1, 1932, in Vogelsang, *Reichswehr*, pp. 482–84.

... **a precedent ... set by the republican cabinet in ... Württemberg** ... *AdRk/KvS*, p. 299, Simpfendörfer to Schleicher, January 24, 1933. See also Waldemar Besson, *Württemberg und die deutsche Staatskrise 1928–1933* (Stuttgart, 1959), pp. 264–73.

... **remark ... during his off-the-record dinner** ... BAK, Sammlung Brammer, ZSg 101/26, "Informationsbericht vom 14. Januar 1933," by Georg Dertinger; Moscow Document (see Appendix).

... **"Option 1!"** ... *AdRk/KvS*, p. 243, n. 40.

... **warning that the president's son had turned against him** ... Brüning, *Memoiren*, p. 645.

... **improvements in the capacity of the army** ... Wolfram Pyta, "Vorbereitungen für den militärischen Ausnahmezustand unter Papen/Schleicher," *MM* 51 (1992), pp. 393f., 410–28; Kolb and Pyta, "Die Staatsnotstandsplanung," p. 178f; Fritz Arndt, "Vorbereitungen der Reichswehr für den militärischen Ausnahmezustand," *ZfM* 4 (1965), pp. 202f.

... **Schleicher met with Hindenburg at eleven-thirty ... January 23** ... *AdRk/KvS*, p. 284f.

... **Schleicher suggested ... leaders of business and labor** ... This is not recorded in the memorandum on the meeting of January 23 with Hindenburg prepared by the president's office, but Schleicher mentioned it in a talk with two trade-union leaders on January 26: *AdRk/KvS*, p. 303.

... **"If we once get power"** ... Max Domarus, *Hitler: Reden und Proklamationen 1932–1945* (2 vols., Munich, 1965), Erster Halbband, p. 140, speech at Königsberg, October 17, 1932.

... cries of protest from the Centrists and Social Democrats ... "Auflösung ohne Neuwahl?" *VZ*, January 24, 1933 (#39); "Staatsstreich-Pläne," *V*, January 24, 1933 (#39); "Debatte ohne Abstimmung?" *BT*, January 25, 1933 (#41); "Bayerische Volkspartei gegen 'Staatsnotstand'," *VZ*, January 25, 1933 (#41); "Gegen reaktionäre Staatsstreichpläne!" *V*, January 26, 1933 (#43); "Warnung vor Staatsstreich," *BT*, January 26, 1933 (#43).

... Schleicher ... returned to that plan on January 26 ... *AdRk/KvS*, pp. 302f.

... "incitement to treason" ... *ibid.*, pp. 311f.

... trade-union leaders ... now distanced themselves from him ... See Richard Breitman, "On German Social Democracy and General Schleicher 1932–33," *CEH* 9 (1976), pp. 352–78. See also "Für ein sozialistisches Deutschland" *V*, January 25, 1933 (#41), report on a speech by Theodor Leipart, leader of the Free Trade Unions affiliated with the Social Democrats, who had previously adopted a conciliatory posture toward the Schleicher cabinet but now endorsed the party's oppositional stance.

... fixated on defending the letter of the constitution ... On the Center Party, see Detlef Junker, *Die Deutsche Zentrumspartei und Hitler 1932/33* (Stuttgart, 1969), pp. 118–26; Winkler, *Weimar*, p. 593f.

... Only the two small liberal parties ... Winkler, *Weimar*, p. 572; "Eine Erklärung der Deutschen Volkspartei," *FZ*, January 10, 1933 (#24–25); "Volkspartei und Regierung," *G*, January 16, 1933 (#16).

... François-Poncet ... analyzed the reasons ... *DDF, 1932–1939,* series I, vol. 2, pp. 478–81, dispatch of January 19, 1933.

... Schleicher made no attempt to stave off a showdown ... "Wieder Kanzlersturz?" *VZ*, January 27, 1933 (#45); "Der Beschluss des Ältestenrates," *VZ*, January 28 1933 (#47); "Dienstag Reichstag," *V*, January 28, 1933 (#47).

... Planck, informed the minister of finance ... *AdRk/KvS*, pp. 316f.

... "trepidation in the face of ultimate decisions." ... Brüning, *Memoiren*, p. 649.

... Theodor Wolff ... invincible master of ... intrigue ... See the excerpts from Wolff's unpublished manuscript, "Grabmal," quoted in Bernd Sösemann, *Das Ende der Weimarer Republik in der Kritik demokratischer Publizisten* (Berlin, 1976), p. 229f., n. 155.

... **When [Schleicher] met with Brüning two weeks later** ... Brüning, *Memoiren*, p. 648.

... **"That's how it always is:"** ... IfZ, ZS 37, Hermann Foertsch in interview with Wolfgang Sauer, January 28 and 31, 1953, p. 12. Another aide, Eugen Ott, recalled Schleicher's saying essentially the same thing: IfZ, ZS 279/270/52, interview of February 22, 1952.

... **[Schleicher] complained to Ambassador François-Poncet** ... *DDF, 1932–1939*, series 1, vol. 2, p. 375f.

... **Harsh press criticism** ... **stung Schleicher painfully.**... See his outburst of anger at a critical article in a rightist newspaper at the dinner for journalists on January 13: BAK, Sammlung Brammer, ZSg 101/26, "Informationsbericht vom 14. Januar 1933," by Georg Dertinger.

... **[Schleicher] confessed to feeling out of place** ... British Ambassador Sir Horace Rumbold reported on December 21, 1932, that Schleicher had that day told him he was not happy in the Chancellery and would prefer to return to the Defense Ministry: *DBFP, 1919–1939*, 2d series, vol. 4, p. 384. Otto Braun recalled a similar remark by Schleicher in their conversation of January 6, 1932: Braun, *Von Weimar*, p. 437. Ewald von Kleist-Schmenzin told Reinhard Quaatz on January 12, 1933, that Schleicher was making the same sentiment known: Weiss and Hoser, eds., *Deutschnationalen*, pp. 221f. On January 21, 1933, Meissner told Quaatz that Schleicher had spoken of returning to the Defense Ministry: *ibid.*, p. 224. See also the reminiscences of his aide at the Defense Ministry, Eugen Ott: "Ein Bild des Generals Kurt von Schleicher," *PS* 10 (1959), p. 371.

... **"Too bad that I have no propensity for megalomania"** ... Vogelsang, *Reichswehr*, p. 310, n. 1470.

... **rumors ... that Hindenburg intended to reappoint Papen** ... "Papen mit Hitler?" *VZ*, January 27, 1933 (#46); "Hugenberg am Werke," *BT*, January 27, 1933 (#45); "Wieder Kanzlersturz?" *VZ*, January 27, 1933 (#45); "Nochmals Papen?" *BT*, January 28, 1933 (#47); Rudolf Morsey, ed., *Die Protokolle der Reichstagsfraktion und Fraktionsvorstands der Deutschen Zentrumspartei 1926–1933* (Mainz, 1969), p. 610; Turner, *German Big Business*, pp. 318f.

... **January 27 ... Hammerstein, called on Schleicher** ... See the account written in 1935 by Hammerstein: Bracher, *Die Auflösung*, p. 733. Hammerstein dated this conversation and the meeting with Hindenburg that followed as January 26, but Bussche-Ippenburg (see next note) placed their meeting with Hindenburg on January 27, which seems more probable, since Bussche-Ippenburg's regular weekly conferences with Hindenburg took place on Fridays.

... Later on the morning of January 27, Hammerstein joined ... *Ibid.;* also the later accounts of the other general present, Erich Freiherr von dem Bussche-Ippenburg, "Hammerstein und Hindenburg," *FAZ,* February 5, 1952 (#30); IfZ, ZS 217, Aktenvermerk, dated April 7, 1951, on interview with Bussche-Ippenburg on March 30, 1951, p. 4.

... January 28, Schleicher informed his ministers ... *AdRk/KvS,* pp. 306–8.

... He began ... last meeting with Hindenburg ... *ibid.,* pp. 310f.

... Earlier that morning, Hindenburg had been visited by Papen ... Ribbentrop, *Zwischen,* p. 41; Papen, *Gasse,* p. 267.

... Hindenburg ... offended by an editorial ... *ibid.*

... Schleicher returned to inform the ... cabinet ... *AdRk/KvS,* pp. 308f., 317.

... final approval to ... job-creation program ... *ibid.,* pp. 309f.

... nearly two million unemployed ... found jobs ... *Statistische Beilage zum Reichsarbeitsblatt 1933,* no. 34, p. 1. In a forthcoming study, Professor Dan P. Silverman of Pennsylvania State University convincingly argues, on the basis of a close analysis of these statistics, that the numbers were not, as some scholars have contended, significantly inflated by the Nazi regime.

6. *Papen Leads the Plunge into the Abyss*

... January 28, the president commissioned Franz von Papen ... *SEG* (1933), p. 30.

... Since Hitler had gone to Munich ... Ribbentrop, *Zwischen,* p. 39. Ewald von Kleist-Schmenzin recalled in 1934 that on January 25 Papen had admitted that he was seeking to win Hindenburg's approval of Hitler as chancellor; see his "Die letzte Möglichkeit," p. 90.

... The Stahlhelm had dabbled in politics ... See Volker R. Berghahn, *Der Stahlhelm* (Düsseldorf, 1966).

... Seldte ... harbored political ambitions ... See Hermann Punder, *Politik in der Reichskanzlei* (Stuttgart, 1961), p. 125.

... friction between the Stahlhelm's leadership and the Defense Ministry ... See Geyer, *Aufrüstung oder Sicherheit*, p. 303; Berghahn, *Stahlhelm*, pp. 192ff., 233, 238.

... A stodgy, vain man ... See Leopold, *Hugenberg*.

... "His round gold-rim spectacles" ... François-Poncet, *Souvenirs*, p. 30.

... "He has no political sex appeal" ... Reinhold Quaatz's diary entry of December 23, 1932: Weiss and Hoser, eds., *Deutschnationalen*, p. 219.

... Upon Hitler's return to Berlin, Ribbentrop explained ... Ribbentrop, *Zwischen*, p. 40.

... Hitler, Frick and Göring met with Hugenberg ... *ibid.;* Schmidt-Hannover, *Umdenken*, p. 332f.; Weiss and Hoser, eds., *Deutschnationalen*, p. 228; Goebbels, *TbJG*, part 1, vol. 2, p. 353. On the Prussian police, see Christoph Graf, *Politische Polizei zwischen Demokratie und Diktatur* (Berlin, 1983).

... Furious ... Hitler broke off ... negotiations ... Ribbentrop, *Zwischen*, p. 40.

... Papen agreed to support Hitler's demands ... *ibid.*, p. 41.

... Papen expected to succeed Schleicher as commissar for Prussia ... *ibid.*

... January 28, Papen met with Hindenburg ... *ibid.*

... Papen asked Ribbentrop to locate Hitler ... *ibid.*

... Hitler now raised the stakes ... *ibid.*, pp. 41f.

... Papen set out to break Hugenberg's resistance ... Papen, *Gasse*, pp. 269f.; Schmidt-Hannover, *Umdenken*, p. 334.

... Papen won endorsement ... from most ... conservative ... ministers ... See the diary of Schwerin von Krosigk in *AdRk/KvS*, pp. 317f.

... Fritz Schäffer, approached both Hitler and Papen ... See Schäffer's testimony at Papen's de-Nazification trial on January 27, 1947: Amtsgericht München, Spruchkammerakten F. von Papen, Bl. 49, 56.

... Schäffer met with no greater receptivity from Papen ... *ibid.*, Bl. 49,

55, 56, 57. Later, when Schäffer had become a prominent figure in postwar German politics, he denied having proposed Catholic participation in a cabinet led by Hitler and claimed he had offered support only for a Papen cabinet, a version accepted by a number of historians. For a reliable account, see Falk Wiesemann, *Die Vorgeschichte der nationalsozialistischen Machtübernahme in Bayern 1932–1933* (Berlin, 1975), pp. 162–64; Otto Altendorfer, *Fritz Schäffer als Politiker der Bayerischen Volkspartei* (Munich, 1993), part 2, pp. 686–88.

... Goebbels found [Hitler] at the Kaiserhof Hotel ... *TbJG,* part I, vol. 2, pp. 353f.

... republican press ... issued repeated warnings ... "Auflösung wahrscheinlich unvermeidlich," *FZ,* January 26, 1933 (#70); "Hoffnung auf Hindenburg," *VZ,* January 27, 1933 (#45); "Acht nutzlose Tage," *BT,* January 27, 1933 (#46); "Warnung vor dem Staatsstreich," *V,* January 28, 1933 (#47); "Kanzlersturz und dann?" *VZ,* January 29, 1933 (#49); "Auf gefährlichem Wege," *BT,* January 29, 1933 (#49).

... Oskar ... won over ... after returning to Dahlem ... Ribbentrop, *Zwischen,* pp. 39f.

... similar advice from ... Oldenburg-Januschau ... Meissner, *Staatssekretär,* pp. 265f. In his own memoirs, Oldenburg-Januschau referred only very generally to conversations with Hindenburg: *Erinnerungen* (Leipzig, 1936), pp. 218f.

... the president received a reassuring message from Göring ... NAUSA, RG 238, Case 11, pp. 4617f., testimony on May 4, 1948 by Meissner (who said that he had relayed the message from Göring to Hindenburg).

... evening of the 28th, Papen called on Hindenburg ... Papen, *Gasse,* p. 271.

... Hindenburg passed over a general proposed by Papen ... *ibid.* Göring confirmed in 1938 that Blomberg had been chosen by Hindenburg, not by the Nazis: Anton Hoch and Christoph Weisz, "Die Erinnerungen des Generalobersten Wilhelm Adam," in *Miscellanea: Festschrift für Helmut Krausnick zum 75. Geburtstag,* edited by Wolfgang Benz et al. (Stuttgart, 1980), p. 41.

... Papen later recalled, ... promise to serve as vice chancellor ... Papen, *Gasse,* p. 271.

... instructing his son to telephone General von Blomberg ... See Oskar von Hindenburg's testimony at his de-Nazification trial on January 28, 1947: NSHSAH, Nds. 171, Lüneburg Uzn/11363, Bl. 107. See also Kunrat von Hammerstein, "Schleicher, Hammerstein," p. 167.

... general had made a favorable impression on the president ... Dorpalen, *Hindenburg,* p. 427.

... Earlier in January ... [Blomberg] visited Hindenburg in Berlin ... Otto Meissner claimed Blomberg had been ordered to Berlin on this earlier occasion without Schleicher's knowledge: *Staatssekretär,* p. 266. There is, however, evidence that Blomberg met with Schleicher on that occasion: Bennett, *German Rearmament,* p. 295.

... Blomberg ... had clashed repeatedly with Schleicher ... Hermann Foertsch, *Schuld und Verhängnis* (Stuttgart, 1951), p. 29; IfZ, ZS 37, interview with Foertsch by Wolfgang Sauer, January 28 and 31, 1953; Geyer, *Aufrüstung oder Sicherheit,* pp. 192, 208–13.

... Blomberg ... under ... influence of pro-Nazi elements ... Thilo Vogelsang, "Hitlers Brief an Reichenau vom 4. Dezember 1932," *VfZ* 7 (1959), pp. 429–33; Vogelsang, *Reichswehr,* p. 375; Thomas Martin Schneider, *Reichsbischof Ludwig Müller* (Göttingen, 1993), pp. 78, 91f.; Bennett, *German Rearmament,* pp. 296–301; Klaus-Jürgen Müller, *Das Heer und Hitler* (Stuttgart, 1969), pp. 49–52.

... Hitler ... kept his appointment at Papen's apartment ... Ribbentrop, *Zwischen,* p. 42.; Papen, *Gasse,* pp. 271f.; Ewald von Kleist-Schmenzin, "Die letzte Möglichkeit," p. 91.

... Hitler then introduced a new demand ... Ribbentrop, *Zwischen,* p. 42.

... afternoon of the 29th Papen set out to complete ... Schmidt-Hannover, *Umdenken,* pp. 329, 334; Schmidt-Hannover convincingly argues that this meeting is erroneous dated as January 26 in Düsterberg's memoir *Der Stahlhelm und Hitler* (Wolfenbüttel and Hanover, 1949), pp. 38f.

... Düsterberg and ... conservative figures ... vehemently opposed ... Kleist-Schmenzin, "Die letzte Möglichkeit," pp. 91f.; Schmidt-Hannover, *Umdenken,* pp. 334–36; Papen, *Gasse,* p. 272.

... Papen informed ... Nazis ... last obstacles ... removed ... Ribbentrop, *Zwischen,* p. 42.

... **"We'll box Hitler in"** ... Düsterberg, *Der Stahlhelm,* p. 39.

... **"What do you want?"** ... Kleist-Schmenzin, "Die letzte Möglichkeit," p. 92.

... **"You're mistaken."** ... Lutz Graf Schwerin von Krosigk, *Es geschah in Deutschland* (Tübingen, 1951), p. 147.

... **"If Hitler wants to establish a dictatorship"** ... Meissner, *Staatssekretär,* p. 247.

... **Schleicher discussed the situation with a group of generals** ... IfZ, ZS 217, Aktenvermerk, dated April 7, 1951, on interview with one of those present, Erich Freiherr von dem Bussche-Ippenburg, on March 30, 1951; see also Bussche-Ippenburg's article, "Hammerstein und Hindenburg," *FAZ,* February 5, 1952 (#30); also *AdRk/KvS,* pp. 320, n. 4.

... **"I am a general, Hindenburg is field marshal"** ... Gottfried Treviranus, *Das Ende von Weimar* (Düsseldorf, 1968), pp. 347f.

... **Hammerstein ... met secretly with Hitler** ... Hammerstein described this meeting in his "Niederschrift" of January 28, 1935, published in Bracher, *Die Auflösung,* pp. 733f. See also the quoted portion of a 1953 letter from Hammerstein's aide, Adolf-Friedrich Kuntzen, in Kunrat von Hammerstein, "Hammerstein, Schleicher," p. 165. Göring recalled the offer relayed by Hammerstein on Schleicher's behalf in his postwar testimony at Nuremberg on March 13, 1946: IMT, *Der Prozess gegen die Hauptkriegsverbrecher vor dem Internationalen Militärgerichtshof* (Nuremberg, 1947), vol. 9, p. 283.

... **Hammerstein went to Schleicher's residence to report** ... Hammerstein, "Niederschrift," in Bracher, *Die Auflösung,* p. 734.

... **Hitler, Goebbels and Göring had ... been alarmed** ... *ibid.;* also Goebbels, *TbJG,* part I, vol. 2, pp. 355f.

... **Göring notified Papen and Meissner** ... Papen, *Gasse,* p. 273; Meissner, *Staatssekretär,* p. 268.

... **Schleicher was alleged to be mobilizing troops** ... Düsterberg, *Der Stahlhelm,* pp. 39f.; Kunrat von Hammerstein, *Spähtrupp* (Stuttgart, 1963), p. 59; Gereke, *Landrat,* pp. 226–28.

... **Papen secured Hindenburg's agreement ... evening of the 29th** ... Papen, *Gasse,* p. 273; Meissner, *Staatssekretär,* pp. 268f. Meissner erroneously stated in his book that the incumbent minister of justice, Franz Gürtner, was included in the list of cabinet members, *ibid.*, p. 269.

... **Papen had resorted to a ruse** ... Papen later claimed, implausibly, that he had, on the morning of January 30, extracted a promise from Hitler to seek inclusion of the Catholic parties in order to secure a parliamentary majority: Papen, *Gasse,* p. 276. The minutes of the Hitler cabinet's first meeting reveal, however, that there was no intention whatever of including the Catholics: *Akten der Reichskanzlei: Regierung Hitler,* part 1, edited by Konrad Repgen and Hans Booms (Boppard, 1983), pp. 1–4.

... **François–Poncet heard ... Papen had abandoned his effort** ... *DDF, 1932–1939,* series 1, vol. 2, p. 542.

... **Similar reports reached ... Count Schwerin von Krosigk** ... See his diary, *AdRk/KvS,* p. 321.

... **Meissner, ... was awakened at 2:00 A.M.** ... *ibid.,* p. 322.

... **Sir Horace Rumbold indicated to his government** ... *DBFP, 1919–1939,* 2d series, vol. 4, pp. 395–98.

... **Planck, ... telephoned Count Schwerin von Krosigk** ... See Schwerin von Krosigk's diary, *AdRk/KvS,* p. 321.

... **General von Blomberg arrived in Berlin** ... See the testimony of the officer sent by Hammerstein to meet Blomberg, Major Adolf-Friedrich Kuntzen, on March 17, 1949, at the de-Nazification trial of Oskar von Hindenburg: NSHSAH, Nds. 171 Lüneburg Uzn/11363, Bl. 299–303.

... **Blomberg was sworn in by the president** ... Schmidt-Hannover, *Umdenken,* p. 339.

... **Schleicher telephoned Meissner** ... See Schwerin von Krosigk's diary, *AdRk/KvS,* p. 322.

... **Hugenberg arrived at Papen's apartment** ... Schmidt-Hannover, *Umdenken,* pp. 338; Düsterberg, *Der Stahlhelm,* p. 39.

... **"If the new cabinet is not installed by eleven"** ... *ibid.*

... **Schmidt-Hannover ... Düsterberg still had ... reservations** ... Schmidt-Hannover, *Umdenken,* pp. 338f.

... **Oskar von Hindenburg ... railed** ... *ibid,* p. 338; Düsterberg, *Der Stahlhelm,* p. 39.

... Düsterberg found ... Hitler and Göring had arrived ... *ibid.*

... [Düsterberg] ... discovered ... one of his grandfathers ... *ibid.*, p. 34; Berghahn, *Der Stahlhelm*, pp. 239—43.

... Hitler ... acted to dispel the Stahlhelm leader's resentment ... *ibid.*, p. 248f.; Düsterberg, *Der Stahlhelm*, p. 40.

... Papen then led Hitler ... *ibid.*, p. 40; Papen, *Gasse*, p. 275.

... Only after arriving did ... Schwerin von Krosigk finally learn ... See his diary, *AdRk/KvS*, pp. 322f.

... Hitler announced ... he must have a commitment on that point ... Düsterberg, *Der Stahlhelm*, pp. 40f.; Papen, *Gasse*, pp. 275f.; Meissner, *Staatssekretär*, pp. 269f.

... Meissner broke the deadlock ... Düsterberg, *Der Stahlhelm*, p. 41.

... Schwerin von Krosigk approached Papen ... See his diary, *AdRk/KvS*, p. 323.

... Catholic Center Party responded defensively ... See "Hitler vereidigt," *G*, January 31, 1933 (#31).

... Social Democrats found themselves without a plan ... See Hagen Schulze, ed., *Anpassung oder Widerstand?* (Bonn-Bad Godesberg, 1975), pp. 131—53.

... *Vossische Zeitung* **quoted the words ...** "Der Sprung," *VZ*, January 30, 1933 (#50).

... "With the appointment of this cabinet," ... "Hitler—Papen Kabinett," *V*, January 30, 1933 (#50).

... Others assumed real power lay ... with Papen or Hugenberg ... "Kabinett Hitler-Papen-Hugenberg," *VZ*, January 30, 1933 (#50); "Die neuen Männer," *DB-Z*, January 31, 1933 (#26); Hans Zehrer, "Nationaler Sozialismus?" *TR*, January 31, 1933 (#26); *Der Deutsche*, quoted in: Josef Becker, " 'Der Deutsche' und die Regierungsbildung des 30. Januar 1933," *Publizistik* 6 (1961), p. 197; BAK, Sammlung Brammer, ZSg 101/26, "Informationsbericht vom 2. Februar 1933," by Georg Dertinger. In a speech in Augsburg on February 4, 1933, Kurt Schumacher, leader of the Social Democrats after the Second World War, proclaimed Hugenberg the key member of the cabinet and dismissed Hitler as a decoration: Josef and Ruth Becker (eds.), *Hitlers Machtergreifung* (Munich, 1983), pp. 45f.

... **veteran political analysts initially assumed** ... *DBFP, 1919–1939,* 2d series, vol. 4, p. 400, Rumbold to Simon, January 31, 1933; Ernst Lemmer, "Der Anfang einer neuen Entwicklung," *NFP,* January 31, 1933 (#24564); Walther Schotte, in *Der Ring,* February 3, 1933, quoted in Yuji Ishida, *Jungkonservativen in der Weimarer Republik* (Frankfurt, 1988), pp. 234f.; *Deutsche Tageszeitung,* quoted in "Die Meinung der Anderen," *DAZ,* January 31, 1933 (#51); "Herr Hitler," *The Times* [London], January 31, 1933.

... **If the new cabinet lost ... majority, predicted Theodor Wolff** ... "Es ist erreicht," *BT,* January 31, 1933 (#51).

... **In a newsreel** ... BA/FA, Deulig Tonwoche Nr. 57 (1933).

... **"without the slightest feeling,"** ... Curt Riess, *Das waren Zeiten* (Vienna, 1977), pp. 151f.

... **"Most people had no idea what had befallen them"** ... Friedrich Stampfer, *Die vierzehn Jahre der ersten deutschen Republik* (Offenbach/Main, 1947), p. 670.

... **"No Nazi government,"** ... Diary of Camill Hoffmann for January 30, quoted in Johann Wilhelm Brügel and Norbert Frei, eds., "Berliner Tagebuch 1932–1934," *VfZ* 36 (1988), p. 159.

... **"difficult to see how they are to achieve"** ... *DBFP, 1919–1939,* 2d series, vol. 4, p. 399, Rumbold to Simon, January 30, 1933.

... **"Have President von Hindenburg and his 'comrade' "** ... Wickham Steed, "Can Hitler Do It?" *Sunday Times* [London], February 5, 1933.

... **François-Poncet betrayed bewilderment** ... *DDF, 1932–1939,* series 1, vol. 2, p. 542.

... **akin to admitting a wolf to the sheepfold** ... *ibid.,* p. 552.

... **"A bear is still a bear"** ... Quoted from the *Baseler Nachrichten* in: Gerd H. Padel, *Die politische Presse der deutschen Schweiz und der Aufstieg des Dritten Reiches 1933–1939* (Zurich, 1951), p. 15.

... **Hitler ... marveled at how ... he had been rescued** ... According to Heinrich Brüning (*Memoiren,* p. 648), Schleicher told him on Feb. 11, 1933, that Hitler had expressed that thought upon their parting, presumably on

January 30th, when Schleicher came to the Chancellery to hold a brief final cabinet meeting after Hitler's appointment (*AdRk/KvS*, pp. 319f.).

7. Determinacy, Contingency, and Responsibility

... **"coup d'état by installments"** ... Konrad Heiden, *Der Fuehrer* (Boston, 1944), p. 579.

... **different from his brother, Otto Strasser** ... See Kissenkoetter, *Gregor Strasser*, pp. 41–46.

... **possibility of a military regime ... Hitler ... feared** ... See his views on the subject as recorded in the memoirs of Otto Wagener: *Hitler—Memoirs of a Confidant*, ed. by H.A. Turner (New Haven, Conn., 1985), pp. 233, 238, 323; also Henry Picker, *Hitlers Tischgespräche im Führerhauptquartier* (Stuttgart, 1976), p. 325.

... **By gaining credit for the economic upswing** ... A recent study finds that Hitler's regime had little to do with the initial stages of recovery, which were already well under way when he took office: Christoph Buchheim, "Zur Natur des Wirtschaftsaufschwungs in der NS-Zeit," in *Zerissene Zwischenkriegszeit*, ed. by Harold James, Christoph Buchheim and Michael Hutter (Baden-Baden, 1994), esp. p. 104.

... **gauleiter ... warned ... an "invisible front"** ... Hambrecht, *Der Aufstieg*, pp. 370, 563, n. 58. See also "Bewegung im Abstieg," *Regensburger Anzeiger*, January 24, 1933 (#24).

... **How much difference would it have made ... ?** I have developed the following reflections more fully in my *Geissel des Jahrhunderts* (Berlin, 1989).

... **leading generals ... territorial aims were modest** ... See Gaines Post, *Civil-Military Fabric*, pp. 98–100.

... **Nazis dampened their anti-Semitism** ... See Gerhard Paul, *Aufstand der Bilder* (Bonn, 1990), pp. 113, 236–39.

... **republican government of ... Prussia ... several ... studies** ... See, for example, Robert M.W. Kempner (ed.), *Der verpasste Nazi-Stopp* (Frankfurt, 1983).

... **"I yesterday committed the greatest stupidity ..."** quoted from the papers of the fellow German-National who recorded his words, Carl

Goerdeler, in: Gerhard Ritter, *Carl Goerdeler und die deutsche Wider-standsbewegung* (Stuttgart, 1954), p. 60; see also Larry Eugene Jones, " 'The Greatest Stupidity of My Life'," *Journal of Contemporary History* 27 (1992), pp. 63–87.

... Oskar von Hindenburg ... radio address ... Quoted in Dorpalen, *Hindenburg,* p. 483.

... Adenauer ... "an extremely ambitious person ..." Adenauer, *Briefe 1945–1947,* p. 350.

... [Papen] "probably one of the most consummate liars ..." Moritz J. Bonn, *Wandering Scholar* (New York, 1984), p. 336.

... Papen was classified as heavily implicated ... Petzold, *Papen,* p. 273f.

... [Papen] sniped at the policies of the postwar ... republic ... While forbidden to publish in West Germany by the verdict of a de-Nazification court, Papen published articles in the press of Franco Spain; at the expiration of the publishing ban, he republished a selection of these in German under the title *Europa was nun?* (Göttingen, 1954).

... [Papen] received an honorific title from the Vatican ... In 1959 Papen was appointed a papal privy chamberlain by Pope John XXIII: Adams, *Rebel Patriot,* p. 475.

BIBLIOGRAPHY

Adams, Henry M., and Robin K. Adams. *Rebel Patriot: A Biography of Franz von Papen*. Santa Barbara, Calif., 1987.

Adenauer, Konrad. *Briefe 1945–1947*. Bonn, 1983.

Allen, William Sheridan. *The Nazi Seizure of Power*. Rev. ed. New York, 1984.

Altendorfer, Otto. *Fritz Schäffer als Politiker der Bayerischen Volkspartei*. Munich, 1993.

Arndt, Fritz, "Vorbereitungen der Reichswehr für den militärischen Ausnahmezustand." *Zeitschrift für Militärgeschichte* 4 (1965).

Bach, Jürgen A. *Franz von Papen in der Weimarer Republik*. Düsseldorf, 1977.

Becker, Josef. " 'Der Deutsche' und die Regierungsbildung des 30. Januar 1933." *Publizistik* 6 (1961).

Becker, Josef, and Ruth Becker, eds. *Hitlers Machtergreifung*. Munich, 1983.

Bendersky, Joseph W. *Carl Schmitt*. Princeton, N.J., 1983.

Bennett, Edward W. *German Rearmament and the West*. Princeton, N.J., 1979.

Berghahn, Volker R. *Der Stahlhelm*. Düsseldorf, 1966.

Berndorff, Hans Rudolf. *General Zwischen Ost und West*. Hamburg, 1951.

Bessel, Richard. *Political Violence and the Rise of Nazism*. New Haven, Conn., 1984.

Besson, Waldemar. *Württemberg und die deutsche Staatskrise 1928–1933.* Stuttgart, 1959.

Bloch, Michael. *Ribbentrop.* London, 1992.

Böhnke, Wilfried. *Die NSDAP im Ruhrgebiet.* Bonn, 1974.

Bohrmann, Hans, ed. *NS-Presseanweisungen der Vorkriegszeit,* 4 vols. Munich, 1984.

Bonn, Moritz J. *Wandering Scholar.* New York, 1984.

Bracher, Karl Dietrich. *Die Auflösung der Weimarer Republik.* Stuttgart and Düsseldorf, 1957.

Braun, Magnus von. *Weg durch vier Zeitepochen.* Limburg/Lahn, 1965.

Braun, Otto. *Von Weimar bis Hitler.* New York, 1940.

Breitman, Richard. "On German Social Democracy and General von Schleicher 1932–33." *Central European History* 9 (1976).

Brügel, Johann Wilhelm, and Norbert Frei, eds. "Berliner Tagebuch 1932–1934." *Vierteljahrshefte für Zeitgeschichte* 36 (1988).

Brüning, Heinrich. *Memoiren, 1918–1934.* Stuttgart, 1970.

Buchheim, Christoph. "Zur Natur des Wirtschaftsaufschwungs in der NS-Zeit." In *Zerissene Zwischenkriegszeit,* edited by Harold James, Christoph Buchheim and Michael Hutter. Baden-Baden, 1994.

Bullock, Alan. *Hitler: A Study in Tyranny.* London, 1952ff.

Caro, Kurt, and Walter Oehme. *Schleichers Aufstieg.* Berlin, 1933.

Childers, Thomas. "The Limits of National Socialist Mobilisation." In *The Formation of the Nazi Constituency, 1919–1933,* edited by Thomas Childers. Totowa, N.J., 1986.

Ciolek-Kümper, Jutta. *Wahlkampf in Lippe.* München, 1976.

Cline, Theodore Albert. "The Chancellorship of General Kurt von Schleicher." Ph.D. diss., University of Texas, 1976.

Craig, Gordon A. "Brief Schleichers an Groener." *Die Welt als Geschichte* 11 (1951).

Demant, Ebbo. *Von Schleicher zu Springer.* Mainz, 1971.

Dietrich, Otto. *Mit Hitler in die Macht.* Munich, 1934.

———. *12 Jahre mit Hitler*. Cologne, [1955].

Domarus, Max. *Hitler: Reden und Proklamationen 1932–1945*. 2 vols. Munich, 1965.

Dorpalen, Andreas. *Hindenburg and the Weimar Republic*. Princeton, 1964.

Düsterberg, Theodor. *Der Stahlhelm und Hitler*. Wolfenbüttel and Hanover, 1949.

Erdmann, Karl Dietrich and Hans Booms, eds. *Akten der Reichskanzlei. Kabinett von Schleicher* (Boppard, 1986).

Erdmann, Karl Dietrich, and Hans Booms, eds. *Akten der Reichskanzlei: Kabinett von Papen*. 2 vols. Boppard, 1989.

Eschenburg, Theodor. *Die improvisierte Demokratie*. Munich, 1963.

Fest, Joachim. *Hitler*. New York, 1974.

Fischer, Conan. *Stormtroopers*. London, 1983.

Fischer, Rudolf. *Schleicher: Mythos und Wirklichkeit*. Hamburg, 1932.

Foertsch, Hermann. *Schuld und Verhängnis*. Stuttgart, 1951.

François-Poncet, André. *Souvenirs d'une ambassade à Berlin*. Paris, 1946.

Gereke, Günther. *Ich war königlich-preussischer Landrat*. Berlin, 1970.

Geyer, Michael. "Das zweite Rüstungsprogramm (1930–1934)." *Militärgeschichtliche Mitteilungen* 17 (1975).

———. *Aufrüstung oder Sicherheit*. Weisbaden, 1980.

Gies, Horst. "NSDAP und landwirtschaftliche Organisationen in der Endphase der Weimarer Republik." *Vierteljahrshefte für Zeitgeschichte* 15 (1967).

Goebbels, Joseph. *Die Tagebücher von Joseph Goebbels: Sämtliche Fragmente,* edited by Elke Fröhlich. Munich, 1987ff.

———. *Vom Kaiserhof zur Reichskanzlei*. Munich, 1934.

Graf, Christoph. *Politische Polizei zwischen Demokratie und Diktatur*. Berlin, 1983.

Haken, Bruno Nelissen. *Stempelchronik*. Hamburg, 1932.

Hale, Oren J. *The Captive Press in the Third Reich*. Princeton, N.J., 1964.

———. "Adolf Hitler: Taxpayer." *American Historical Review* 60 (1955), pp. 830–42.

Hambrecht, Rainer. *Der Aufstieg der NSDAP in Mittel- und Oberfranken (1925–1933)*. Nuremberg, 1976.

Hammerstein, Kunrat von. *Spähtrupp*. Stuttgart, 1963.

————. "Schleicher, Hammerstein und die Machtübernahme 1933." *Frankfurter Hefte* 11 (1956).

Hanfstaengl, Ernst. *Hitler: The Missing Years*. London, 1957.

Hayes, Peter. " 'A Question Mark with Epaulettes'? Kurt von Schleicher and Weimar Politics." *Journal of Modern History* 52 (March 1980).

Heiden, Konrad. *Der Fuehrer*. Boston, 1944.

Hentschel, Volker. *Weimars letzte Monate*. Düsseldorf, 1978.

Hoch, Anton, and Christoph Weisz. "Die Erinnerungen des Generalobersten Wilhelm Adam." In *Miscellanea: Festschrift für Helmut Krausnick zum 75. Geburtstag,* edited by Wolfgang Benz et al. Stuttgart, 1980.

Horkenbach, Cuno. *Das Deutsche Reich von 1918 bis heute*. Berlin, 1932.

Horn, Wolfgang. *Führerideologie und Parteiorganisation in der NSDAP*. Düsseldorf, 1972.

Hüls, Hans. *Wähler und Wahlverhalten im Land Lippe während der Weimarer Republik*. Detmold, 1974.

International Military Tribunal. *Der Prozess gegen die Hauptkriegsverbrecher vor dem Internationalen Militärgerichtshof*. 24 vols. Munich, 1984.

Ishida, Yuji. *Jungkonservativen in der Weimarer Republik*. Frankfurt, 1988.

Jäckel, Eberhard. *Hitler's Weltanschauung* Middletown, Conn., 1972.

Jacobsen, Hans-Adolf. *Nationalsozialistische Aussenpolitik, 1933–1938*. Frankfurt, 1968.

Jonas, Erasmus. *Die Volkskonservativen, 1928–1933*. Düsseldorf, 1965.

Jones, Larry Eugene. " 'The Greatest Stupidity of My Life'." *Journal of Contemporary History* 27 (1992).

————. "Why Hitler Came to Power." In *Geschichtswissenschaft vor 2000,* edited by Konrad H. Jarausch, Jörn Rüsen and Hans Schleier. Hagen, 1991.

Junker, Detlef. "Die letzte Alternative zu Hitler." In *Das Ende der Weimarer Republik und die nationalsozialistische Machtergreifung,* edited by Christoph Gradmann and Oliver von Mengersen. Heidelberg, 1994.

————. *Die Deutsche Zentrumspartei und Hitler 1932/33.* Stuttgart, 1969.

Kempner, Robert M. W., ed. *Der verpasste Nazi-Stopp.* Frankfurt, 1983.

Kissenkoetter, Udo. *Gregor Strasser und die NSDAP.* Stuttgart, 1978.

Kleist-Schmenzin, Ewald von. "Die letzte Möglichkeit." *Politische Studien* 10 (1959).

Knickerbocker, Hubert R. *The German Crisis.* New York, 1932.

Koehl, Robert Lewis. *The Black Corps.* Madison, 1988.

Kolb, Eberhard, and Wolfram Pyta. "Die Staatsnotstandsplanung unter den Regierungen Papen und Schleicher." In *Die Deutsche Staatskrise 1930–33,* edited by Heinrich August Winkler. Munich, 1992.

Kracauer, Siegfried. *From Caligari to Hitler.* New York, 1960.

Krebs, Albert. *Tendenzen und Gestalten der NSDAP.* Stuttgart, 1959.

Leopold, John A. *Alfred Hugenberg.* New Haven, Conn., 1977.

Longerich, Peter. *Die braunen Bataillone.* Munich, 1989.

Ludecke, Kurt. *I Knew Hitler.* New York, 1937.

Marcon, Helmut. *Arbeitsbeschaffungspolitik der Regierungen Papen und Schleicher.* Frankfurt, 1974.

Meissner, Hans-Otto. *30. Januar '33.* Esslingen, 1976.

Meissner, Otto. *Staatssekretär unter Ebert—Hindenburg—Hitler.* Hamburg, 1950.

Mommsen, Hans. *The Rise and Fall of Weimar Democracy.* Chapel Hill, N.C., 1996.

Morsey, Rudolf. "Die deutsche Zentrumspartei." In *Das Ende der Parteien 1933,* edited by Erich Matthias and Rudolf Morsey. Düsseldorf, 1960.

————, ed. *Die Protokolle der Reichstagsfraktion und Fraktionsvorstands der Deutschen Zentrumspartei 1926–1933.* Mainz, 1969.

Müller, Klaus-Jürgen. *Das Heer und Hitler.* Stuttgart, 1969.

Münchner Stadtmuseum. *München—"Hauptstadt der Bewegung."* Munich, 1993.

Muth, Heinrich. "Das 'Kölner Gespräch' am 4. Januar 1933." *Geschichte in Wissenschaft und Unterricht* 37 (1986).

———. "Schleicher und die Gewerkschaften 1932." *Vierteljahrshefte für Zeitgeschichte* 29 (1981).

Neliba, Günter. *Wilhelm Frick.* Paderborn, 1992.

Noakes, Jeremy. *The Nazi Party in Lower Saxony, 1921–1933.* London, 1971.

Noakes, Jeremy, and Geoffrey Pridham, eds. *Documents on Nazism 1919–1945.* New York, 1974.

Oldenburg-Januschau, Elard. *Erinnerungen.* Leipzig, 1936.

Orlow, Dietrich. *The History of the Nazi Party.* 2 vols. Pittsburgh, 1969–73.

Ott, Eugen. "Ein Bild des Generals Kurt von Schleicher." *Politische Studien* 10 (1959).

Padel, Gerd H. *Die politische Presse der deutschen Schweiz und der Aufstieg des Dritten Reiches 1933–1939.* Zurich, 1951.

Papen, Franz von. *Der Wahrheit eine Gasse.* Munich, 1952.

———. *Europa was nun?* Göttingen, 1954.

———. *Vom Scheitern einer Demokratie.* Mainz, 1968.

Patch, William L., Jr. *Christian Trade Unions in the Weimar Republic.* New Haven, Conn., 1985.

Paul, Gerhard. *Aufstand der Bilder.* Bonn, 1990.

Petzold, Joachim. *Franz von Papen.* Munich and Berlin, 1995.

Picker, Henry. *Hitlers Tischgespräche im Führerhauptquartier.* Stuttgart, 1976.

Plehwe, Friedrich-Karl von. *Reichskanzler Kurt von Schleicher.* Esslingen, 1983.

Post, Gaines, Jr. *The Civil-Military Fabric of Weimar Foreign Policy.* Princeton, N.J., 1973.

Pridham, Geoffrey. *Hitler's Rise to Power.* New York, 1974.

Pünder, Hermann. *Politik in der Reichskanzlei.* Stuttgart, 1961.

Reiche, Eric G. *The Development of the SA in Nürnberg, 1922–1934.* New York, 1986.

Repgen, Konrad, and Hans Booms, eds. *Akten der Reichskanzlei: Regierung Hitler.* Part 1. Boppard, 1983.

Ribbentrop, Joachim von. *Zwischen London und Moskau.* Leoni am Starnberger See, 1961.

Riess, Curt. *Das waren Zeiten.* Vienna, 1977.

Ritter, Gerhard. *Carl Goerdeler und die deutsche Widerstandsbewegung.* Stuttgart, 1954.

Rolfs, Richard W. *The Sorcerer's Apprentice: The Life of Franz von Papen.* Lanham, Md., 1996.

Rosenhaft, Eve. "The Unemployed in the Neighborhood." In *The German Unemployed,* edited by Richard J. Evans and Dick Geary. London, 1987.

Schmidt-Hannover, Otto. *Umdenken oder Anarchie.* Göttingen, 1959.

Schneider, Michael. *Das Arbeitsbeschaffungsprogramm des ADGB.* Bonn-Bad Godesberg, 1975.

Schneider, Thomas Martin. *Reichsbischof Ludwig Müller.* Göttingen, 1993.

Schön, Eberhard. *Die Entstehung des Nationalsozialismus in Hessen.* Meisenheim am Glan, 1972.

Schröder, Arno. *"Hitler geht auf die Dörfer."* Detmold, 1938.

———. *Mit der Partei Vorwärts.* Detmold, 1940.

Schulze, Hagen, ed. *Anpassung oder Widerstand?* Bonn-Bad Godesberg, 1975.

———. *Otto Braun oder Preussens demokratische Sendung.* Frankfurt/Main, 1977.

Schwerin von Krosigk, Lutz Graf. *Es geschah in Deutschland.* Tübingen, 1951.

———. *Staatsbankrott.* Göttingen, 1974.

Semmler, Rudolf. *Goebbels—the man next to Hitler.* London, 1947.

Severing, Carl. *Mein Lebensweg.* 2 vols. Cologne, 1950.

Sösemann, Bernd. *Das Ende der Weimarer Republik in der Kritik demokratischer Publizisten.* Berlin, 1976.

Sontheimer, Kurt. "Der Tatkreis." *Vierteljahrshefte für Zeitgeschichte* 7 (1959), pp. 239–60.

Stachura, Peter. *Gregor Strasser and the Rise of Nazism.* London, 1983.

―――. "Der Fall Strasser." In *The Shaping of the Nazi State,* edited by Peter Stachura. London, 1978.

Stampfer, Friedrich. *Die vierzehn Jahre der ersten deutschen Republic.* Offenbach/Main, 1947.

Stelzner, Fritz. *Schicksal SA.* Berlin, 1936.

Stokes, Lawrence D. *Kleinstadt und Nationalsozialismus.* Neumünster, 1984.

Struve, Walter. *Aufstieg und Herrschaft des Nationalsozialismus in einer industriellen Kleinstadt.* Essen, 1992.

Treviranus, Gottfried. *Das Ende von Weimar.* Düsseldorf, 1968.

Turner, Henry Ashby, Jr. *German Big Business and the Rise of Hitler.* New York, 1985.

―――, ed. *Hitler—Memoirs of a Confidant.* New Haven, Conn., 1985.

―――. *Geisel des Jahrhunderts: Hitler und seine Hinterlassenschaft.* Berlin, 1989.

Vogelsang, Thilo. *Kurt von Schleicher: Ein General als Politiker.* Göttingen, 1965.

―――. "Neue Dokumente zur Geschichte der Reichswehr." *Vierteljahrshefte für Zeitgeschichte* 2 (1954).

―――. *Reichswehr, Staat und NSDAP.* Stuttgart, 1962.

―――. "Zur Politik Schleichers gegenüber der NSDAP 1932." *Vierteljahrshefte für Zeitgeschichte* 6 (1958).

Weiland, Ruth. *Die Kinder der Arbeitslosen.* Berlin, 1933.

Weiss, Hermann, and Paul Hoser, eds. *Die Deutschnationalen und die Zerstörung der Weimarer Republik.* Munich, 1989.

Werner, Andreas. "SA und NSDAP." Ph.D. diss., Erlangen-Nürnberg, 1964.

Wessling, Wolfgang. "Hindenburg, Neudeck und die deutsche Wirtschaft." *Vierteljahrschrift für Sozial- und Wirtschaftsgeschichte* 64 (1977).

Wheeler-Bennett, John W. *The Nemesis of Power.* London, 1956.

Wiesemann, Falk. *Die Vorgeschichte der nationalsozialistischen Machtübernahme in Bayern 1932–1933.* Berlin, 1975.

Winkler, Heinrich August. *Der Weg in die Katastrophe*. Berlin, 1987.

———. *Weimar 1918–1933*. Munich, 1993.

Wörtz, Ulrich. "Programmatik und Führerprinzip: Das Problem des Strasser-Kreises in der NSDAP." Ph.D. diss., Erlangen–Nürnberg, 1966.

INDEX